# ANCIENTS AND MODERNS

General Editor: Phiroze Vasunia, Reader in Classics, University of Reading

How can antiquity illuminate critical issues in the modern world? How does the ancient world help us address contemporary problems and issues? In what ways do modern insights and theories shed new light on the interpretation of ancient texts, monuments, artefacts and cultures? The central aim of this exciting new series is to show how antiquity is relevant to life today. The series also points towards the ways in which the modern and ancient worlds are mutually connected and interrelated. Lively, engaging, and historically informed, *Ancients and Moderns* examines key ideas and practices in context. It shows how societies and cultures have been shaped by ideas and debates that recur. With a strong appeal to students and teachers in a variety of disciplines, including classics and ancient history, each book is written for non-specialists in a clear and accessible manner.

ESTHER EIDINOW is Reader in Ancient Greek History at Newman University College, Birmingham. She is the author of *Oracles, Curses, and Risk Among the Ancient Greeks* (Oxford University Press, 2007).

# ANCIENTS AND MODERNS SERIES
ISBN: 978-1-84885-200-6 • www.ancientsandmoderns.com

THE ART OF THE BODY: ANTIQUITY AND ITS LEGACY • MICHAEL SQUIRE

DEATH: ANTIQUITY AND ITS LEGACY • MARIO ERASMO

DRAMA: ANTIQUITY AND ITS LEGACY • DAVID ROSENBLOOM

GENDER: ANTIQUITY AND ITS LEGACY • BROOKE HOLMES

LUCK, FATE AND FORTUNE: ANTIQUITY AND ITS LEGACY • ESTHER EIDINOW

MAGIC AND DEMONS: ANTIQUITY AND ITS LEGACY • TO BE ANNOUNCED

MEDICINE: ANTIQUITY AND ITS LEGACY • CAROLINE PETIT

PHILOSOPHY: ANTIQUITY AND ITS LEGACY • EMILY WILSON

POLITICS: ANTIQUITY AND ITS LEGACY • KOSTAS VLASSOPOULOS

RACE: ANTIQUITY AND ITS LEGACY • DENISE McCOSKEY

RELIGION: ANTIQUITY AND ITS LEGACY • JÖRG RÜPKE

SEX: ANTIQUITY AND ITS LEGACY • DANIEL ORRELLS

SLAVERY: ANTIQUITY AND ITS LEGACY • PAGE DUBOIS

SPORT: ANTIQUITY AND ITS LEGACY • TO BE ANNOUNCED

WAR: ANTIQUITY AND ITS LEGACY • ALFRED S. BRADFORD

ANCIENTS AND MODERNS

# LUCK, FATE AND FORTUNE
# ANTIQUITY AND ITS LEGACY

ESTHER EIDINOW

Published in 2011 by I.B.Tauris & Co Ltd
6 Salem Road, London W2 4BU
175 Fifth Avenue, New York NY 10010
www.ibtauris.com

Copyright © Esther Eidinow, 2011

The right of Esther Eidinow to be identified as the author of this work has been asserted by the author in accordance with the Copyright, Designs and Patent Act 1988.

All rights reserved. Except for brief quotations in a review, this book, or any part thereof, may not be reproduced, stored in or introduced into a retrieval system, or transmitted, in any form or by any means, electronic, mechanical, photocopying, recording or otherwise, without the prior written permission of the publisher.

ISBN (HB): 978 1 84511 842 6
ISBN (PB): 978 1 84511 843 3

A full CIP record for this book is available from the British Library
A full CIP record is available from the Library of Congress

Library of Congress Catalog Card Number: available

Typeset in Garamond Pro by Ellipsis Books Limited, Glasgow
Printed and bound in Great Britain by CPI Antony Rowe, Chippenham

# CONTENTS

FOREWORD:     vii
    Phiroze Vasunia

INTRODUCTION:     1

CHAPTER I:     PHILOSOPHIES OF FATE     12

CHAPTER II:     A MINISTRY OF MISFORTUNE     25

CHAPTER III:     OEDIPUS: A TRAGEDY OF FATES     53

CHAPTER IV:     CULTURAL MODELS AND SHIFTING MEANINGS     66

CHAPTER V:     THE ARCHAIC POETS: POLITICS OF FORTUNE     76

CHAPTER VI:     HERODOTUS: PATTERNS OF FATE     93

CHAPTER VII:     THUCYDIDES: RHETORICS OF COINCIDENCE     119

CHAPTER VIII     THE RESURRECTION OF CHANCE     143

NOTES     163

INDEX     209

# FOREWORD

*Ancients and Moderns* comes to fruition at a propitious moment: 'reception studies' is flourishing, and the scholarship that has arisen around it is lively, rigorous, and historically informed; it makes us rethink our own understanding of the relationship between past and present. *Ancients and Moderns* aims to communicate to students and general readers the depth, energy, and excitement of the best work in the field. It seeks to engage, provoke, and stimulate, and to show how, for large parts of the world, Graeco-Roman antiquity continues to be relevant to debates in culture, politics, and society.

The series does not merely accept notions such as 'reception' or 'tradition' without question; rather, it treats these concepts as contested categories and calls into question the illusion of an unmediated approach to the ancient world. We have encouraged our authors to take intellectual risks in the development of their ideas. By challenging the assumption of a direct line of continuity between antiquity and modernity, these books explore how discussions in such areas as gender, politics, race, sex, and slavery occur within particular contexts and histories; they demonstrate that no culture is monolithic, that claims to ownership of the past are never pure, and that East and West are often connected together in ways that continue to surprise and disturb many. Thus, *Ancients and Moderns* is intended to stir up debates about and within reception studies and to complicate some of the standard narratives about the 'legacy' of Greece and Rome.

All the books in *Ancients and Moderns* illustrate that *how* we think about the past bears a necessary relation to *who* we are in the present. At the same time, the series also seeks to persuade scholars of antiquity that their own pursuit is inextricably connected to what many generations have thought, said, and done about the ancient world.

Phiroze Vasunia

# INTRODUCTION

'Nothing is written'
From *Lawrence of Arabia*[1]

Lawrence of Arabia, Sherif Ali and their men have almost finished crossing the blazing Nefud desert, the so-called 'Sun's Anvil', on their mammoth trek to the city of Aqaba, when they notice that one of the camels in their party is riderless – one of their companions, Gasim, is missing. Without pausing, Lawrence turns back towards the desert to search for him. Sherif Ali tries to dissuade him, protesting: 'What for? To die with Gasim? In one hour comes the sun. In God's name, understand! We cannot go back!' and 'Gasim's time is come, Lawrence. It is written!' But Lawrence disagrees: 'Nothing is written.' And when he finally returns from the desert, bringing Gasim, still alive, he proclaims this again to Ali: 'Nothing is written.'[2]

In the 1991 cult film, *Terminator 2: Judgment Day*, the heroine, Sarah Connor, is on the run with her son and the cyborg that has been sent from the future to protect them. They are fleeing from a 'Terminator', another machine from the future, but sent by enemies to kill Sarah and her son. The fugitives arrive at a farm, where they pause to collect crucial provisions and plan their next move. Sitting at a wooden table, watching her son play with the cyborg, Sarah falls asleep – and has a vision of the terrible future that she is trying to prevent. At first, in her dream everything seems peaceful, even joyful. She watches herself and her children playing in a small park, her vision lingering on a small girl, who is laughing as she plays on a swing. In the dream, Sarah runs to the park fence to try to warn those inside of the dangers they are in, but cannot make a sound. She can only watch as their happiness turns to horror. With a searing flash, a nuclear explosion devastates the city; the bodies of those around her burst into flames and then dissolve into ashes, which flutter away in the wind. When the vision ends and Sarah finally wakes she finds she has carved the words 'NO FATE' into the table before her.

These are powerful scenes, each of which turns, very differently on a single theme: Fate. Each episode shows a hero determined to resist what, for others, must happen – indeed, has already happened – even though it means facing terrible risks to their own lives. Members of the audience may never experience such dramatic situations; nevertheless, the underlying circumstances still appeal to a common set of ideas and emotions. Who has not wished they could change what they believe must happen; and who has not, at some point, felt (even if only to reject the notion) that there is something in control of their lives, setting them to follow a particular direction, bringing good luck or bad, directing them towards a final outcome?

And yet we are meant to have progressed far beyond such concerns, to a wholly different conception of future uncertainty and our relationship to it: 'the revolutionary idea that defines the boundary between modern times and the past is the mastery of risk'.[3] Risk has become the lens through which we view and discuss the uncertain future: for some, the growth of the importance of risk is a story of almost unmitigated success, although others have seen a darker side to its increasing dominance.[4] Whichever position on risk we take, in terms of our day-to-day experiences, we are increasingly used to the language of risk and its management in most professional settings. This is a discourse of action and control in which the unknown is rationalised, and then taken firmly in hand: risk 'issues' are identified, assessed, prioritised, monitored, and managed.[5] Risk management is an arena of expertise: specialised education, training, and professional development offer practitioners knowledge and technical proficiency, while the opportunity for qualifications indicates the rapid growth of professionalisation. Nevertheless, as

# INTRODUCTION

the films above suggest, another and contrasting set of concepts survives alongside, challenging the post-enlightenment discourse of risk management to evoke the sense of a powerful agency (or several, simultaneously) acting in our lives. As their dictionary definitions reveal, these concepts are multivalent, overlapping and interconnecting to spin a web of implied, but often ambiguous (and portentous) meanings – often shading into an intriguing sense of agency.[6]

Since it has already been mentioned, let us start with 'fate'. The word originates in a Latin word, *fatum*, which literally means not, as Lawrence's dialogue with Sherif Ali might suggest 'what is written', but 'what has been spoken', and was used to refer to prophetic declarations. However, even in antiquity it held a darker meaning, indicating bad fortune, ill fate, ruin, or even death.[7] A similar, perhaps even wider, range of meanings persists nowadays, from 'disaster, especially death' to 'inevitable and often adverse outcome, condition or end', to even just, the 'expected result of normal development'. However, it can also mean 'the will or principle or determining cause by which things in general are believed to come to be as they are or events to happen as they do'.[8] Synonyms for 'fate' include 'destiny', 'lot', 'portion' or 'doom', each of which conveys a particular nuance – and introduces further terms, as well as connections between those terms. Thus, 'destiny', which has its origins in the Latin verb *destinare* ('to make fast or firm, to establish') implies 'something foreordained and often suggests a great or noble course or end'; while 'lot' and 'portion' 'imply a distribution by fate or destiny'; and 'lot' alone suggests 'blind chance'.

Instead of 'fate', some people might prefer to use the term 'fortune', which seems to cover a similar range of meanings, from the final outcome (e.g., 'a prediction of fortune'), to a 'hypothetical force or personified power', reminding us of the word's origins in the Latin term *fortuna*, which was also personified by the Romans as a goddess. 'Fortune' may convey an additional element of precariousness, since, in this sense, it 'unpredictably determines events and issues favourably or unfavourably'. Used in the plural, it can also mean the 'turns and courses of luck accompanying one's progress (as through life)', so 'her fortunes varied but she never gave up'. It may come as a surprise then to find that we also use it to mean 'prosperity attained partly through luck' or, with no reference to how it was obtained, simply 'a store of material possessions': 'the family fortune'.

'Fortune' introduces another term, 'luck', a word whose precise origins are unknown, but which is thought to have originated as a gambling term.[9] Its range of meaning is relatively wide: it can evoke either 'a force that brings good fortune or adversity' or, as above, indicate 'the events or circumstances that operate for or against an individual'. 'Luck' can also be described as 'favouring chance', which leads us on to yet another term: 'chance' or 'something that happens unpredictably without discernible human intention or observable cause' – 'they met by chance'. With its origins in Latin *cadere*, 'to fall', chance seems to have a strong sense of incalculable contingency, but again, it may also indicate some sense of agency: 'an assumed impersonal purposeless determiner of unaccountable happenings'.

When we turn from dictionaries to daily life, we find that these notions of luck, fate and fortune are ubiquitous, from the simple wish to experience 'good luck!', to the labelling of someone as particularly lucky or unlucky, to the vague sense of reassurance gained from carrying a particular special object. These concepts lurk unexamined behind myriad everyday phenomena, from the daily gestures of crossed fingers and 'knocking on wood' for luck, to buying a lottery ticket or checking our horoscope to see 'what's in store'. While sports reporters debate the luck of teams and players – Will current good luck run out? Are events the result of bad luck or poor decision-making? – mention of destiny, fate, and fortune implicitly enhances the promises of some political rhetoric.[10] It seems that modern theories of risk and trust may not have totally supplanted the older concepts of luck, fate and fortune, as some commentators have suggested.[11]

Indeed, in many arenas, we can also observe our own reflexive fascination with these concepts: many novels and films offer subtle explorations of the key role that chance or coincidence – or is it luck, fate or fortune? – play in people's lives (and further examples will appear throughout the book). Recently, some scientists have made attempts to identify the causes of luck: Professor Richard Wiseman has analysed the psychological attributes and

## INTRODUCTION

approaches of people who consider themselves lucky or unlucky, arguing that the behavioural techniques of lucky people can be learned and applied by us all.[12] Wiseman narrows it down to four main principles of luck (and 12 sub-principles) – and even provides exercises so that readers can assess their current 'luck profile' and then practise the techniques that will help them develop a new, lucky approach to life. Richard Wiseman's *Luck Factor* reveals something of our post-enlightenment attitude to luck, fate and fortune: the refusal to submit to the idea, let alone the impositions, of a powerful, external force. Wiseman attempts to replace a traditional idea of luck with a scientific methodology designed to increase individual control. Somewhat similarly, our two film heroes, Lawrence of Arabia and Sarah Connor, resist the notion of fate, fighting for the freedom to shape their own future.

Nevertheless, even in this brave new world of self-direction, the old questions remain. Across the burgeoning literatures of futures studies, change management and strategic planning, to the statistical labyrinths of risk studies, to soothing guides for self-help and New Age lifestyles, to more recent anxieties about the meaning of genetic inheritance we trace similar concerns: are the events of the future malleable or set fast? Who has the authority or power to decide what is to come? What techniques can provide, if not control over, then perhaps a helpful glimpse of, future events? And, perhaps above all, why have I suffered this misfortune, and how can I avoid it in the future? Human vulnerability to uncertainty about the future and the need to at least make sense of, if not avoid, inexplicable, unpredictable events has been a prevalent concern throughout history. Modern responses reveal a rich legacy of ideas, from many different cultures, ancient and modern. This book explores some of the key ideas of ancient Greek culture that resonate with modern conceptions of luck, fate and fortune, and, in turn, looks at how modern approaches may help us to understand some of those ancient ideas and their role in society.

The evidence suggests most ancient Greeks paid close attention to the uncertainty of the future, and the risks this presented. Epigraphic and archaeological evidence draws our attention to the range of supernatural forces and beings that many of the ancients understood to be involved in manipulating the events and outcomes of their daily lives. As well as temples to the gods where individuals and communities might simply pray to the gods to grant them safety and prosperity in the future, the landscape was strewn with oracular sanctuaries, where men and women, slave and free, sought a glimpse of what was actually in store for them. If you were unable to visit a sanctuary, then doubtless an itinerant seer or oracle-seller would knock on your door sooner or later, bringing oracle-books or some other device with which to tell you about your future.[13] Similarly, moving from the physical to the imaginary, the ancient Greek literary landscape teems with stories that, with a variety of different emphases, illustrate and reinforce the wholly unpredictable, and yet (if one only had the power) utterly foreseeable, nature of future events.

This book will explore some aspects of how some ancient Greeks imagined the future to be structured and organised, and how this was connected to events in their own lives – in particular, I would argue, their experiences of misfortune. This aspect of life seems to have demanded a startling range of explanations, which, for the purposes of initial simplicity we might divide roughly into two groups. The first group consists of experiences of misfortune caused by acts of supernatural violence: these can be divided into acts perpetrated by mortals against mortals (attacking each other with spells, for example), and assaults on mortals by the supernatural entities themselves.[14] These supernatural entities comprised a vast bureaucracy, ranging from the gods to the dead, with a host of uncanny and bizarre office-holders in between, including, for example, the multitudes of heroes or the more monstrous, vengeance-seeking, justice-dealing creatures, the *Erinyes*.[15] Both mortal and immortal assaults were often explained as being motivated by *phthonos* or jealousy,[16] but some supernatural entities might pursue individuals or communities for particular offences; for example, the *Erinyes* were said to avenge the violent deaths of relatives, especially parents.[17]

Alongside this supernatural civil service, operating concurrently, sometimes very closely, was what we might imagine as a 'Ministry of Misfortune'. This provides the second group of explanations of mortal experiences of misfortune. The Ministry of Misfortune comprised a set of entities whose supernatural status still remains somewhat mysterious to modern imaginations. The ways in which these different entities worked, separately and together, give some idea of the complexity and richness of concepts and imagery that, even at this relatively early date (to our eyes), were already part of the imagined operation of luck, fate and fortune. These include ideas of apportioning or of a lottery, spinning or weaving, or being snared. Some of this vocabulary describes a general fortune for all mankind, other vocabulary emphasises the idea of personalised fortune, both good and bad. Over time, it becomes apparent that individualised fortunes might belong not only to individuals, but also to groups and communities, including cities.

Although I hope some of the similarities between ancient and modern ideas are already becoming apparent, the focus of this book is not intended to suggest that the ancient Greeks alone are directly responsible for what most people now believe about fate and fortune. Nor is it, because it cannot be, an attempt to chart the reception of ancient Greek ideas about luck, fate and fortune in modern-day philosophies. Such a simplistic approach is impossible: we, whoever we are, stand in a long corridor of time bustling with ideas and influences originating from many and diverse cultures, including, for example, such concepts as the (different ideas of) *karma* of various south and southeast Asian cultures.[18]

Ideas about the structure and organisation of luck, fate and fortune vary markedly across cultures. For example, we find that in the Western tradition luck may be described as a 'secular faith', one which concerns itself with 'the worldly or temporal as distinguished from the spiritual and the eternal', whereas luck is part of some Japanese Shinto religious traditions – indeed, small objects or *engimono* (e.g., 'good luck arrows' or *fukukasane*) are produced and sold, often but not necessarily at shrines, for use in the home, in order to help bring luck to households.[19] In the Western tradition, we find that, traditionally, there is thought to be little that one can do to avert misfortune, whereas in the Japanese context, with its heritage of Buddhist beliefs about karmic causality, it may be possible to change one's fortune by taking spiritually significant action. This is to talk of luck, fate and fortune very generally, in terms of the beliefs of different cultures. When we turn to individuals' beliefs about, and attitudes towards, luck, fate and fortune, these will not only depend on what they have been brought up to believe, but also the ideas that they have come into contact with since then.

The variety of beliefs we find in modern society may also have been true of 'the ancient Greeks'. Although, for reasons of space and evidence, this book will tend towards generalisations about ancient society, it is important to remember that groups and individuals in the same period may have espoused very different ideas. For example, the ancient philosopher Aristotle relates how, in his time, there were people who believed that 'chance is a cause, but that it is inscrutable to human intelligence, as being a divine thing and full of mystery', while at the same time, others said that 'everything which we ascribe to chance or spontaneity has some definite cause.'[20]

In the ancient Greek arena, this study will focus on the relationships between, and gradual developments of, two particular members of the Ministry of Misfortune – *moira* and *tuche* – during the Archaic and Classical periods (that is from the eighth to roughly the fourth centuries BCE). Scholarly focus on what these terms represented and how they developed within Greek culture have waxed and waned.[21] In general discussions of Greek religion, they are usually simply translated as, respectively, 'fate' and 'fortune' or 'luck' or 'chance', with little clarification, although, as we have seen above, our own concepts are far from unambiguous. (Are we evoking final outcomes or the events that shape them, material possessions or spiritual entities, personifications or abstract forces?) Investigations into both *moira* and *tuche* have tended to describe them in terms of progress – or not – towards a more modern, rational mindset. Discussions of *moira* frequently focus on the development of ancient ideas about free will and agency vs. fatalism or determinism; while consideration of *tuche* may be coloured by post-enlightenment impatience with such irrational notions as 'luck'. Confused by the parallel existences of *moira* and *tuche* as both divinities and abstract impersonal powers, scholars have been markedly reluctant throughout the years to credit either figure with authentic religious significance, even when there is evidence for a widespread cult (as we shall see is the case for *tuche*, at least). Instead, the tendency is to see them as expressions of a sense of human vulnerability to the uncertain future.[22] While this is no doubt part of what *moira* and *tuche* expressed for ancient Greek men and women, this makes for a very limited view of the multi-dimensional roles these entities played in the ancient Greek imagination, their various characteristics in different contexts, their use in different discourses.

In contrast, I want to use this study to introduce a different approach to thinking about the concepts of *moira* and *tuche*, that is as 'schemas', or 'cultural models', in a cognitive structure. More will be said about this in detail in a later chapter, suffice to say here that this approach draws on theories of cognitive anthropology, which explore how we make meaning out of our experiences, and communicate that meaning to each other. Schemas or cultural models are cognitive configurations of objects and relations, which provide a system for describing how the world works that is culturally learned and shared, and used to represent, organise and evaluate experiences.[23] They reflect the regularities of a culture, but are flexible, evolving over time in response to developments within that culture. Understood as schemas, the terms '*moira*' and '*tuche*' no longer need be considered as each indicating a single concept, but instead as having activated a mental pattern of connections, a network of associations, dependent on both the context of their use and the experiences of those using and apprehending the terms. If this seems vague, then compare how hard it is to pin down the precise meaning of our own modern terms for luck, fate and fortune: as their dictionary definitions, above, demonstrate, this is at least partly because each of these terms does not symbolise a single concept, but evokes a set of (sometimes inconsistent) experiences.

This study will attempt to identify the nature and characteristics of ancient cultural models of *tuche* and *moira* by analysing a number of ancient discourses. It will mean using the analytical approach of one discipline, cognitive anthropology, to explore the evidence of another, ancient history. Admittedly, such an approach is usually used to analyse the discourse of living people, and usually depends on a larger sample than that used here.[24] Nevertheless, although the data set available to the ancient historian may not allow her to plumb the depths of a culture in any one moment, it may offer sufficient material for identifying changes in concepts across a period of time, and offer a useful approach to the question of how to think about religious belief in the ancient world.

What this approach is not intended to achieve is a single, simple account of ancient Greek luck, fate and fortune. Quite apart from the multiplicity of views that are likely to have been held in any society, and the difficulties of sifting through fragmentary evidence, cultural models are rarely neat or unambiguous structures, but are 'continually in modification, continually adapting to reflect the current state of affairs'.[25] This study is intended to elicit insights into specific texts, and the cultural models that they suggest, and, in turn, provide some idea of the development of ideas about and attitudes towards concepts of luck, fate and fortune across the period represented by these texts.[26]

The first part of this book will investigate the similarities and differences between ancient and modern views of luck, fate and fortune. The study will start with a brief overview of modern popular and academic approaches to luck, fate and fortune, to remind the reader of the many different ways in which modern minds grapple with these issues. For comparison, Chapter II will then introduce the personnel that represent the ancient Greek concepts of luck, fate and fortune, a bustling department of abstractions, personifications and supernatural entities, with a variety of complex roles and responsibilities. In Chapter III, an analysis of the ancient and modern meanings of Sophocles' *Oedipus the King* will suggest that ancient Greek approaches to these concepts were not concerned with questions of free will and determinism as we understand them. It will explore how the characters' conceptions of luck, fate and fortune seem to change as the terrible events of the play unfold, and examine ways in which the language of luck, fate and fortune can be used differently to respond to changing circumstances. This chapter will suggest another way of approaching the discourse of luck, fate and fortune in ancient Greek literary texts – not as offering insights about free will, but as a discourse about responsibility that could be deployed in a variety of ways. Chapter IV will then offer some theoretical bases for this approach, drawing on cognitive anthropology and introducing ideas about storytelling and cultural models. This will be followed by a series of case studies that

## INTRODUCTION

examine the discourse(s) of luck, fate and fortune deployed in particular texts. Alongside the detailed examination of ancient Greek concepts, the book includes a selection of modern examples of references to luck, fate and fortune: these are not intended to provide an in-depth examination of contemporary concepts, but rather to suggest to the reader that the ideas of the Greeks are perhaps not so far from some of our own. The final chapter will examine some modern ideas about the uncertain future, and the possible resurrection of luck, fate and fortune and related concepts among contemporary cultural models.

# CHAPTER 1

# PHILOSOPHIES OF FATE

'If, after the tea has been drunk and the swirling and twirling ritual has been done, the leaves are in a rounded pile against the side of the cup opposite to the handle, there is trouble coming. This trouble is not of the Enquirer's own doing and it will come without warning.'

S. Fenton, *The Fortune Teller's Workbook*[1]

'Principle One: Maximise your chance opportunities. Lucky people create, notice and act upon the chance opportunities in their life.'

R. Wiseman, *The Luck Factor*[2]

We start with some reminders of the complexity of our modern approaches to ideas of luck, fate and fortune: the first quotation above is from a section of useful tips on how to read tea-leaves – one of 19 forms of fortune-telling offered in *The Fortune-Teller's Workbook* by Sasha Fenton. The tips hail from the grandmother of a friend of the author. She describes the techniques of the trade, and also offers hints not only for the skilful practitioner, but also the competent recipient. Thus we find out that, in her experience, only 'intuitive people' actually ask for a reading, and when they do so, they tend to receive good news. In contrast, when she felt compelled to offer someone a reading, then it meant bad or sad news for the recipient. The unspoken notion of luck, fate and fortune that underpins the information in *The Fortune-Teller's Workbook* describes a future that is mapped out and simply waits to be discovered. Implicit in the grandmother's comments is a tacit epistemology of how this process of discovery works: the role of intuition, the prodding of a bad fortune that must be revealed. In contrast, the second quotation above presents a very different picture of the nature of future events, one where nothing is set in stone, and the future is up for the making! This quotation is the first of 'four principles of luck', as identified by the psychologist Richard Wiseman in his research on what it means to be lucky. Wiseman's work suggests that good or bad luck, far from being external forces or unchangeable 'gifts', are to a great extent created by the people who experience them, and their particular attitudes to life. The four principles that he identifies embody the psychological mechanisms that underpin the differences between living a lucky and unlucky life.

These two quotations begin this chapter's brief review of (some) contemporary views of luck, fate and fortune. Both, in their different ways, raise one of the most persistent concerns of these themes: that is, to what extent can our futures be said to be controlled by external forces — and what does that mean for the concept of free will? This chapter will explore, albeit briefly, contemporary approaches, both popular and philosophical, to this aspect of luck, fate and fortune, tracing its roots in ancient philosophical developments. Together, these will then provide a useful context for our exploration of the nature and evolution of the models of *moira* and *tuche* in ancient Greek culture.

Nowadays, we might think that many, if not most, of us are less likely than ancient Greek men and women to think of supernatural or metaphysical forces influencing our actions. But, as an experiment, plug the term 'fate' into a search engine: the result includes computer games, dress designers and rock bands. At first, this seems to suggest the inevitable and irreversible dilution of this word, but, amidst this wealth of webpagery there are plenty of stories in which the word appears to evoke the unknown destiny of some individual (e.g., 'so-and-so awaits their fate'). Even more to our point, there are sites that offer to help you 'find your fate', via a vast variety of techniques for revealing the future ('personalised fate-finding services'), including astrology, numerology, gemology, graphology or dream analysis. Obviously (and as the initial quotation of this chapter itself suggests) this is not a strange new phenomenon of the Internet: a vast variety of techniques to discover what the future has in store has existed from earliest times across most cultures. Perhaps modern media simply makes it easier to find, to share – and to enjoy. *Fate Magazine* ('True Reports of the Strange and Unknown') has been going strong since 1948, and is aimed at an audience 'seeking both answers and entertainment.' *Chat! It's Fate* was started in 2001 as a biannual, but went to a monthly circulation only five years later, in response to demand. It offers a mixture of insights and personalised advice, usually alongside accounts of a wide array of other paranormal events and experiences. Both magazines provide ample opportunities for readers to write in about their own experiences. The editor of *Chat! It's Fate* tells me that her readers, while fully appreciating that they have free will, love the idea of Fate, especially in relation to 'meeting their life partners': she says that 'They seek answers as their destiny and their lifepath'.[3] Underpinning these magazines and their web relations, there appears to be a conception of fate that might be described as encompassing some form of philosophical 'determinism' – a 'family of views' that hold that a causal chain of factors generate both what we choose to do and what we do.[4]

Throughout history, ideas about the origin of such controlling causal factors have ranged from the supernatural or metaphysical (e.g., fate, god, *karma*), to aspects of us as individuals (e.g., character, psychology, genetic make-up), to our role as members of a particular community (e.g., social and cultural conditioning). Most approaches, like that expressed by the editor of the magazine, *Chat! It's Fate*, allow for some overlap between individual choice and an established fate. Nevertheless, in the realm of philosophy, there are (still) some classical hard determinists, who simply deny the possibility of free will at all. This position takes three forms: i) natural determinism, which is closest perhaps to the views based on genetics above, which holds that the laws of nature, combined with past states, can lead to only one future state; ii) logical determinism, which holds that every proposition is either true or false, and that holds true of future statements; and finally, iii) 'epistemic determinism', which can be described as a variety of logical determinism, and turns on the foreknowledge of a god or other supernatural/higher power.[5]

The doctrines of divine foreknowledge and/or divine providence both threaten to lead to fatalism, which can be described as a form of determinism, insofar as it suggests that an individual's deliberations and decisions bear not at all on his/her actions and what happens to him/her.[6] The difference is, however, that fatalism does not explain the causal chain that has led to events; it simply asserts that what happens (or has happened) must happen (or have happened). Nowadays, it is generally understood to encompass 'the refusal of modernity – a repudiation of a controlling orientation to the future in favour of an attitude which lets events come as they will.'[7] Cast like this, fatalism is simply incompatible with the idea that any form of deliberation, decision-making or action is relevant to the course of events. For fatalism to work effectively, there is no need for a divine figure at its centre: the idea of *karma* in Buddhism is fatalistic, but does not utilise any form of agency.[8]

More recently, many New Age beliefs include the idea that a higher power (called by a variety of names, ranging, for example, from 'the Universe' to the 'Universal Mind' or 'Cosmic Consciousness', to 'All That Is' to 'God' and/or 'Goddess') is directing events so that the cosmos is universally interconnected, benevolent and in (morally) perfect balance; there are no mistakes, no accidents, and human judgement on any event or action is unnecessary (and counter-productive). This vision of the interconnected, directed and evolving universe usually exists side-by-side with a philosophy of individual self-empowerment, which encourages the search for/evolution towards one's 'higher self', one's real identity, which is linked to or comprises the higher power, and which follows the cosmic plan and directs our behaviour.[9]

Some of these themes can be traced in contemporary self-help books. Sandra K. Dolby sees in them a response to certain concepts of the 'self' current in American culture, such as individualism, competition and control. The prevalence of self-help books suggests that these concepts are increasingly a focus of concern and reflection; nevertheless, their values and roles in daily life remain ambiguous. The solution offered by these self-help writers includes the idea that the universe and all in it are one, and are to be trusted and accepted. As Wayne Dyer puts it in *Staying On the Path* 'Everything that is happening is supposed to be happening'.[10]

This may seem to have a strongly deterministic aspect. However, in most self-help books, this is balanced by the belief that once we realise the difference between our higher and more mundane selves, then we will realise how we create our own reality – and take responsibility for it. Back to Dr Dyer, 'Believe it and you'll see it; know it and you'll *be* it!'; or, in more detail, the guidance of Mihaly Csikszentmihalyi: 'The more psychic energy we invest in the future of life, the more we become a part of it. Those who identify with evolution blend their consciousness with it, like a tiny creek joining an immense river, whose currents become as one. Hell in this scenario is simply the separation of the individual from the flow of life. It is clinging to the past, to the self, to the safety of inertia … within an evolutionary framework, we can focus consciousness on the tasks of everyday life in the knowledge that when we act in the fullness of the flow experience we are also building a bridge to the future of our universe.'[11]

Some recent studies of ideas about luck offer similar notions of being at one with a higher power. Modern rational descriptions of luck may portray it as an unstable, external and uncontrollable factor. But a study conducted in 1997 suggested that some people think of luck as something personal, stable and dependable, consistently bringing them success day-to-day, and continuing to do so in the future.[12] Holding these beliefs did not indicate that these people necessarily thought of themselves as 'fortunate', or that they would simply trust to luck: like those who believe in fate, as described above, those who believed in luck in this way, still thought that personal qualities and skills were important in the conduct of their daily lives. A number of studies have suggested that such beliefs may offer those who hold them both a source of hope for the future and a sense of control over daily events.[13] As Wiseman's work, mentioned above, suggests, it seems that simply holding a set of beliefs like this can actually give rise to a lucky life, since they shape how we act and behave.

In our modern society, it appears that people can believe that fate, a higher power, and luck all play a role in directing their lives, while still believing in, if not stressing the importance of, their own autonomy. Serious questions about free will do arise when we come to new scientific discoveries such as the role of the genetic code, or a greater understanding of the influence of social conditioning on behaviour – and we see these expressed vividly in fiction, for example Aldous Huxley's *Brave New World*, which famously depicts a society whose members appear to make choices, but have in fact been programmed from birth. In *Brave New World Revisited*, Huxley described how he feared his vision becoming a reality as a result of 'ever more effective methods of mind-manipulation', as 'more and more of every nation's affairs are managed by the bureaucrats of Big Government and Big Business'.[14] More recently, the activist magazine *Adbusters* campaigns against just such mind-manipulation, revealing widespread popular concern about the power of commercial forces to manipulate actions and decisions.

While quantum physics may appear to have banished the idea of certainty from the realm of the physical sciences, (scientific) exploration of the mechanisms of the human mind and body suggest quite the opposite, implying or reinforcing the idea that our deliberations and actions – our futures – are somehow predetermined by past facts and laws of nature.[15] Although some popular debates in these areas rest on technical misunderstandings (for example, about the significance of particular discoveries in genomics), this does not hold for all of them, nor are they to be simply dismissed as unimportant. Not only do they show something of the range of attitudes towards these technologies, but they also illuminate widely held values and beliefs – and profound uncertainties – not only about how individuals make decisions and the nature of autonomy and causation, but also about how we allocate blame, accountability and responsibility.[16] Here, perhaps, we may find the greatest overlap between popular questions about free will and determinism, and philosophical approaches to those concerns.

Since the seventeenth century, philosophers have argued over the nature of the relationship between free will and determinism.[17] Incompatibilists hold that determinism and free will simply cannot both exist. This leads to one of two basic positions: either determinism is true, in which case possibilities for action are dictated by laws of nature and past events – so we have no free will and no responsibility for our actions. (This is the Consequence Argument, and holding it leads to a 'hard determinist' position.[18]) Alternatively, although free will and determinism are incompatible, nevertheless we can still believe in the existence of free will ('soft determinism').[19] As a result, one argument is that all actions must be free and there is no such thing as determinism (the 'libertarian view'[20]); but this leaves open the puzzling question of what an undetermined life – one entirely the result of chance – must look and feel like.[21] Alternatively, we can argue that free will is possible because of something about the nature of determinism (the 'indeterminist view'). Indeterminism usually takes one of three basic approaches: non-causal theories, event-causal theories and agent-centred accounts: all three turn on a common idea that an agent may take action without that action being caused deterministically, but they take very different approaches. Agent-centred explanations link the performance of an action to the inherent power of an individual; non-causal explanations deny the need to link the performance of an action to an individual's reasons for acting; and 'event-causal' may link an individual's reason and action, but undeterministically.[22]

But perhaps the conflict between free will and determinism is an illusion? This is the argument of the compatibilists, an umbrella term for those who hold a wide range of views that free will and determinism can co-exist. Classical compatibilists argued that so long as we have the capacity and the opportunity to do otherwise, then we have free will (the principle of alternative possibilities, or PAP).[23] But this was seriously undermined by the Consequence argument of the determinists. It is after all possible for us to act according to our own will or desire, even when that will or desire is somehow manipulated by some other force, be it some kind of mental disorder, genetic code or cultural conditioning, or even in situations where we lack an alternative course of action. This concern has led to the development of a variety of other compatibilist approaches. The primary focus of most of these modern discussions is the relationship between freedom/determinism and moral responsibility. Although some still argue that freedom and responsibility are one and the same, others now hold that moral responsibility need not entail free will in the sense of alternative choices for action. For example, Daniel

Dennett argues that even if an individual feels compelled to act by his or her character and circumstances, then s/he has the kind of free will that matters, and still counts as morally responsible. This compatibilist approach recognises determinism in the individual's characters and motives, but stresses the presence of free will and moral responsibility.[24] Harry Frankfurt offers a different approach that turns on circumstance rather than character: he has used a variety of intriguing examples to show how, even in situations where there is no alternative possibility for action, individuals can still be held to be responsible for their actions.[25] To explain how this might work, he has gone on to develop a theory of action that turns on reflective self-evaluation, in which a person's different desires interact with each other. He argues that so long as our desires do not conflict then we have free will, even if some of those desires are determined.[26]

Building on these so-called 'Frankfurt examples', John Martin Fischer has argued for a 'semi-compatibilist' position, in which moral freedom is compatible with determinism, because it does not depend on an individual having alternative choices for action. Nevertheless, a lack of alternatives may still mean lack of freedom.[27] In contrast, other philosophers, such as David Widerker, have argued against Frankfurt's examples: for example, Widerker has argued that if an individual cannot avoid acting in a particular way, then he/she cannot reasonably be held to blame.[28] Taking another approach, Galen Strawson, meanwhile, has argued for compatibilism on the grounds that our concepts of moral responsibility are a result of our belonging to moral communities and being the agents and recipients of morally reactive attitudes.[29]

Meanwhile, the philosophical problem of 'moral luck' raises some similar questions – and poses some new problems. First raised in 1976 by Bernard Williams and Thomas Nagel, the notion of moral luck focuses on the question of moral assessment in apparently contingent circumstances – how can we evaluate morality if events and actions are the result of luck?[30] Apparently, Bernard Williams actually intended the phrase, 'moral luck', to evoke an oxymoron, but one that crucially challenged widespread modern ideas of 'the immunity of morality to luck'.[31] This notion may seem to offer what

Williams called 'a solace to a sense of the world's unfairness', but even so, there are situations in which we hold individuals responsible, despite the significant role played by luck – this is moral luck.[32] For example, under the Nazi regime, German citizens could choose to co-operate or to oppose their government, and we hold them responsible for that choice. However, the notion of moral luck raises the possibility that we cannot hold those German citizens responsible: they were simply unlucky enough to be living in Germany at this particular time, whereas citizens of other countries were never placed in this position (they were morally lucky in this sense). This is one of the examples given by Thomas Nagel to illustrate one of the four kinds of moral luck he identified as impacting objective moral assessment. These are: constitutive (the kind of person you are); circumstantial (the kind of situation one faces – for example, living under a Nazi regime, as above); luck in the way things turn out; and the luck of those circumstances that precede and influence a particular action. When we think about events and actions in these terms, then the actor's scope for moral agency and responsibility becomes sharply diminished. As Nagel noted, 'when the seemingly natural requirement of fault or responsibility is applied in light of these facts . . . Ultimately, nothing or almost nothing about what a person does seems to be under his control.'[33]

Many responses to this assessment of moral luck focus on dismantling the four particular types of luck. For example, a number of philosophers have dismissed the idea of constitutive luck, arguing that the question of what kind of person one is cannot be considered a matter of luck – it is not out of one's control.[34] Others have argued against the idea of resultant moral luck by pointing out the difference between moral and social judgements. For example, consider our moral response to two negligent drivers, one of whom kills a child who jumps out in front of them, while the other does not. Our moral evaluation of these drivers is the same, the argument runs, although society may feel very differently about them, and treat them quite differently.[35] The Nazi question posed above (circumstantial luck) has been tackled in a variety of ways that emphasise the moral significance of the collaborator's wicked character.[36]

Another approach to denying moral luck is to consider it as a question about the nature of agency and free will (if all events are a matter of luck, then to what extent can we be considered as making free choices?). As discussed above, some indeterminist agent-centred explanations of action deny the need to explain actions beyond the individual. Others involved in the free will debate accept moral luck, arguing that it can still be compatible with free will, so long as one can distinguish the agent's capacity to exert control.[37]

Those who argue for the significance of moral luck usually argue for some kind of shift in society's idea of morality. The most famous of these takes us back to Bernard Williams, who considered the question of moral luck from the point of view of the subject – asking how luck might influence an individual's moral choices. As his example, he (famously) considered the painter Gauguin, and his choice to abandon his family for his art. Williams argued that Gauguin's choice could only be morally evaluated in retrospect: since it succeeded because of lucky extrinsic events, then it provides an example of moral luck. Although, or perhaps because, this article appeared to reveal morality's vulnerability to luck, in a later crucial postscript to his work Williams argued that, in taking this approach, he intended to preserve morality's immunity to luck, and highlight the realm of ethics, as concerned with situations in which luck plays a role.[38]

In modern philosophy, problems of moral luck and morality, and free will and determinism are concerned with the conditions that create moral responsibility, and the identification of the nature of moral agency. In ancient philosophy, the question of free will vs. determinism, in the sense that a modern philosopher might recognise, only really begins to emerge with the later philosophers – in the teachings of Epicurus, for example, and in the beliefs of the Cynics and Stoics, whose philosophies took shape towards the end of the fourth century BCE.[39] The Cynics, Epicureans and Stoics also sought to find a way of realising a life of value that was not susceptible to luck. These ideas were also discussed before them by the philosophers Plato and Aristotle, each of whom took very different approaches to this question.[40] Plato argued for the achievement of a good life, immune from luck; Aristotle suggested, in contrast, that a good human life is necessarily full of incident and experience – and this will, by necessity, be susceptible to the vagaries of luck. In Aristotle's approach one may exert control over one's virtue (*arête*), but not over one's achievement of the good life (*eudaimonia*).

This does not mean that pre-Hellenistic Greeks did not raise philosophical questions about the nature of right conduct and responsibility. Such concerns do appear in philosophical writings much earlier – although they take some intriguing forms. It is worth briefly exploring these, because some of the themes they raise will appear again in discussions of the members of the Ministry of Misfortune. For example, the earliest writers of what we now call philosophy – the pre-Socratics, or Ionian naturalists – seem not to have explicitly discussed the question of free will as we now recognise it, but appear more concerned with the nature of the physical world. So, for example, Anaximander, in his description of the principle and element of existing things, what he called 'the unbounded' (*to apeiron*), wrote about how things come into being and are destroyed 'according to necessity' (*kata to chreon*).[41] Heraclitus used a similar phrase in a fragment in which he describes how 'all things happen by strife and necessity' (*kat' erin kai chreon*).[42] Parmenides described 'what must be' in a slightly different sense, insofar as his 'what is' exists, and there is no alternative other than non-existence.

However, aspects of these discussions certainly imply some kind of ethical stance: all three writers gave descriptions of the natural world in terms of the natural correction, and punishment, of injustice.[43] The fragment of Anaximander mentioned above, continues 'for they pay penalty and retribution to each other for their injustice according to the assessment of Time'. In turn, Parmenides explained that Justice controls 'what is', which is limited, restrained by strong Necessity, and bound by *Moira*/Fate 'to be whole and motionless'.[44]

This metaphor of crime and punishment as part of the role of natural justice is put even more vividly in the writings of Heraclitus, who, in one fragment describes how the *Erinyes*, supernatural creatures who were responsible for administering mortal justice, and whom he calls 'ministers of justice', maintain the route of the sun. But further fragments suggest that perhaps this was not so much a metaphor as an expression of the way he understood cosmic justice to encompass the operation of all things, extending beyond natural phenomena to human interaction. So the fragment describes how 'Those who speak with sense must put their strength in what is common to all, as a city in law – and much more strongly. For all human laws are nourished by one, the divine [law]; for it controls as much as it wishes, and it is sufficient for all, and is left over.'[45] Moreover, if mortals transgress, then Justice 'will catch up with the fabricators and purveyors of lies'.[46] However, there is still a gap between cosmic and mortal comprehension of justice: 'To God everything is fine and good and just; but men have taken some things to be unjust and others to be just.'[47] This last fragment, especially if taken with his comments about the necessity of strife, above, do suggest a world view rather similar to those found among some contemporary New Age philosophies, that everything is accounted for by a higher power. It is a position that easily confuses descriptive with prescriptive laws – Heraclitus appears to be arguing that there is a cosmic law – and it must be followed. In this context, one final tantalising fragment should also be introduced: it states simply 'Man's character is his *daimon*',[48] where *daimon* seems to mean a man's personal divine guide. We will discuss the role of *daimones* in the next section, but what this suggests is that Heraclitus may have understood this cosmic certainty to operate, in some way, at the level of the individual. This brief statement may indicate that an individual has some control over his future – through his own character.[49] But it could also be read as meaning just the opposite: that *even* a person's character comprises a divine allocation. Either way, as we will see, it prefigures some popular models of luck, fate and fortune that we will find in many later texts.

Indeed, a number of these ideas will prove influential – for example, the notion of 'what must be' in accordance with cosmic law will reappear in the work of the atomists and Stoics, playing a crucial part in the modern philosophical problem of free will and determinism.[50] More immediately, for our purposes, we find, more or less spelled out in these writers, ideas about the relationship between the divine, justice, cosmic necessity and day-to-day mortal life. As we will see, these ideas will prove fundamental to our understanding of, in particular, the initial and developing nature and role of *moira*.

Besides these assertions of moral authority, there is little evidence in the pre-Socratic writings of any questioning of the nature of moral responsibility.[51] Explicit philosophical discussions of responsibility emerge most overtly in literary evidence from Athens in the fifth century – and perhaps this is not surprising, bearing in mind the extensive role of litigation in this ancient city – alongside the rise of the sophist movement, which comprised travelling teachers who questioned traditional ideas. A number of the early discussions of moral responsibility by the sophists are written in the form of speeches of defence: for example, Antiphon's *Tetralogies*, four law court speeches, two for the prosecution and two for the defence; while Gorgias' *Helen* gives a comprehensive explanation of why Helen is not to be considered responsible for the events that led to the Trojan War.[52] Debating these matters alongside the sophists, the famous philosopher Socrates and his companions famously analysed questions of virtue and the nature of goal-directed action, while, on the Athenian stage, the tragic writers presented complex problems of responsibility.[53]

We should not regard these investigations as appearing out of nowhere: as we will see, the question of mortal relationships with the gods, and the role of mortal character in assessing attributions of responsibility are already a theme of Greek literature. Nor are they limited to philosophical settings; questions of moral responsibility continue to be debated and explored in a variety of ways, across different forums and a range of literary genres. It may be the effect of evidence, but it appears that during the fifth century we are witnessing what we might call a 'first enlightenment', during which traditional conceptions of how the world worked and the locus of authority, divine as well as mortal, were questioned.[54] It is in this environment that we find the concept of *tuche* beginning to come into its own.

## CHAPTER II

# A MINISTRY OF MISFORTUNE

They call you Lady Luck
But there is room for doubt
At times you have a very unladylike way
Of running out

You're on this date with me
The pickin's have been lush
And yet before this evening is over
You might give me the brush

You might forget your manners
You might refuse to stay
And so the best that I can do is pray

Luck be a lady tonight
Luck be a lady tonight
Luck if you've ever been a lady to begin with
Luck be a lady tonight

From *Guys and Dolls* [1]

In a sewer in New York city, the tough-talking, high-rolling gambler, Sky Masterson, stands poised among a crowd of hoodlums, ready to roll dice. In love with Sergeant Sarah Brown of the Save-A-Soul Mission, Sky must make good his promise to deliver 'one dozen genuine sinners' to be saved by the good sergeant, or lose her forever. And so, when he stumbles on Nathan Detroit's craps game, now being held in a sewer (as the only place safe from the law) Sky issues a bet: if he wins, then his fellow hustlers must attend a prayer meeting at the Mission; if he loses, he must pay them one thousand dollars each. It all depends on the dice – and the attitude of 'Lady Luck'. The setting of this scene in the musical *Guys and Dolls* may be quintessentially the New York of the 1930s, as depicted, originally, by the writer Damon Runyon, but the image of Lady Luck goes back much further . . .

Swathed in a cloak and wearing a mural crown, a female figure sits, one foot hidden beneath her tunic, the other resting on the shoulder of a naked man swimming, or perhaps flailing, at her feet. Relaxed, yet alert, she leans slightly forward, her right elbow propped on her knee, and gazes out into middle distance. Her left hand rests calmly on the rock beside her; the position of her right hand indicates that she was holding something. Originally, it was probably a palm leaf, symbolising the victory of the founder of a city, but over time other things may have replaced the leaf – a sheaf of corn, perhaps – which linked this figure and other aspects of her power to the people she worshipped and the city she represented.[2] This was the *Tuche* of Antioch, originally cast in bronze, created by the artist Eutuchides, probably shortly after 300 BCE.[3] The rock she sits on is Mount Sipylos, the naked male figure is the Orontes River: this was the guardian of Antioch's fortunes, that city's Lady Luck, its *Tuche*.

During the Hellenistic period, the cult of *Tuche* diffused and developed throughout the Mediterranean, proving especially popular in eastern cities. Although we find her combined with local divinities, mythical figures or even local rulers (in one case, she appears as a man), as guardian of a city she usually worked alone – and she worked hard.[4] Most cities in the Hellenistic period seem to have acquired a guardian *Tuche*: her statue would occupy a prominent public position in the city; her image would appear on the local currency.[5] Eutuchides' original statue of the *Tuche* of Antioch is now lost, but we know what it looked like because, after about the first century BCE, this image became increasingly popular.[6] Many cities used the *Tuche* of Antioch as the model for their *Tuche*, adapting her attributes to the local context; she appeared not only on coins from Antioch but also those of other cities.[7] Individuals might carry their own *Tuche* – images of the goddess carved into gemstones and worn as jewellery – or collect souvenirs of Eutuchides' statue cast in bronze, or shaped as glass bottles.[8] Her image was everywhere, revealing the extent of her influence across the Mediterranean – and the development of a shared understanding of, and approach to, the uncertain future.

But behind this Hellenistic Lady Luck lurks a crowd of older concepts, found in the Homeric poems onwards, that are perhaps even more mysterious, and whose responsibilities extended beyond the simple allocation of fortune, to the maintenance of order in the entire universe. The ideas and associations that surround concepts of luck, fate and fortune at this early stage continue to resonate throughout later periods – and, as we will see, can even find echoes in modern times. The most well known of these is *M/moira* ('Fate'), who quickly developed a multiple personification, as the *Moirai* ('The Fates') still referenced in contemporary sources, albeit often in a pseudo-mythological setting.[9]

But *M/moira* also had some relatively less well-known colleagues including *moros*, *A/aisa*, *H/heimarmene* and *P/potmos*. Although these concepts operated in the same general area, they should not necessarily be taken as synonymous: their uses suggest particular nuances and emphases with regard to fate and fortune. In the description that follows, we will take a closer look at *M/moira* and some of these less well-known accomplices, before investigating *T/tuche*'s rise to power.

But, first, a few words about those C/capitals (above), and what they represent: that is, the personification (or not) of some of these concepts.[10] Let us start with a gentle warning: although this capitalisation is a neat device to suggest personification, it had no equivalent in the ancient world, and presents a more definite modern categorisation than the ancient language itself supplies. We may feel more certain about typing a capital if there is evidence for the personification in question receiving cult in the appropriate period, but even in these cases, there is still the lingering concern that its appearance in the text just represents a particular use of a particular metaphor

– essentially, a poetic flourish. In turn, as this last description illustrates, English lacks a fundamental component of ancient Greek – an explicit gender structure. We can talk about 'it' when we refer to an abstract concept: for the Greeks, whether it was personified or not, 'it' always had a gender.[11] This describes some of our semantic difficulties in identifying personification, but we also have to admit to conceptual difficulties.

Scholars have offered a variety of explanations for the personification of abstract concepts in the ancient world. On the one hand, it has been taken to be part of a process of rationalisation, bridging the gap between traditional religious beliefs and developing secularisation.[12] Such an approach risks valorising the traditional, leading to some puzzling criticisms of personified abstracts. In the case of *Tuche*, this has ranged from accusations of instigating cultural deterioration,[13] to celebration as a mark of increasing secularisation, an indication of a move towards more morally challenging concerns: the acknowledgement of personal responsibility and the complex question of free will.[14] The common thread among these arguments is that these abstract concepts, as goddesses, lacked religious meaning. As one scholar neatly put it, 'personification of *tykhe* can be treated more as a grammatical than as a theological phenomenon'.[15]

An alternative approach argues that an ancient perspective on the world would have understood it as filled with divinity – making the personification of abstract concepts a perfectly natural process.[16] Even so, it is still important to examine the context in which certain personifications make their appearance, and to recognise not only that the personification of a particular abstract concept may have answered the needs of a particular moment, but also that it/she/he was likely to have been religiously significant. These two aspects are likely to have been linked, timing and need reinforcing meaning, and vice versa.[17]

When these aspects can be seen to coincide, they can offer very satisfying historical explanations for personifications. For example, the concepts that acquire personifications across cultures in the Archaic period tend to cluster in 'the sphere of power and justice, of moral admonition and intensive pleading.'[18] They are concepts that strengthen community values, reinforce the idea of order; give legs to these ideals. All of this fits well within a context in which communities were taking shape, and community values were gaining increasing attention. This insight may help to explain the rise of *M/moira(i)*, especially those aspects related to ideas of cosmic order. Meanwhile, the plethora of personifications in the last quarter of the fifth century in Athens may be explained by people's need to 'compensate for the poor performance of the traditional gods.'[19] This in turn may provide a context for understanding the development of *Tuche*.

Nevertheless, we should neither lose sight of the cognitive messiness that leads to and underpins these neat explanations, nor try to elude it. The evidence suggests that both the process of personification and the development of cult in honour of that personification are processes of the individual and cultural imagination, which are responsive to context. Such processes may take time; they may not occur immediately nor simultaneously, but gradually and piecemeal.[20] Some personifications and/or cults may form part of a response to particular circumstances; others may be attributed to a more general human experience. As an example, consider the multiplication of ancient Greek personifications relating to Death, a range that probably offered mortals (and, indeed, might illustrate for modern observers) something of the variety of responses that death may have provoked. *Thanatos*, 'Death' himself, although personified from early on, is usually described as not being worshipped, whereas personifications of the various phases of dying do seem to have received cult. Such a variety of personifications may have offered people a way to think about the different forces or events in mortal lives that were (still are?) otherwise inexplicable or unavoidable.[21]

This leads to a final point: in ancient Greece, people tended to imagine certain experiences and emotions that we think of as internal events as attacking an individual from outside his or her body. The evidence suggests that the ancients in any particular time or place did not need to categorise such incidents as clearly as the modern scholar demands. Would it have been necessary to present these concepts/gods always as fully personified, or enough to indicate in particular situations a sense of them as somehow being embodied? Abstract concepts that were only sometimes, somehow, animate may simply have offered greater scope for the expression and understanding of a particular and intense experience. In this respect, were the Greeks so unlike us?

Fate, in both her ancient and modern guises, might provide us with a particularly good example of this phenomenon. As we shall see, in contrast to luck, 'fate' in the singular is seldom wholly personified in the ancient world – and this is also the case nowadays. Indeed, I have found only one modern 'personification' who lays claim to Fate as his identity. Dr. Fate (from the DC Comics stable of superheroes) was invented by Gardner Fox (who was heavily influenced by H. P. Lovecraft) and drawn by Howard Sherman, and first appeared in *More Fun Comics* #55 (May 1940). He has since been repeatedly reincarnated – wearing diverse versions of his original fabulous blue and gold costume.[22] He was certainly mysterious. For the first year of his existence at least, he had no backstory, and no alter ego: 'Dwelling apart from mankind in his lonely tower north of ghost-ridden Salem is the mysterious Dr. Fate, who calls upon secret and ancient sources for the power with which he fights unusual crimes.'[23] For later readers, there was more information but perhaps even less clarity: in one account, one 'Kent Nelson' gained his powers from an ancient Egyptian magician/ alien/supernatural being, in another, he was the protégé of ancient gods.[24] But, despite his splendid name, costume, occult powers and isolation, Dr. Fate does not offer any connection to future uncertainty.[25] His remit remains limited, as he himself says: 'Such is my lot – to guard mankind from the weird threats of eerie evil!'[26] And yet, we still might see in this cartoon character an accurate depiction of modern attitudes to fate, in which Fate is a something of a cipher – a mysterious figure of great power, but with little explicit character. As we will see, this modern incarnation may also capture something of the nature of the ancient vision, as well. In what follows, I will use a lower-case letter for the supernatural entities under discussion, except where they are clearly personified.

## *Moira*

Starting with the great epic poems of Homer, conceptions of fate in earlier Greek literary sources are dominated by *moira*.[27] As noted already, most scholars hold that this conception of fate arose from the idea of a 'share' or 'allocation' – the literal translation of the Greek word – which carries with it a further sense of the natural, and right, regulation of all things. This meaning is apparent in simple phrases that use the term, such as '*kata moiran*', which is used to indicate that something has happened 'as it should', in a way that conforms to, and maintains, social and cosmic order; an act that does not conform may be regarded as a dangerous act of transgression.[28]

In the *Iliad*, *moira* tends to be found in connection with death, either in phrases that mean 'it was fated (for someone) to die';[29] or alongside *thanatos* (death) itself (they are described as 'prepared' together for someone[30]); or accompanying the fatal machinations of a god.[31] It has been argued that these uses reveal an active agent or deity of death, and certainly there are cases when *moira* could be characterised in such a way, for example, when death and *moira* are described as 'overpowering' a mortal.[32] However, this is not true of all uses of the term in the Homeric epics; as some of the examples above suggest, sometimes *moira* seems closer to a neutral meaning of 'a share'.

Moreover, to describe *moira*'s remit as confined to death does not convey the full range of its role as we find it in other passages. Elsewhere we find *Moira* seemingly personified, not so much an agent or angel of death as an engineer of situations.[33] For example, in the *Iliad* we find Lycaon, a young prince of Troy, blaming *Moira* for placing him (for a second time) in the hands of the fearsome warrior Achilles; in a second passage the narrator cites *Moira* as the reason why the Trojan prince Hector is caught outside the city gates to face Achilles, although his fellow soldiers have all managed to flee.[34] But not all the situations in which *Moira* is named are fatal either: in his apology to Achilles, King Agamemnon blames *Moira*, alongside the *Erinyes* and Zeus, for the bad behaviour that led to his insulting Achilles; again, *Moira* has helped bring this situation about, afflicting Agamemnon with the *Ate* (madness) that caused him to act, rather than doing anything directly.[35]

*Moira* may have something of a larger sphere of activity in the *Odyssey*: it retains its fatal associations, still leading particular individuals to their deaths, while extending and reinforcing its other roles. So, the phrase 'it is fated', largely used to describe death in the *Iliad*, is used to describe, for example, the travels (and eventual return of) Odysseus.[37] However, the term is most frequently used in the phrase *kata moiran* to describe how appropriately people have spoken, or how they have conducted particular daily rituals (the allocation of meat, the fitting of oars, the division of spoils); Odysseus uses the same phrase to berate the Cyclops, after he has consumed some of his fellow sailors.[38] *Moira* seems to be understood to provide some kind of structure for the activities of mortal life: so Penelope, Odysseus' lonely wife, says of the mortal need for sleep, 'the gods have made for mortals a *moira* for each thing'.[39]

This last example introduces the vexing question of the relationship between *moira* and the gods, which is shifting and ambiguous in both *Iliad* and *Odyssey*. The gods sometimes appear to be in charge of fate, especially Zeus – perhaps most famously in the image of the urns and the lots, which Achilles describes as he comforts Priam, father of Hector, the Trojan prince whom Achilles has butchered. As Achilles tells it, Zeus sits with two urns, one containing ills, the other blessings, and it is he that allocates these lots to mortals. But in other examples, the relationship between Zeus and *moira* is more equivocal; for example, Zeus may be implementing events, but the pattern of those events has already been devised – by *moira*.[40] The gods are also found to be subject to *moira* and described as themselves appealing to fate when they are rescuing particular individuals or trying to change the course of events.[41] There is possibly a greater emphasis on the role of the gods rather than *moira* in the *Odyssey*.[42] But how difficult this relationship is to define can be illustrated by the variety of interpretations of the significance of the phrase, '*moira* of the god/gods' a formula that first appears in that poem.[43] For some scholars, it has indicated that *moira* is simply a part of the gods; others have argued that it may represent the exact opposite: that the gods are the agents of *moira*; finally, an alternative reading interprets this phrase as simply evoking the boundaries of divine power.[44]

In addition, we should not forget mortal relationships with *moira* and the course of events. Not only can mortals dramatically transgress *moira* (see above), they are also instrumental in bringing *moira* about. In the *Odyssey*, Zeus complains about the way mortals blame the gods for their misfortunes, when in fact their own behaviour means they suffer more than their lot. In the *Iliad*, mortals are part of a complex web of causality – so the death of Achilles' companion Patroclus is attributed to Zeus; the purpose of Zeus; the gods; Apollo; Zeus and Apollo; – and *moira*; and Apollo, Euphorbus and Hector.[45]

What can we conclude? First some impressions about *moira*: the lack of a single clear theory in these poems is probably to do, at least partly, with the method of their composition, which means that they encompass a range of different beliefs held at various times – as we have noted, we can see a similar process at work in contemporary references to luck, fate and fortune. However, it also carries an important indication of the nature of the exploration to come, and the difficulties of interpreting these ancient concepts in a way that satisfies any current desire for distinct categories.

Perhaps more importantly, we can observe how the complex relationships between mortal, divine and supernatural provide an account of events that offers both flexibility (who *does* what, why?) and what we might call overdetermination (who *did* what, why?) that is powerful in terms of both evoking human experience and constructing the poems' narratives. In the *Iliad*, there is an episode in which the gods discuss the *moira* (literally 'allotted share' of mortals): Zeus is looking down on his mortal son Sarpedon, unable to decide whether he should let him be killed on the battlefield of Troy, or snatch him away from death. Hera, his wife and sister, notes that if Zeus chooses to save him, then other gods may also want to do this . . . It has been observed that this suggests a notion of fate that is more like the 'rules of the game' than 'a natural law or a Calvinistic predetermination'.[46] But the possibilities that it raises presumably mean that there is a reason why mortals may pray to the gods (as both Greeks and Trojans pray to Zeus before the duel between Paris and Menelaus) or simply attempt to change a situation (as Hector tries to persuade Paris to take up arms, and not sit in his royal apartments with Helen while the battle rages around the city).[47] In turn, we find Zeus can vacillate (for example, as he watches Patroclus fighting Hector) and, as we have seen, may be moved to compassion or even pity by the experiences of the mortals he watches.[48] By revealing divine and mortal responses to the constraints of fate, these descriptions help to shed light on the character of individuals, both mortal and divine.[49]

The workings of fate are seldom revealed to common mortals. The artistry of Homer maintains a hauntingly opaque veil between mortal and god: whereas the poems of the epic cycle may contain oracles and prophecy aplenty, they are not a feature of the *Iliad* and *Odyssey*.[50] We should not be surprised, then, to find Homer's characters talk of endurance: for example, in the *Iliad*, the enduring soul that the *Moirai* have given to men is described by the god Apollo as he chides the other deities for allowing Achilles to abuse Hector's corpse; in comparison, Achilles instructs Priam to endure because grieving will not bring back his son. In the *Odyssey*, Nausicaa prettily lectures the stranger washed up on the beach (Odysseus) on the need for him to endure his fate, before inviting him home to her father's palace; while on his return home, Odysseus gives the suitor Amphinomus one last moral lesson about the importance of enduring one's fate.[51] The rhetoric that surrounds fate is already one of caution and consolation. In terms of the former, the message seems to be that one should not trust the gods;[52] of the latter, the comfort that misfortune is inevitable is a rhetorical trope that will run and run.[53] But endurance is not the same as resignation: across the epics, as well as their strong belief in the power of gods and/or fate, individuals reveal their determination to play an active part in creating future events – and this also provides the narrative with a rich source of characterisation.[54]

Mortal comment on *moira* and/or the gifts of the gods are always at some level explanatory – a way of making sense of what has happened – but this explanation is treated in different ways. The gifts of the gods are a source of pride for the Trojan prince Paris;[55] and provide an explanation of events for Priam, king of Troy, that means he need not blame Helen for what has happened, and can find surprising compassion for her plight;[56] Hector offers Andromache some thoughts on fate, not only as a comfort for her, but also as a way of explaining why he cannot yield to her entreaties not to go outside the city and fight.[57] As noted, an interesting use of fate offered as an excuse for behaviour occurs in Agamemnon's speech of apology to Achilles in the *Iliad*, where, alongside the *Erinyes* and Zeus himself, *Moira* is said to have cast into his mind *Ate*, a supernatural being who, in turn, caused him to insult Achilles.[58] Is the excuse intended to excuse his actions entirely? Not for the audience: the king has admitted his guilt to Nestor earlier.[59] But it certainly suggests that he had little room for choice in the moment. And the reason for this supernatural ambush? On the one hand, Zeus can be deceptive: for example, when he sends a dream messenger to tell Agamemnon to send his troops to fight in the absence of Achilles, so that the Greeks will suffer terrible losses; or when he instructs Athene to go in disguise among the Trojans and persuade one of them to break the ceasefire.[60] On the other hand, *Moira* and the *Erinyes* seem not to have this capacity for deception, so does their presence indicate the justice-wielding, order-enforcing aspect of Zeus here? If so, it might suggest that, for some unnamed offence, Agamemnon was being punished; even, that this is what Agamemnon himself is trying to suggest. Or is he, in fact, doing what people who apologise somewhat grudgingly often do, that is, bring up what they perceive to be the other person's offence within their own apology: is Agamemnon, in fact, not so subtly telling Achilles that he understands *Achilles'* behaviour to be a result of *Ate*?

# The *Moirai*

In the Homeric epics, *moira* remains for the most part a single, powerful but mysterious entity: there are only two indications of its later, more popular and well-known guise as three spinning sisters, and they occur, as it were, separately – as spinning in one episode, as sisters in another. The first significant mention of spinning occurs as Queen Hecuba describes to Priam how the circumstances of their son Hector's death was established at his birth, when *Moira* spun his thread of life. *Moira*'s activities are clearly associated with imagery of weaving, binding and spinning rope or thread[61] (although in her guise as the *Moirai*, this activity is represented as belonging to only one of the three sisters, Clotho, see below).[62] This imagery (often explicitly) evokes the active creation of a human life and may also provoke the idea that these supernatural entities bind man to his destiny.[63] This, in turn, may have some bearing on the imagery of binding found in binding spells, in which people attempt to control their enemies using formulaic spells: 'I bind so-and-so . . .', aiming their curse specifically at parts of the body or the mind of their victims or other aspects of them that pose some kind of threat.[64]

The three sisters make their one and only appearance in the Homeric epics in a speech by the god Apollo as he berates the other gods for allowing Achilles to abuse Hector's body: it may be that Achilles was distraught over the death of Patroclus, but there is a limit to mourning 'for the *Moirai* have given to men a spirit that endures'.[65] This is the only mention of the *Moirai* in Homer's poems, but other early evidence, albeit slightly later than Homer, indicates a parallel tradition in which *Moira* has multiplied. In Hesiod's *Theogony*, the fateful siblings are even introduced by their names – Clotho ('the Spinner'), Lachesis ('the allocater of lots'), and Atropos ('the one who cannot be turned') – names that obviously evoke important aspects of their activities and relationships with mortals.[66] We also learn a little about their families: their father, Hesiod tells us, is Zeus, but in two different parts of the poem they appear as the daughters of different mothers, with very different implications. Relatively early on in the poem they are daughters of Night, who is also, in this passage, mother of, among others, *Moros* (another word often translated as 'fate', usually with associations of doom, misery or death[67]), *Ker* (a goddess of death), *Momos* ('blame') and *Nemesis* ('retribution'). We are told here that these *Moirai* 'give good and bad to men at their birth to have', that they 'pursue men and gods when they overstep the limits', and do not 'relinquish their anger, until they have extracted vengeance from the man who has erred.' However, later on in the poem they are granted a much happier family: their mother is Themis, and their sisters are the *Horai* ('the Hours' or 'Seasons'), *Dike* ('Justice'), *Eirene* ('Peace'), and *Eunomia* ('Good Order'); here, their responsibilities are limited to giving out good and bad to men.

There is no need to see this conflicting genesis as problematic, or even as mutually exclusive. In some ways, it usefully summarises the conceptual families to which *Moira* in her single or triple personification belongs. These two genealogies neatly evoke her fundamental association with a crowd of characters, sinister or beneficent that were, according to the ancient Greek imagination, involved in maintaining cosmic order and imposing justice.[68] As we have seen, this set of associations, in which *Moira* is linked with the *Erinyes*, and with *Dike* in the pursuit of cosmic justice begins in Homer; it will become more fully developed in the plays of Aeschylus.[69] The combination of justice and order introduces the notion of unavoidability, and *Ananke* or 'necessity' will also join this alliance: the relationships between the three are well summarised by an interchange from Aeschylus' play *Prometheus Bound* in which Prometheus, who dared to oppose the gods, describes to the curious chorus how his ambitions are, indeed must be, restrained by fate.[70] Over time, *Ananke* acquires increasing independence, and sometimes seems to stand in for fate itself.[71]

Only the plural aspect of *Moira*, the *Moirai* appear to have received cult.[72] We might connect this distinction between *Moira* and the *Moirai* with the discussion for reasons of personification at the beginning of the chapter. *Moira* appears to have been regarded as an unalterable force, whereas the *Moirai* could be imagined as overlooking the course of a life, active in shaping its different aspects before it even began. As we might expect, the *Moirai* are found in connection with *Eileithyia*, the goddess of birth,[73] and, at least in Athens, receiving marriage sacrifices, alongside Hera *Teleia*, and Artemis.[74]

The evidence for cults of the *Moirai* starts in the fifth century BCE, and some scholars have taken this as indicative of the beginning of the cult itself (and argued that this kind of personification marked a corruption of the traditional religion, an argument that, we will see, resurfaces around the emergence of cults of *Tuche*).[75] However, others have persisted in positing a much earlier date, arguing that the lack of later evidence is due to older rituals being subsumed by the worship of the Olympian gods.[76] Whichever viewpoint on their age we find most persuasive, information about the cult rituals does seem to hint at a rich and complex ideology. However, since much of this is from incidental descriptions by the second century CE travel-writer Pausanias, it is hard to assemble a fuller picture.

Some of the cults indicate chthonic or negative associations. At Sicyon, the altar of the *Moirai* was in a grove within the sanctuary of the *Semnai/Eumenides* – the 'kindly ones' – who were the transformed versions of their fearsome sisters, the *Erinyes*.[77] Pausanias tells us that both sets of gods received the same sacrifice – involving a pregnant ewe, libations of honey and water or milk (not wine, as comprised the usual libation), and flowers instead of wreaths. The inclusion of the pregnant animal, as well as the odd libation (along with what we know of sacrifice to the *Eumenides* at Athens, conducted at night in silence) indicates that this might be regarded as a 'negatively valued context'.[78] The position of the sanctuary at Sparta, apparently by the grave of the hero Orestes, may also indicate a similar context.[79]

At other cults the lack or inaccessibility of cult imagery is suggestive. For example, Pausanias tells us that there were no images of the *Moirai* in the cult at Thebes, where the sanctuary of the *Moirai* stood in a group alongside the sanctuaries of Themis and Zeus *Agoraios*.[80] In the cult at Corinth on the Acro-Corinth, the images of the *Moirai* were not in view and Pausanias tells us that this was also the case at the temples of Demeter and Persephone. It may be that this indicates some kind of mystery ritual at this sanctuary, and the continued concealing of the cult statues in Pausanias' time was a hangover from these original ritual events. Could the same be true of the *Moirai*?[81]

Other evidence points to close associations with particular gods. Not surprisingly, there were explicit connections with Zeus. At Olympia and Delphi, the *Moirai* were depicted alongside Zeus *Moiragetes*, 'the bringer of fate'. The altar to Zeus with this epithet is on the way to the starting point for the chariot race, and close by is an oblong altar of the *Moirai*; while at Delphi, statues of two *Moirai* stood by an altar of Poseidon, and were accompanied by images of Zeus *Moiragetes* and Apollo *Moiragetes*.[82] Near Acacesium, Arcadia, the *Moirai* and Zeus *Moiragetes* were represented in a relief, set in a portico in the entrance to the temple of the Mistress (*Despoina*).[83] At Megara, they were above the head of the unfinished statue of Zeus, along with the *Horai*. Pausanias reported that this showed how Zeus is 'the only god to be obeyed by fate [*to pepromenon*] and that this god arranges the seasons as is necessary.'[84]

*Moirai* were also part of a cult image of Aphrodite in Amyclae, which comprised a statue seated on a throne. The statue's pedestal was shaped like an altar and adorned with images of gods; the *Moirai* were grouped with Demeter, Persephone, Pluto, the *Horai*, Aphrodite, Athena and Artemis.[85] An even more explicit connection with Aphrodite was found in Athens, where, we are told, there was a statue of Aphrodite, square like a herm, with an inscription that announced that Aphrodite *Ourania* ('Heavenly') was the oldest of those called *Moirai*.[86] This may be connected to stories that link Aphrodite and the *Moirai*, describing them both as the children of Zeus, which can be traced in fragments of Epimenides, a mysterious sixth-century BCE philosopher and poet from Crete.[87]

## The *Moira(i)* and the Afterlife

Although, from about the fourth century BCE, *moira/Moirai*'s role in managing events is somewhat superseded by *Tuche* (see below), its/their strong appeal to the religious imagination of the Greeks appears to continue. Moreover, perhaps unsurprisingly bearing in mind fate's association with death and cosmic order (and punishment), it appears, in the singular and plural, in a vast variety of formulations in funerary inscriptions. Most of these date from after the fourth century, and most evoke a personification of *Moira*, although impersonal forms appear as well. Many of these involve Homeric formulae, which may be a literary conceit, but should also be considered as expressive of popular feeling and belief.[88] These inscriptions usually blame, and protest against, the fate that has caused the death in question, and in that light some scholars have made a convincing case that they are an expression of the ritual lament against fate and death that is also to be found in ancient Greek tragedy.[89]

It makes eminent sense that *moira*'s associations with death and cosmic order/justice might also draw it into the realm of the Orphic mystery cults. Across Greece, a variety of mystery cults existed. Although they may have focused on different gods, they seem to have shared two salient characteristics. First, they were concerned with preparing their members for the afterlife, promising to liberate individuals who joined from the fear of death by revealing secret knowledge and conducting special rituals; secondly, they insisted on secrecy. Those who were initiated into these cults took an oath of silence, which means that, nowadays, relatively little is known about their operations.[90]

Among these cults were some that used Orphic literature, that is, poetry concerning eschatology and theogony, relating myths, ritual instructions and hymns, all of which were attributed to the mythical singer Orpheus.[91] Evidence for the kinds of beliefs and rituals espoused by these cults is found in a number of sacred texts, including a half-carbonised papyrus scroll, found among the remains of a fourth-century BCE funeral pyre at Derveni in Macedonia, which appears to provide a commentary on an Orphic creation story, and a number of inscribed gold leaves, found in graves across the Mediterranean, providing instruction to initiates on what they should do after death.

Most date the Derveni papyrus to the second half of the fourth century, but its contents are thought to be as much as 200 years older. *Moira* makes two major appearances in the text. In the first (col. 18), the author elaborates on most people's understanding of *Moira* and explains that although their understanding is not wrong (that *Moira* 'spun for them and that those things which the *Moira* has spun will be') they lack a proper understanding of the true nature of either *Moira* or spinning. The author's explanation is that 'Orpheus called wisdom *Moira*', where the wisdom in question is that of Zeus, which existed even before Zeus received his name.[92] The author of the Derveni papyrus is anxious to explain the language of the Orphic poem, digging beneath the apparently conventional terms to unearth their real (in his eyes) meaning.[93] The passage is unclear about the genealogy of *Moira*, suggesting that it existed before the gods, as one of the primaeval forces. However, the close relationship between Zeus and *Moira* that it suggests is supported by the second discussion of *Moira* in the text (col. 19, 5–7), which elaborates how 'when they say that the *Moira* spun they say that the wisdom of Zeus ordains how the things that are and the things that come to be and the things that are going to be must come to be and be and cease'.[94]

*Moira* appears to have a similar role in its appearance in at least one of the Orphic gold leaves. It may be described in the text of one tablet with the epithet *pammestoi* or *pammestori*, meaning 'all-inventive'. However, others have read this as the adjective *pamnestoi*, meaning all-remembering, and as applied to *Moirai* in the plural.[95] One suggestion is that the appearance of the Fates in this text is to show how all the events of a person's life are taken into consideration by the gods, who decide on how he will be treated after his death.[96] In another text, *Moira* appears in a more familiar role as a destructive force. The speaker of this text, representing the soul of the initiate, claims his death came about in the following way: 'but *Moira* subdued me and Zeus who wounds with lightning'.[97] The formulation referring to *Moira* first and then to a god is familiar from the Homeric poems.[98] The effect may be to liken the speaker in the text to a Homeric hero, whose life has been brought to its fated end through divine action by *Moira* and Zeus.[99]

Intriguingly, iconographic evidence for fate's role in some kind of initiatory mystery religion may also be apparent on a three-sided relief, believed to originate from Lokroi-Epizephyrioi in S. Italy, and dated to the second half of the fifth century.[100] The figures on the relief may be interpreted as follows: a winged youth holds a set of scales (he may be either the god *Eros*, companion to Aphrodite, or the god *Thanatos*, or 'Death', accompanying the goddess Persephone, or a nameless *daimon*). He is holding a set of scales on which he is weighing two young men; on the lighter side of the scales, a sorrowful Persephone, accompanied by a seated, lyre-playing Orpheus; on the other side, a joyful Aphrodite, and at her side, Clotho spinning. Sourvinou-Inwood argues that this curious assortment of actors corresponds to a scene of rebirth, after a period of purgatory, a crucial part of the Pythagorean cult. This was a mystery cult that drew on Orphic texts and was popular in S. Italy.

In addition to *moira* meaning death, doom or fate, a further aspect is added with the development of the concept of *theia* ('divine') *moira*, meaning 'divine dispensation', which acquires a specific meaning within Plato's philosophy, describing the divine allocation of virtue.[101] Gradually, as we have seen (above), among the philosophers, the role of fate is subsumed within a technical discussion of free will and determinism. Nevertheless, the attributes and personalities of the *Moirai* become increasingly well defined, and evidence of cult continues well into the Graeco-Roman period. As *Tuche* finds a Roman *alter ego* in the Roman goddess of fortune, *Fortuna*, *Moira* will become identified with the Roman *Fatum*, and her three sisters with the *Parcae*.[102]

# Friends of Fate

Among the other words for fate occurring first in Homer's epics, we find *moros* and *morsimos*, *aisa*, *heimarmene* and *potmos*. Like *moira*, the first four of these also seem to have their roots in the idea of a lot or allocation (and all appear with this straightforward meaning in the epic poems), and thus some of them carry more or less explicit associations with notions of social and/or cosmic justice.[103] *Moira, moros, morsimos* and *heimarmene* are thought to originate from various forms of the verb *meireo*, 'to take one's portion', and its passive form *meiromai*, 'to be allotted one's due'. In the Homeric epics, forms of this verb are most commonly found describing the honour due to a particular mortal or semi-divine character; although it does appear, in impersonal form, as a way of describing an individual's time to die.[104] Its appearances in the fifth century are largely in tragedy, where it appears to be used to describe events that have been prepared at the level of the divine, to maintain cosmic order.[105] Thus, in Aeschyhus' *Agamemnon* the murderous Queen Clytemnestra uses the term of the bloody events that will follow her husband King Agamemnon's entrance into the palace: they are *heimarmena dikaios sun theois*, that is 'fated justly/rightly with the gods' and this follows her exhortation to her maids to prepare the infamous purple robe for her husband, so that 'Justice will usher him into the house.' Deianeira's use of the term in Sophocles' *Trachiniae* (l.169) is even more explicitly in this vein – and yet, at the same time, it raises interesting questions for our understanding of ancient 'fate'. Deianeira describes how, before Heracles left on his final journey he produced an oracle tablet he had been given at the oracular sanctuary at Dodona. Such tablets were used both to present questions to the oracle, and, it seems, to receive its answers. This tablet described for him his future – and yet the events that are described in this passage as foretold by the oracle, and therefore as fated (*heimarmena*), do not comprise a single prediction, but two alternative possible futures. On the one hand, the oracle stated, Heracles may die, but on the other, if he survived a year and three months, he could expect a peaceful and untroubled life.

*Potmos* summons a slightly different image of fate's activities: the verb seems to originate in *pipto*, 'I jump or fall', and so could indicate the allocation of a lot, although some scholars have argued for its connection to the falling of a body, that is, to death.[106] Although this idea might itself suggest a sense of doom, in Pindar we find the term used interchangeably with *theos* and *moira* to indicate the origins of goods that include wealth, blessedness and honour.[107] *Potmos* becomes increasingly rare: when used in fifth-century literature, it seems to be intended to invoke a deliberately archaic ideal of fate.[108]

The use of these different terms suggests subtle nuances of meaning: both *moros* and *morsimos* tend to be found in Homer associated with death or a doom-laden event – whether they are being described as occurring or not.[109] In the Homeric epics, *aisa* tends to occur in similar contexts to that of *moira*, but is used more specifically to describe the life-courses and expectations of individuals – *aisa* is described as having spun the thread of life of the Trojan hero Achilles – and is also found in this sense alongside *moira* referring to death.[110] It may be that the seemingly more personal nature of this concept accounts for its association with a *daimon*, a divine entity that often seems to work as some kind of personal assistant of fate (see further below), in the account of the death of Elpenor, a companion of Odysseus who dies falling off a roof that he had drunkenly clambered on to the night before.[111] Later, the term is found in tragedy but rarely used in Attic Greek otherwise, and rarely, if ever, seems to indicate a personified entity.[112]

In contrast, *heimarmene* gradually develops into a distinct personification of fate, gaining an increasingly explicit association with justice. This seems to start with Plato, who is aware of the use of the word in the tragedians.[113] Elsewhere in Plato's works, the term is used without explicit reference to its poetic ancestry to express the existence of an imperative cosmic order, one which ordains the course of events in individual and civic life, until it calls men to their deaths, and organises not only the itinerary of their afterlives, but the events that will occur in the lives they embark on next.[114] Woven throughout the dialogues, the term, in its different forms, adds a sombre note of cosmic causation to discussions.[115] *Heimarmene* occurs again, both in impersonal form, and as a noun, in some of the law court speeches that survive, usually to indicate a prearranged and unavoidable, generally unpleasant event, although, as we will see, with some interesting variations.[116] But the term really comes into its own, as we have seen, in the Hellenistic period when it is adopted by Stoicism to indicate that philosophy's all-encompassing view of fate.[117]

Among all the fates discussed, most appear as impersonal forces, but there is evidence for a personification of *heimarmene*. A pointed amphoriskos of the middle to late fifth century BCE is decorated with a scene showing Helen and Paris attended by a number of personifications of powerful, relevant abstract concepts.[118] The goddess *Himeros* ('Desire') demands Paris' full attention, holding his arm and gazing into his eyes. Helen, meanwhile, is seated in Aphrodite's lap with the goddess *Peitho* ('Persuasion'), standing close by; *Nemesis* ('Retribution') and *Tuche* ('Luck or 'Fortune', the difficulties of translating the term are discussed in more detail below) stand on one side of the goddess and her favourite, while *Heimarmene* is on the other, accompanied by another female figure, who may be *Themis* ('Justice'). This is the name-vase of the *Heimarmene* painter.

## *Daimon(es)*

Sometimes working with these characters, sometimes working alone, *daimones* were part of the divine bureaucracy of the ancient Greeks. In some sources, we find their status and role fairly tightly defined: in Plato's philosophical dialogue, the *Symposium*, for example, the philosopher Diotima defines them as beings 'halfway between mortals and gods'. However, in many other contexts, their precise role (in particular, their status with regard to 'the gods') is more difficult to ascertain.[119]

The best we can do is to observe the number of different supernatural dimensions which the term may represent: i) an unnamed god; ii) an unnamed external and supernatural force that interposes some kind of unexpected event, experience or action on an individual; iii) an unnamed external and supernatural force that works with named gods or other named supernatural personnel (especially *Tuche*);[120] iv) the dead themselves;[121] v) a personified abstract concept, e.g., see above for Agamemnon's fingering of *Ate* as the cause of his treatment of Achilles (sometimes *Tuche* herself is given the status of a *daimon*[122]); vi) an unnamed external supernatural force attached to a particular individual, responsible for representing their individual personal fortunes.[123] It has been argued that the ancients preferred to attribute favourable events to *theoi* or gods, while *daimones* tend to get saddled with less pleasant interventions. This can perhaps be seen most clearly in Homer's poetry – and some scholars have argued that this is also the case in later literature, in particular with the use of *tuche*.[124] However, the exceptions suggest that there is, in fact, no simple division of power in either Homer or the later writers; *daimones* cannot be taken to provide a simple solution to the problem of representing 'evil' – indeed, nor can *tuche*.[125]

## *Tuche*

Slowly rising through the ranks over the centuries, from literal obscurity to Universal Administrator, is Lady Luck herself: *Tuche*. The term has a range of meanings including: a lucky hit in archery/shooting, success, good or bad fortune, an unexpected or unplanned event, a chance happening, and the outcome of an event.[126] Personified or otherwise, *tuche* does not appear in Homer, although the use of the verb *tunchanein* ('to happen') in that text may provide some intimations of her later appearances. Other writers know her as having some minor myth, or at least allot to her some kind of genealogy, but it varies over time. According to Pausanisas her earliest mention in ancient literature is her appearance as a nymph, or Nereid, playing alongside Persephone in the *Homeric Hymn to Demeter*.[127] In fact, the list of characters in Persephone's retinue seems to rely on Hesiod's *Theogony*, in which *Tuche* is listed as an Oceanid, one of 3000 water nymphs.[128] The seventh-century poet Alcman describes her as the sister of *Peitho* ('Persuasion') and *Eunomia* ('Good Order'), and daughter of *Promatheia* ('foresight').[129] Not until Pindar, and his suggestion that *Tuche* is one of the *Moirai*, does her genealogical connection with fate and fortune become explicit.[130]

Unfortunately, she appears only briefly in the literature of the seventh and sixth centuries; her literary persona only really comes into its own in the fifth century. Then, she exhibits very similar characteristics – a certain whimsical unpredictability – to those of the Lady Luck invoked by this high-rolling gambler Sky Masterson, described at the beginning of the chapter, as he shoots dice for the souls of the local hoodlums in the musical *Guys and Dolls*.

Perhaps unsurprisingly, it is Pindar, famous for his victory odes, who provides us with detail about the role *Tuche* was understood to play in daily life. The relevant fragments of his poetry come from a lost hymn – some say to *Tuche* herself, others to the goddess Persephone. In one, he mentions that *Tuche* wielded a rudder, an intimation of how she was understood to steer men's lives. He also offers a much more detailed resume of her divine role and responsibilities in *Olympian Ode* 12. This poem ostensibly celebrates the victory of Ergoteles of Himera in the long foot race in the Olympic Games of 472 BCE; but another of its themes may explain its particular preoccupations with fortune. Ergoteles was originally from Knossos, but was deprived of his homeland by a political faction (l. 16). In the poem, Pindar describes *Tuche*'s key role in guiding the decisions of those involved in navigation – of ships and of people in war and politics (ll. 2-3). These are, perhaps, particularly relevant to Ergoteles, an immigrant from Crete. So too, perhaps, Pindar's evocation of *Tuche* to watch over the city of Himera, a city recently troubled with political unrest.[131]

In this poem, *Tuche* appears already in a number of roles that later evidence suggests would become key parts of her persona. She is a guide to navigation; she is a city-guardian (in another brief fragment Pindar describes *Tuche* as *pherepolis* or 'city-guardian'[132]); but, perhaps above all, she is unpredictable. Despite emphasising her role as a guide in decision-making, Pindar is at pains to point out that she offers no assurances for men of their safety, and rehearses what we will see is a common trope found throughout Greek literature – the unexpected reversal of men's fortunes.

Pindar's references to *Tuche* as a city-guardian is supported by some early evidence for her cult worship, in particular with connection to the welfare of cities: Pausanias reports that Boupalus of Chios sculpted a *Tuche* for the city of Smyrna – dated to the mid-sixth century.[133] Material evidence also supports Pausanias' account of an archaic period temple in Sikyon, near a sanctuary of the *Dioskouroi*, on the acropolis. He also mentions a number of other cult images of *Tuche*, which he describes as *archaion*, 'ancient', but just how old this means they really were is far from clear.[134] There is also evidence for a temple of *Tuche* in Syracuse that gave its name to the northern part of that city.[135]

In the rest of the book we will explore some of the ways in which *T/tuche* is portrayed and put to use in literature during the fifth century. During this period, as we will see, *tuche* is increasingly acknowledged as a powerful force, but rarely seems to achieve the full, consistent personification that later develops. In texts we find the idea of trust in *tuche* set against the exercise of intellectual attributes such as *gnome*, *techne* and *pronoia* (insight, skill and foresight). It suggests that, as in our own time, some preferred to plan, rather than simply trusting in 'Lady Luck'. In fact, some have argued that *tuche* was actually unpopular in the Classical period – after all, not only did she represent irrationality and uncertainty, but her decisions overruled those of the other gods and could not be undone.[136]

Balancing this impression and reminding us of the limitations of our modern understanding is evidence for the realisation of these characters. In this period there seems to have been images of *Tuche* appearing on fifth-century vases: among the earliest are the name-vase of the *Heimarmene* painter described above, where *Tuche* is coupled with *Nemesis* ('Retribution'); and a red-figure acorn lekythos now lost. Attributed to the Meidias Painter, this vase apparently showed a similar crowd of abstract concepts, including *Harmonia* ('Harmony'), *Peitho* ('Persuasion'), *Hygieia* ('Health') and *Tuche*.[137] It has been stated that 'degrees of "personifiedness" are not in question' in the visual arts.[138] Yet the representations here suggest one way in which this might be possible. Certainly these goddesses are represented as persons, but the extent to which they are characterised is very limited. The naming of the figures on both vases suggests that, at this stage, they were not well known enough (or distinguished sufficiently by their attributes) to be recognised otherwise. Nevertheless, these images do seem to represent some kind of investment in thinking about these forces in anthropomorphic terms during this period.[139] This is similarly supported by the evidence for other abstract concepts appearing on the stage in Greek drama, both tragedy and comedy.[140]

Dedicatory inscriptions suggest the gradual spread of the cult of *Tuche* throughout Greece in the fourth century. In these she often appears alongside other divinities, including, unsurprisingly, the *Moirai*, Zeus and Aphrodite, but also more unexpected divinities such as Dionysus.[141] But there is also evidence for her significance as an individual goddess, perhaps even for her development as a city guardian. A mid-fourth-century silver didrachm from Salamis, Cyprus, may show an image of the *Tuche* of that city.[142] Praxiteles is said to have created a figure of *Tuche* for the city of Megara; an Athenian sculptor, Xenophon, and his Theban colleague, Callistonicus, made one for Thebes.[143] This *Tuche* was depicted carrying Plutus ('Wealth') and it is not clear if she was intended as a city-guarding goddess or not (the association with Wealth may indicate that was *Agathe Tuche*, 'Good Fortune').[144] Other sources report that Praxiteles created a statue of *Agathe Tuche* for the city of Athens; the story goes that the beauty of this image was so great that one young man was willing to die for love for her.[145]

Briefly, it is worth emphasising that *Agathe Tuche* and *Tuche* were two separate personifications, although, as we will see, over time they seem to develop a close, if not symbiotic relationship. The earliest iconography for each of these two goddesses emphasises the fundamental difference between them: '*Agathe Tuche*' is a young woman depicted carrying a cornucopia[146] while '*Theos Tuche*', similarly young and female, carries a rudder, an attribution that she also bears in some of her earliest literary appearances.[147] Differences between the two goddesses are also underlined by their relationships with other divinities. *Agathe Tuche* is found in partnership with *Agathos Daimon* in cults across Greece, the islands and the eastern Mediterranean,[148] a coupling focused on good fortune. In contrast, as we have seen, *Tuche* is found in literary sources alongside, or sharing attributions with, other personifications that represent the fragile nature of 'opportunity' (*Kairos*) or the inevitability of 'retribution' (*Nemesis*).[149] In iconography, she gradually begins to appear in combination with female members of the traditional Greek pantheon, and, in particular, with Isis.[150]

By the fourth century BCE, she has gained sufficient stature to appear on the Athenian stage, for example, in the *Prologos* of Menander's *The Shield*. In that play, *Tuche*'s speech suggests that she has engineered a complicated situation (the sister of a soldier believed dead will have to marry her greedy uncle instead of her betrothed), in order to resolve it, thus bringing to light the wicked uncle's grasping character. It gives us one idea of how *Tuche* was understood to function and what she oversaw: she may create confusion and suffering, but this is because she intends to bring about justice, bringing down the arrogant because they deserve it. She does not actually reveal who she is until near the end of her speech, but then explains that she is 'mistress of all', 'organiser and judge' of everything that will happen in the play.[151] Although her revelations in this speech mean that the audience now knows what is going to happen, they can now appreciate the irony of what follows. Although *Tuche* does not appear again, she nevertheless dominates what follows.[152]

Menander offers us a number of other reflections on *tuche* that, although fragmentary and largely context-free, may give us a better idea of the family of ideas and experiences with which she/it was associated. From a play called *The Achaeans* there is a comment on *Tuche*'s ability to reverse a man's fortunes, and perhaps the right attitude to take to these experiences: 'But *Tuche* trained him / To poverty and meekness in his troubles, / So when things changed he might regain his glory.'[153] From *Girl Pipers* a more pessimistic observation: 'And in between *Tuche* ... / Destroys all logic and runs counter to / Our expectations, planning other outcomes. / *Tuche* makes all efforts futile'[154] A similar sentiment is found in a fragment from *The Changeling*, along with general contempt for man's ability to control his own future: 'Stop reasoning; for human reason adds / Nothing to *Tuche*, whether *Tuche* is divine / Spirit or not. It's this that steers all things / And turns them upside down and puts them right, / While mortal forethought is just smoke and crap. / Believe me; don't criticise my words. / All that we think or say or do is *Tuche*; / We only write our signatures below.'[155]

Further gnomic statements expressing similar views can be found among the *Menandri Sententiae*, 'The Proverbs of Menander' – a collection of sayings that, for the most part, probably had little to do with the playwright, although they were collected under his name.[156] Meanwhile, *Tuche*'s growing role in the epitaphs reveals another aspect of the goddess – one in which she provides a popular explanation for death. In these inscriptions she is, in general, described as a snatcher of life, hateful, or filled with hate, unreasonably cruel and, of course, unavoidable.[157]

From what she says, Menander appears to have portrayed *Tuche* empty-handed and without distinctive dress – which is how she appears in her earliest surviving (classical) iconography.[158] Over time, *Tuche* gradually acquires a number of attributes, some of which draw attention to her unpredictable personality, while others bring her closer to (and may be shared with or even inherited from) *Agathe Tuche*.[159] Unsurprisingly, perhaps, she is usually associated with the former in literary texts, which tend to meditate on the uncertainty of life; while cult iconography, although it may acknowledge her unpredictability, tends to show her with attributes that emphasise her more beneficent aspect.[160] Hesiod's placing of *Tuche* in his *Theogony*, just after *Eudora* ('good gifts'), suggests that there was an aspect of her that was associated with giving good things.[161] On the other hand, it is also possible that some of the images that we have assumed to be *Tuche* should instead be read as representing *Agathe Tuche*.

So, in literary texts we find *Tuche* described in terms and with imagery that evoke her random, unstable, swiftly changing personality[162] but these rarely, if ever, occur in her physical representations. These tend to depict her standing or sitting, with attributes that evoke her generosity (so, with a cornucopia; during the Hellenistic period combined with a phiale or sceptre[163]) or her power to influence the direction of events (e.g., holding a rudder[164]); after the second century BCE these attributes may appear together.[165] Generosity is also, presumably, the point of depicting her with the infant Plutus, sometimes in combination with a cornucopia. A number of Roman copies place her on a globe.[166] In addition to these features that reveal her inherent character, she begins to gain attributes that indicate a growing political role. During the Hellenistic period, *Tuche* remains bare-headed: towards the middle of the second century BCE, she starts to wear the mural crown,[167] and a little later (end of the second century BCE) the *polos* – a cylinder used to indicate fertility[168] – although *Agathe Tuche* appears with this slightly earlier (third–second centuries BCE).[169]

As these changing attributes might suggest, *Tuche*'s remit is changing over time. The evidence suggests that, however influential she may have been, during the fourth century BCE, *Tuche* was largely perceived as operating in the lives of individuals. But in the years to come, *Tuche* gradually evolved into an increasingly powerful, political presence. Her ascent coincides with the rise of the Macedonian empire, which triggered momentous changes in the social and political structures of the Mediterranean. According to the Hellenistic historian Polybius, the fourth-century governor of Athens, Demetrius of Phaleron, was moved to write a treatise, 'About *Tuche*', perhaps in an attempt to make sense of the violent transformations he saw around him. Contemplating the destruction of the Persian dynasty by the Macedonian King Alexander, Demetrius is reported to have argued that 'by endowing the Macedonians with the whole wealth of Persia, . . . *Tuche* makes it clear that she has only lent them these blessings until she decides to deal differently with them . . .'[170]

During the Hellenistic and Roman periods, *Tuche*'s influence and importance continued to grow. In this period of change, the figure of *Tuche* seemed to answer some widespread existential need: 'Every individual and every social group no doubt feels anxiety at one time or another when faced with the uncertainties of life, but social conditions in the Hellenistic age seem to have made this anxiety so intense that its personified source, Fortune [Tuche], became an obsession.'[171] The spread of localised *Tuche* cults alongside, and despite, an existing pantheon of traditional divinities, can be seen to map changes in the political situation even more directly. This was a world in which decisions by distant political powers could bring unpredictable and devastating change. Perhaps as well as, perhaps instead of, those gods who traditionally occupied higher positions in the hierarchy of the Greek pantheon, cities and their citizens required a local goddess who would be able to pay particular attention to their local fortunes, who specialised, as it were, in the experiences of their daily lives.[172]

For citizens and rulers, a cult of *Tuche* offered practical benefits: for individuals living in cities crowded with cultures, the cult of *Tuche* offered a stable point of commonality and cohesion with fellow citizens.[173] For rulers, *Tuche* was a powerful and unifying source of propaganda. Individuals who wanted to claim a relationship with *Tuche* might assume her attributes: for example, Marcus Vipsanius Agrippa is depicted on gold and silver coins from Rome (13/12 BCE), wearing not only the rostral crown to signify his naval victories and status, but also the mural crown of *Tuche*.[174] Under the Ptolemaic empire, the personal *tuchai* of Ptolemaic queens received cult – and this practice was later incorporated into Roman imperial cult.[175]

If this was how she appeared and was used, how was she understood? Polybius may offer us some sense of how, at an intellectual level, *Tuche* offered a route for making sense of what did not make sense in the world. Indeed, in his eyes, this is the purpose of history: alongside providing an education and training for a political career, it will help a student to bear the changes brought about by *Tuche*, by reminding him of the disasters suffered by other people. The historian states explicitly that *Tuche* is responsible for those things that are 'impossible or difficult for a mortal to understand'; in turn, when it *is* possible to find mortal causes for an event 'we should not, like fools, speak simply of *Tuche*'.[176] But the two explanations are not mutually exclusive: he appears to feel no inconsistency in explaining a single event by mentioning *Tuche* alongside a practical account.[177] *Tuche* is an operational force in life – creating coincidences, imposing long-awaited retribution, or, in particular, inflicting devastating reversals of fortune – whether she was depicted as an impersonal power, or personified as a whimsical engineer.[178] The actions of the latter, as he notes at the end of his work, may have no clear cause: '*Tuche* is apt to envy men and she shows her power particularly where one thinks that one is especially fortunate and successful in his life.'[179]

Polybius seems to have felt that this aspect of history had a particular lesson for his Roman audience: as mentioned above, Polybius cites Demetrius of Phaleron's warning of the disaster awaiting the Macedonians, a premonition that Polybius himself saw realised at Pydna in 168, when, in turn, the Romans brought down the Macedonian Empire.[180] Polybius was not the only one who felt that Rome needed to remain on friendly terms with *Tuche*. Even with the advent of Christianity, the fickle goddess remained important: Constantine ensured that there was a temple of *Tuche* in his new or renewed city of Constantinople, matching the *Fortuna Romana* of the city of Rome; and, as late as the fourth century CE, Julian the Apostate sacrificed to the *Tuche* of Antioch.[181]

CHAPTER III

# OEDIPUS: A TRAGEDY OF FATES

> The name that you were given at birth and the day you were born cannot change. You may change your name through marriage or through choice, but the God-given talents and the 'life lesson' numbers cannot change.
>
> S. Fenton, *The Fortune Teller's Workbook*[1]

The quotation above, from the *Fortune Teller's Workbook*, illustrates some of the ways in which our culture approaches the idea of individual destiny. This example highlights two aspects of a person – birthdate and name – as a way of understanding what that fate must be. The implicit beliefs here are complex, including aspects of, at least, astrology, theology, numerology, and some notions of *karma* (the 'life-lessons' to be gleaned). Underpinning all this is a sense that one's fate is already established – and is unchangeable.

In contrast, when we turn back to our modern cinematic heroes, Sarah Connor and Lawrence of Arabia, we find examples of individuals who refuse to accept the presence, let alone the power, of fate. In comparison, let us examine an ancient hero, still famous in modern times, for his struggle with his fate. Sophocles' play, *Oedipus Tyrannos*, translated as *Oedipus Rex*, or *Oedipus the King*, is famously rich in meanings, and has prompted an immense variety of interpretations. In this chapter we will use it to take a first look at some of the ways in which ideas and language about luck, fate and fortune might change in response to the different needs of different contexts.

The story of Oedipus is well known: he grew up a prince of Corinth, but fled that city after the Delphic oracle revealed that he was doomed to kill his father and marry his mother. He travels to Thebes, and by saving that city from the scourge of the monstrous sphinx, he gains its throne, and marries its queen, Jocasta, whose husband, Laius, happens to have been killed in a fight on the road to Delphi. When Sophocles' play opens, we are some years into Oedipus' reign, Thebes is beset by a terrible plague, and his subjects are desperate for their King's help. A consultation of the Delphic oracle reveals that the source of the pestilence is the presence in the city of Laius' murderer – and Oedipus sets out to find him. But this manhunt takes on a very different meaning as Oedipus slowly and agonisingly realises that he murdered Laius. And this brings him to a terrible truth: the king and queen of Corinth were not his real parents; he was born into the royal house of Thebes, but given away by his parents because of an oracle about his future, an oracle that he has now fulfilled. The man he has killed, Laius, was his father, and Jocasta, now his wife, is his mother.

How does Oedipus compare to the cinematic heroes Sarah Connor or Lawrence of Arabia, and their valiant rejection of fate? Is he, too, a rebel against the dictatorial power of an unwanted and unjust future? Some critics have argued that he is indeed such a figure, battling the forces of society and/or the gods.[2] Others have cast his superhuman struggle in a different light, seeing in it, instead, a reassertion of the religious view of a divinely ordered universe. For some, this means that Oedipus' suffering carries a moral lesson: he is being punished for an offence, a *hamartia*, usually taken to mean 'a flaw of character'.[3] In Oedipus' case, this flaw is thought to be his overweening pride in his own intelligence, which 'blinds' him to the truth.[4] And yet it is difficult to justify such a reading of Sophocles' play, since there is little arrogance in Oedipus' actions or attitudes.[5] He is, in fact, shown to be quite right to trust his intelligence – after all, it is precisely this faculty that leads him to the discovery of the truth of his birth.[6] If instead we read Oedipus' *hamartia* as 'a wrongful decision taken in a state of ignorance' – this leads to a second, and perhaps darker way of understanding the play's assertion of religious power, one which emphasises the distance between human and divine, and the powerlessness of the former against the latter. Oedipus may be innocent because he does not know his circumstances; nevertheless, he must still be punished because his actions have broken cosmic laws of order.[7]

Other readings reject the idea that this play is about fate and fortune in a supernatural sense at all. For Freud, the play concerned man's relationship with his inner self: the 'tragedy of fate' depicted by Oedipus' fall represented our denial of our unconscious knowledge of ourselves, 'and the perception of one's own impotence'. Others have seen a commentary on man's existence within a community: in a marvellous essay, John Gould argued that *Oedipus* has 'nothing to say about responsibility, almost nothing to say about fate, and seemingly very little about the workings of divinity.'[8] Instead he proposed a reading that evokes the distance between human society, with all its rules and values, and the world outside it. In this marginal realm, which wandering seers and shepherds may penetrate, Oedipus, in his state of guilt, is forced to dwell. Something of both these readings can be seen in Karl Reinhardt's interpretation of the alienation of Oedipus as '*the* tragedy of human illusion'.[9] In clinging to his (false) impression of the world, Sophocles' hero becomes increasingly 'lone, uprooted, exiled'. It is this desperate state that confirms the power of the gods: 'it is only at breaking point that his being attains a quality of purity and seems to move from dissonance to a state of harmony with the divine order.'[10] But even if we accept aspects of these readings, *moira* and *tuche* are hard to write out completely, if only because the play's characters themselves use these concepts in a variety of ways to describe what they think is happening to them. Indeed, to take up Freud's description, we might describe this play not so much as a tragedy of a single fate, but as a 'tragedy of fates', evoking all the different ways in which fate (and luck and fortune) are portrayed throughout the play.

Intriguingly, *moira* occurs only six times in the play. Its first appearance is during Oedipus' confrontation with Teiresias the seer (376): Teiresias has announced the dire nature of Oedipus' circumstances, and Oedipus, in turn, is protesting that the old seer cannot hurt him. In response Teiresias asserts that 'it is not your *moira* to fall at my hands' and, in the next line, 'since Apollo, to whom these things matter, is sufficient'. Three hundred and thirty-seven lines later, Jocasta comforts Oedipus, who has told her of Teiresias' attacks. In her attempt to reassure Oedipus she tells him of the oracles that had come to her husband, Laius, and how '*moira* would hold him to die at the hands of his child'. She goes on to tell the story of her husband's death, little knowing that she is recounting the fulfilment of the oracle – and introducing into her husband/son's mind the very questions that will prick his desire to uncover the past.

The next two appearances of *moira* follow quickly and reinforce the role that *moira* was understood to play in ensuring universal order. The chorus' second *stasimon* begins with a plea that *moira* may find the speaker continuing to be pure in words and deeds, obeying the laws of the gods (863). It goes on to describe the kind of character and activities that break those laws, condemning *hubris* or 'pride', and its dangers for the tyrant. The song finishes with a second evocation of *moira*, this time an evil *moira* who will punish those who are haughty and have no thought for justice or avoidance of unholy deeds (887). The crucial importance this correction plays for cosmic order is proclaimed in this chorus' famous final question: 'if such deeds are held in honour, why should we join in the sacred dance?'[11]

*Moira* does not appear again by name until the dreadful secrets have finally been uncovered, and Oedipus is lamenting his situation. The chorus asks Oedipus, in effect, 'Why you?', but their turn of phrase introduces a whole retinue of misfortune-makers all working together: (1297–1302) 'O terrible suffering for men to see! O most terrible of all that I have witnessed! Who is the *daimon* who, with bounds greater than those of the tallest men, sprang on you, you with your badly fortuned fate (*dusdaimoni moira*)?' Finally, Oedipus meditates on his own circumstances, and seems to elicit a strange comfort from what has happened, asserting that he is not likely to suffer any mundane illness, not with a destiny like his (1458). Although his words seem almost to indicate a sense of resignation – 'Let my *moira* go wherever it will go' – this does not seem to indicate a surrender to passivity. He goes on to carefully secure the future of his children, and make arrangements for himself to live safely in the hills.

Although appearing relatively rarely throughout the play, *moira* presents a certain conceptual stability. In its first and last occurrence, by Teiresias and by the chorus, respectively, it seems to be used to represent the personal *moira* of Oedipus. In between, it appears as a more active character, something of an enforcer – holding someone to fulfil a future action, finding someone out, punishing the haughty for breaking cosmic laws of order. In contrast, *tuche*, which makes twice as many appearances, undergoes something of an evolution over the course of the play.

In its initial appearances, *tuche* seems to refer to good events: (52) the priest of Zeus, as he pleads with Oedipus to save the city from the plague, refers to his previous successful struggle with the sphinx, and talks of the *tuche* he provided for the city, 'with good omen'. A little later (80) Oedipus uses it himself with a similarly positive affect in his prayer to Apollo, describing the *tuche* with which his brother-in-law Creon, who has gone to Delphi to consult the oracle on behalf of the city, will arrive as a 'saviour'. However, once Creon arrives and reports the oracle's warning about the murderer, Oedipus uses *tuche* with a slightly different nuance. He asks after the identity of the man whose murder has brought about the pestilence to Thebes, and uses *tuche* to mean the murder referred to by the oracle (102). A little later, Oedipus again uses *tuche* to describe the event of Laius' murder, and this time the imagery is vivid, even chilling: '*tuche* swooped upon him' (263).

As the play proceeds, this changed, more negative meaning of *tuche* starts to dominate. In conversation with Oedipus, Teiresias uses it, as did the priest of Zeus in the first scene, to describe Oedipus' solving the sphinx's riddle (442). However, unlike the priest, Teiresias makes it clear that the outcome of that event would be far from positive for Oedipus: 'It was just that *tuche* that destroyed you', Teiresias asserts, although, as Oedipus points out, it saved the city. Gradually, the meaning of *tuche*, at first so positive, comes to indicate an unpleasant, disruptive, but undefined experience. Jocasta uses *tuche* as she waits to find out 'what has happened' between Oedipus and Teiresias (680); Oedipus asks Jocasta, as he begins the story that frames his current forebodings, 'to whom would I speak more than to you as I go through such a *tuche*' (773). He repeats the word a few lines later as he reveals how his previous happiness was disrupted by a *tuche* that came upon him, a stranger's revelation that he was not his father's son (776). The verb he uses here to describe *tuche*'s arrival is used elsewhere to describe an enemy ambush.[12]

As Oedipus and Jocasta's misapprehensions develop, these multiple aspects of meaning allow *tuche* to evoke a powerful irony for the audience/reader. For example, Jocasta joyfully describes the death of Polybus (the king of Corinth, thought to be Oedipus' father) and the fact that he has not been killed by Oedipus, as Oedipus feared, but '*pros tes tuches*' (949). By this phrase Jocasta means, 'in the course of his natural life', but for the audience, who knows what has happened, this phrase suggests a very different *tuche* – the fortune that the gods have set in place for Oedipus – and so her comment is full of irony. This is reinforced when Jocasta prefaces these words with a joyful, impious cry: 'Oracles of the gods, where are you now?' Little does she know: they are being fulfilled before her unknowing eyes.

Jocasta's ignorance and impiety is emphasised again a little later when she asks 'What should a mortal man fear, over whom the playing out of *tuche* rules, and who has foresight of nothing?' (977). Jocasta means it as a cry of rebellion against the fear imposed by divine prescription, but the audience, knowing to what extent *tuche* is in fact directing proceedings, can also hear the bitter truth it contains. This aspect of *tuche* is reinforced when the Corinthian messenger uses *tuche* to refer to the events that gave Oedipus his name (1036).

In turn, Oedipus' use of *tuche* makes manifest the depth of his misunderstanding as, ignoring Jocasta's desperate pleas not to persist in his questioning, he announces that he is not worried by his possibly humble parentage, and proclaims himself to be the son of '*Tuche*, who gives good'. Following this, the chorus slips into an apparently light-hearted song about the frolicking gods, a song that starts with a disturbing claim to their own mantic authority (in contrast to the invocation of divine power and cosmic order that they made at the end of the second *stasimon*). Their sentiments contradict all their previous observations about the nature of the divine (that is, that Zeus is absolute, eternal, pure and remote (863–73, 903–905). It could be that their contorted expression (1089–95) is intended to suggest oracular speech;

indeed, it may be that it is meant to parody the mystifying speech of itinerant seers.[13] If so, it is another aspect of this chorus that reinforces how very wrong mortals can be about the nature of the gods who direct man's fate. This is the last mention made of *tuche*, before the final horrific events play out: by this point, *tuche* has been transformed from the simple indication of good fortune that she represented at the beginning of the play, and now, as the end draws near, use of this term tends instead to signify mankind's dangerous misunderstanding of the power of the divine.[14]

The idea of the *daimon* also undergoes a shift during the course of this play. Initially, it appears simply as a synonym for 'god(s)'. Sometimes it implies a particular god, for example, Zeus' priest believes that a *daimon* helped Oedipus solve the sphinx's riddle (33); and Oedipus uses *daimon* to refer to Apollo, when he curses the murderer of Laius (244). The plural use tends to describe a group of supernatural beings: for example, when the chorus sings of images of the gods (886); or when Jocasta is going to visit the shrines of the gods (912), whose sacred statues, Oedipus will later announce, he can no longer bear to look upon (1378).

But gradually the term takes on a more personalised sense, relating directly to Oedipus' fate. An intermediate stage in this process is suggested when Oedipus, fearing that he is guilty of Laius' death (but suspecting only that he has murdered a stranger, and so is susceptible to his own curse, not that he is a patricide), raises the idea that these events come 'from a vicious *daimon*' (828). By the end of the play, this personalisation of fate is complete, and *daimon*ic imagery comes thick and fast from both chorus and characters. The *daimon* appears as both attacker and victim: the chorus laments what has happened to Oedipus and his *daimon* (1194), then describes a *daimon* as attacking him – literally as jumping on his 'badly-*daimon*ed *moira*' (1301/2); finally, they ask their king the identity of the *daimon* that led him to blind himself (1327–8). This *daimon*ic ambiguity continues as the messenger reports that when Oedipus is crashing around the palace in his grief, some *daimon* shows him the way, giving him the strength to break down the doors to the bedroom to find his wife – a terrible image, and made more terrible by its sexual double-meaning (1258). Oedipus also maintains the confusion, bewailing his *daimon* – and how far it has 'sprung' (1311). He specifically denies the role of the *daimon* (whom he names as Apollo) in his blinding, which he famously claims as his and his alone (1328 ff.). At the end of the play (1478–9), he wishes Creon good luck, and that *daimon* should prove a better guardian to him than he has to Oedipus, emphasising how the attentions of a god are no guarantee of good fortune. By the end of this play, the identity of, and role played by, a/the *daimon* remains fluid and unpredictable: by turns described as both attacker and victim, director and engineer, anonymous supernatural entity and perhaps even Apollo himself.

The language of the characters themselves reveals their understanding of the central role played by *moira*, *tuche* and *daimon* in the course of events. And yet, these crucial entities are given no explicit meaning or relationship with each other or with mortals. *Daimon*ic ambiguity is matched by what we might call *tuchian* shape-shifting, as *tuche* morphs from a term of success (52, 442, 771–834, 776) to a double-edged significance (773); culminating in Jocasta's claim that *tuche* indicates the upending of cosmic order (977–79).[15] Similarly *moira*, reveals a 'Jekyll and Hyde' character, at one moment a point of stability, at another in pursuit of its quarry, reminiscent of its death-dealing role in a Homeric epic.

Meanwhile, the precise relationship of each of these supernatural entities to the other is never explicitly described: the most we can acquire is some sense of the particular emphasis of their role from the contexts of their appearances. For example, the *daimon* jumping on Oedipus (1302, in the words of the chorus) may describe the shock of a particular moment – the process of discovery or the moment of blinding in the already dreadful, fated course of events – or it may be that we are being told of the power of a particular *daimon* whose attack on Oedipus means that his *moira* has, in that moment, become ill-fated (*dusdaimoni*). The confusion of roles may be the point: whichever way we hear it, this vivid picture of supernatural activity tells us this situation has been engineered – and overdetermined. There has been no chance of escape for Oedipus.

This last example raises the question of the presence of the gods, and their role among these entities. In a play so suffused with supernatural power, we might expect gods to make more of an appearance, but no god actually appears in Sophocles' *Oedipus*.[16] Instead, the audience is *made aware* of divine attention indirectly, through the experiences and comments of the characters. Two gods are named: Apollo and Zeus, but the extent to which they are involved is never clarified. In the case of Apollo, his power is felt throughout the play, through the oracles that structure both the play and events within it (discussed below). At the very end of the play there is a suggestion that the god has been more directly involved than we might think: the chorus asks Oedipus which *daimon* has caused him to blind himself, and (1328) Oedipus famously names Apollo. The statement appears to conflate god and *daimon*, but this is far from an unalloyed allocation of blame, especially when Oedipus goes on to clarify that he alone is responsible for blinding himself. Does Oedipus mean his personal *daimon* (discussed at 1194) is actually Apollo, or is this just a pious acknowledgement of the more general power of the oracular god?

If Apollo seems a remote figure, hard to pin down, yet another power looms even more distantly behind him: throughout the play, with particular attention from the chorus, Zeus is depicted as the embodiment of universal and eternal moral order.[17] It is Zeus that Oedipus calls upon when the world and self he thought he knew start to crumble in the face of his horrified suspicions: 'Zeus, what have you planned to do to me?' (738). The answer arrives, not as direct divine pronouncements, but through the unremitting sequence of events: the play's narrative reveals Zeus' will; its unlikely coincidences demonstrate the inexorable nature of his unavoidable plan.[18]

The consistent presence of the divine, and the inescapability of fate, is marked throughout the play by the three oracles that structure both the play and events within it.[19] But rather than drawing them closer, these divine messages emphasise the distance between man and gods. This is not because they are confusingly phrased. Although oracles, especially those from Delphi, were traditionally tricksy, these oracles are strikingly straightforward.[20] Nevertheless, the recipients of these divine messages persist in understanding them as problems to be worked out, rather than straightforward announcements of the inevitable.

This attitude to the oracles gives us some crucial insights into the role of fate in this play. Much of Sophocles' *Oedipus* concerns not a fight against the gods for the assertion of free will (each decision that Oedipus makes, the play makes clear, he does so freely, often going against the advice of others), but rather, a mortal struggle for understanding. The oracles are in fact only one example of this theme.[21] At the heart of *Oedipus the King*, Sophocles presents us not with a dilemma or a fight, but with a riddle – or rather a series of riddles – with enormous significance for our reflections on the problem of luck, fate and fortune.[22]

Riddles are not tests of factual knowledge, but rather of the capacity to analyse cognitive categories, to recognise the familiar when it is described in unfamiliar terms.[23] As Aristotle defined it: the essence of a riddle is to express true facts in impossible combinations.[24] The riddle that sets the backdrop to *Oedipus the King*, the riddle of the sphinx, is notoriously appropriate for the events that go on to take place in the play.[25] In this drama, the content of this riddle is not spelled out or explained, but the audience is likely to have been well aware of it.[26] Formulated by the mythographer Apollodorus it is: 'What is that which has one voice and yet becomes four-footed and two-footed and three-footed?' The answer is, of course, man. Set by a hybrid monster (according to Apollodorus, the sphinx had the 'face of a woman, the breast and feet and tail of a lion, and the wings of a bird'[27]), the sphinx's riddle draws attention to the shifting physical shape of mankind, breaking him down to his constituent parts, asking the audience, 'what makes a man?'

In solving riddles, it is not enough to be skilled: the riddle-solver needs luck, as well. When it is possible to identify different 'right' answers to a riddle (and it usually is), solving a riddle correctly means finding the response that is in the mind of the riddler.[28] This additional uncertainty heightens the tension attached to resolving the riddle. In the story of Oedipus, there were additional reasons to feel tense: the sphinx would eat those who got the answer to her riddle wrong. This is an example of what is now called a 'neck riddle', one that gives the recipient of the riddle a simple choice – solve it or perish.[29] Once the question is asked, there is no going back.

But solving a riddle also has implications: it rearranges the facts; it can offer transformation.[30] In the case of the sphinx's riddle, it ushers in safety to the city and a period of harmony and peace (as emphasised by the plea for help made by the priest to Oedipus at the very beginning of the play, ll. 14–57). It brings heightened status for Oedipus as the itinerant murderer becomes monarch and saviour.[31] But of course, other changes have also taken place: by answering this riddle, the man who has been fleeing from his fate begins to move towards it. Mother becomes wife; son, husband. As a result, instead of order brought to chaos, the city is gripped by plague. The solving of the final riddle – the question of Oedipus' identity – will bring healing, but also tragedy.

The riddling has happened before the play begins, but we are soon reminded of it. The binary nature of Oedipus' initial choice becomes the trajectory of events. The opening plea of the priest to Oedipus describes his previous success, and summons to mind the monstrous form and weighty symbolism of the sphinx and her riddle to loom over the play. One voice but many forms: the sphinx herself; her riddle; her interlocutor, Oedipus. He is both riddle-solver and riddle; he is the man *with* the answer, who, in turn, *becomes* the answer.[32]

The unfolding of the drama, the discovery of fate's plan, is, for the characters involved, the inexorable resolution of a riddle. The language of clues, signs and symbols that must be pieced together runs throughout the play.[33] And, as discussed above, the resolution of the riddle means the blurring of boundaries between categories.[34] But this is not a harmless, verbal game. The resolution of this riddle is indeed transformative, irredeemable and horrifying. Oedipus is both son and husband of his mother, son and murderer of his father, saviour and destroyer of his city. He is a monstrous hybrid, like the sphinx whose riddle he guessed.[35]

Here are Aristotle's true facts in impossible combinations: resolving a riddle is not a question of knowledge, so much as a challenge to reassemble, review and re-comprehend the knowledge you already possess. The scene between Teiresias and Oedipus underlines this aspect, presenting a confrontation between two men who see the world in such different terms that they literally inhabit different worlds.[36] Oedipus is looking for mortal solutions to a political problem; his fury towards the old seer is perhaps a mark of frustration rather than arrogance.[37] Teiresias, in contrast, sees the plan of the gods, supernatural cause and effect, inevitable mortal suffering; his anger with Oedipus is rooted in the pain of bearing knowledge that benefits no one.[38] When Teiresias reveals what he knows, Oedipus can only recast the information in terms of the world he inhabits, describing his accusations as part of a political conspiracy, disarming their supernatural power with mundane authority . . . for the moment.[39]

In the later philosophical debates of the Stoics and their critics, the oracles in this play will become stock examples in a debate about determinism, the nature of fate and the use of the practice of divination.[40] Should we understand it in the same way: do we see here a preview of our cinematic heroes and the brave struggle against fate? Surely Sophocles' play offers a much more compassionate understanding of the human condition than this reading could provide – along with a more profound insight into ancient Greek attitudes to luck, fate and fortune and their role in daily life.

*Oedipus the King* offers its audience a rare insight: 'divine' knowledge coupled with mortal experience. Sophocles portrays his characters in the act of creating the stories of their lives: they look back to past events and explain where they fit in the current stories of their lives; they describe how they have dealt with past challenges, and how they will deal with future problems. For them, the oracles they are given have either passed without incident or are the stuff of future possibilities. In the process of making sense of their experiences, the characters reveal their understanding through a discourse about luck, fate and fortune: *tuche*, *moira*, *daimon* all appear as ways of making sense of the situations in which they find themselves and each other. There is no discussion here of who is to blame, at a religious or civic level.[41] Luck, fate and fortune instead provide a set of shared concepts, a language, for the characters in the play to explain what is happening to them, and how these experiences affect them.

But the audience knows that their lives are already set. The oracles these characters receive are already fulfilled: they describe not the future, but the past and the present. The life-stories these characters think they are creating have already been written. Thus, each character's hopeful account of events becomes a moment of complicity between author and audience, and the irony is almost unbearable. And yet, although the audience may share the knowledge of the author, of the divine plan, we are far from god-like.[42] While we feel the irony arising from our 'divine' knowledge of the play, we are only too aware of how our own attempts to make sense of events can mirror the struggle that we are witnessing on the stage. Together, these experiences provoke an exquisite sensitivity to the presence and operation of fate and fortune in our own daily lives. Alongside its presentation of mortal struggle, divine knowledge and authorial irony, Sophocles' play provokes compassion and pity for the suffering of our fellow human beings – and, in the end, for ourselves.

CHAPTER IV

# CULTURAL MODELS AND SHIFTING MEANINGS

'... much of the order we perceive in the world is there only because we put it there.'
D. Holland and N. Quinn, 'Culture and Cognition'[1]

*Superstition Increases Japanese Health Costs*
Modern medical care is based on a scientific tradition, but the health beliefs of patients may have a very different basis. Belief in superstitions relating to the six-day lunar calendar is common in Japan and affects many social events. On p.1680 Hira *et al.* report the findings of a retrospective study of hospital discharge dates in Kyoto, Japan. They found that most patients were discharged on Taian, said to be a lucky day, and fewest were discharged on the unlucky day *But-sumetsu*. The authors conclude that patients extend their stay in hospital so that they are discharged on Taian, and calculate that this costs the hospital 7.4 million yen (£31 000) per year. However, they caution against outright dismissal of such superstitions, warning that this may have a negative effect on some patients' health.
*BMJ* Vol. 317 (December 19–26, 1998)[2]

The terms luck, fate and fortune lead modern minds quickly into the midst of an apparent contradiction: we find ourselves torn between ideas of causation that turn on free will (which intuitively feel right) and those that depend on strict laws of necessity (which appeal to our understanding of the workings of the world around us). For the Greeks, however, this dilemma seems only to have emerged later, as the idea of scientific laws of nature (warranting inference and counterfactual inference) began to develop. Why? One answer might be that they just had not developed a sufficiently nuanced understanding of the problems involved in talking about fate and assuming free will. On the other hand, or alongside, it may be that the ancient Greek concepts of *tuche, moira*, etc. were not the kind of explanatory models that we are used to nowadays.

As established above, when characters in Sophocles' *Oedipus the King* use the terms, *tuche, moira*, etc., they do not appear to be referring to a single definition, but instead to be moving among a range of associated meanings, which change over the course of the play, as the characters try to make sense of the circumstances in which they find themselves. (And how different readers interpret these associations also depends on the approach and assumptions they bring to bear.) Thus, we find, *tuche* may indicate the unpredictability of human life, but it may also be used to refer to a force that works in concert with the gods, reinforcing cosmic justice; alternatively, it may indicate the presence of a personified, and perhaps malevolent, goddess.

If this seems too imprecise, we might compare how the terms 'luck', 'fate' and 'fortune' are used in our own culture. As suggested above, these terms tend not to offer a single meaning. Instead, they activate a set of associations and ideas concerning the uncertain future, and our role in it. Consider, for example, some of the modern examples we have mentioned so far: the image of Lady Luck, serenaded by Sky Masterson, before he rolls the dice, alongside Richard Wiseman's salutary analysis of the psychology of lucky and unlucky people. Consider the many different, largely unspoken assumptions, about fate and fortune that underlie the diverse activities in the *Fortune-Teller's Workbook* quoted at the beginning of Chapter II of this book, or the struggles of our cinematic heroes, Sarah Connor and Lawrence of Arabia, against the tacit workings of fate. None of these examples provides a clear and unequivocal definition of the mechanisms of luck, fate and fortune. Indeed, when set side by side, they appear in a number of aspects to be contradictory: can we influence our own fortune or not? Can we escape our fate, or does it simply dictate events? Are luck, fate and fortune external forces or an integral part of who we are?

Nevertheless, these terms still carry a rich array of meaning, and can swiftly convey vast amounts of information. Depending on the emphasis we give them, these concepts may initiate associations with past, present and future events, invoke conceptions of the supernatural, raise ideas of causation and responsibility or praise and blame, or reinforce notions of identity, to name but a few. It will all depend on the kind of story in which they appear, the audience for that story, and the circumstances of the story's telling.

'Luck', 'fate' and 'fortune' are not remarkable in this sense. Take, for example, the word 'bachelor': as a now-famous article has observed, a simple lexical definition of 'bachelor' may provide us with the meaning of a word, but it does not explain why we might not apply this word to the Pope or use it to describe a wolf-boy reared in the wild. To clarify that, we have to turn to a larger set of implicit understandings and assumptions, specific to our culture, within which the word 'bachelor' is embedded, and which we implicitly understand. In this theory, the term 'bachelor' creates for us 'a prototype world' of meaning, which the Pope and wolf-boys do not fit.[3] Prototypes may include not only objects and concepts, but situations and experiences: indeed, in the original article, prototypes were also called 'scenes'. Some cognitive linguists argue that such a process of interpretation with regard to the use of a single term exemplifies a larger process that occurs in our everyday discourse. When a person interprets a text, their first, unconscious, mental response is to create a 'prototype scene' or 'partially specified world', which is innately known to them, and, as they continue to read, they fill in the details; this may mean the introduction of new scenes, or combinations of scenes. However, many of the details of that scene may never be mentioned explicitly in the text, but remain unspoken, implied by our grasp of the scenes as communicated by certain terms.[4]

If cognitive linguists are interested in prototypes as part of a system of meaning acquisition, scholars working in the fields of cognitive psychology and cognitive and psychoanalytic anthropology have built on these ideas to explore cultural knowledge.⁵ They have argued that a similar process may help us understand how humans, within and across different cultures, understand and manage information about the world around them – even as it, and they, change – and then pass on that 'cultural knowledge' to others.⁶ They think that much of our everyday interaction depends on similar kinds of mental processes to those described above, in which a vast amount of shared understanding about how the world works is swiftly transmitted and acted upon. The information conveyed remains tacit and taken for granted. There is no need to make it explicit: this body of knowledge or understanding is shared, and internalised, across a culture, through the activation of 'schemas' and cultural models.

Unlike prototypes, which offer a specific set of criteria, schemas offer a way to describe the cognitive structures that come from organising more complex abstract configurations of objects and relations that represent regularities of events and experiences within our environment. Schemas are both structures and processes. They provide a system for describing how the world works that is culturally learned and shared, and used to represent, organise and evaluate experiences: they are 'culturally shared mental constructs' and they occur in every arena of our lives.⁷ As an example, consider an account of a boy in an exam whose pen ran out of ink, whose pencil broke, who had to borrow a pen from another student and then ran out of time in the exam, so lost points for his messy handwriting. As cognitive anthropologist Roy D'Andrade observes, such a simple story offers no explicit explanation that writing involves making marks on paper, or what those marks may be; it provides no account of what an exam is or what it requires of a student.⁸ Instead storyteller and audience hold this understanding implicitly, and this enables them to make sense of the story.

This transmission of understanding does not have to happen by means of spoken or written words: images can convey information in the same way. Thus, if we see a person swap an object for money with another person, it will trigger what D'Andrade has termed a 'commercial transaction' schema.⁹ Schemas can be and are used to great effect in visual media, where scenes with little, if any, explicit clarification convey key information about characters and plot. Advertising, which has to convey a great deal of information, and often emotional affect, in a very short period of time draws on our implicit cultural knowledge in this way, so that very brief references to schemas mean that we instantly understand what is going on – which can bring both advantages and disadvantages: 'Consider the double-edged challenge of presenting a typical auto dealer ad to a consumer who already does not like car dealers and is also "wise" to the slick promotional techniques these dealers are known to use'.[10]

Schemas help us not only to represent, but also to process information, allowing the rapid and implicit understanding of extremely intricate webs of meaning.[11] Schemas or sets of related schemas working in this way are also referred to as 'cultural models'.[12] Some theorists have classified cultural models with reference to their particular uses: for example, 'explanatory models' (as defined by Arthur Kleinman) describe how individuals think about an illness and its treatment – their assumptions about its causes, their evaluation of its seriousness, their expectations of its course, and how it should be treated.[13] Different groups and individuals may hold very different explanatory models of the same illness – and a single individual may hold multiple models at the same time, and change their model in response to changing events or influences.

We can see the clash of different explanatory models quite starkly when we review responses to the HIV/AIDS epidemic: in some cultures, the epidemic has been attributed to the wrath of God; in others, it is thought to be caused by the jealousy of family and neighbours.[14] One of the ongoing challenges facing those combating HIV/AIDS in many societies is the multiplicity of explanatory models of the disease, which means that sufferers may choose a traditional healer or therapies, rather than Western medicine. Interestingly, rather than simply demanding that everyone adopt the models of Western medicine, many health workers advocate the involvement of traditional healers, alongside Western medicine, in fighting the epidemic.[15]

A schema is not meant to imply the application of a set of rigid rules, but a set of associations, a sort of pattern-recognition, which allows us to find or create meaning. As this suggests, schemas/cultural models describe both the enactment and production of cultural understandings; they both structure the production of meaning, as well as being deployed to explain it, and are used in this way by individuals and groups for their own purposes.[16] When we mentally fill in a schema, we usually turn to a default set of details, or a 'prototype', but some of the most powerful uses of schemas in visual media turn on creating 'atypical' advertising, which does not conform to the expectations created by a prototype. In response, 'Rather than a snap judgment (the general response to schema-consistent information) a detailed and piecemeal judgement process generally results . . . The result is a more objective evaluation of the advertising message, and a more memorable ad.'[17] In fact, the founder and chair of advertising giant TBWA Worldwide, Jean-Marie Dru, has described how his company turned 'disruption' into a highly effective and lucrative creative process, which aims to 'reframe, restage, and reshape, by rejecting the obvious.'[18]

As this suggests, cultural models seem to be fairly fluid, changing over place and time. (As an example, we can revisit our first illustration, the term 'bachelor' and see how the meaning of this term, the schema it triggers and the other schemas and cultural models to which it is related, have shifted over time, encompassing a range of different levels of significance.) Nevertheless, this fluid set of assumptions plays a crucial role in how we apprehend and comprehend the world around us, how we remember or reconstruct past events, and how we form our expectations of and responses to the future – indeed, recent scholarship is exploring how cultural models may inform notions of identity and supply motivational force for action.[19] In the US, the Environmental Protection Agency and National Science Foundation have teamed up to support research into environmental decision-making, and a number of projects in this area are exploring the role of cultural models – how they are involved in people's understandings of their environment; how they might be used to help different groups of stakeholders develop shared perceptions of their environment, and thus help them to make more effective and inclusive decisions at local and state levels.[20]

In this context I am interested in exploring some of the schemas and cultural models that helped to structure the ancient Greek understanding of the uncertain future, in particular those that we tend to translate as 'luck', 'fate' and 'fortune'. As our overview of the ancient 'ministry of misfortune' has revealed, these models were replete with supernatural figures, not only gods and various *daimones*, but also more puzzling abstractions, such as *moira* and *tuche*. Examination of Sophocles' *Oedipus the King* has also demonstrated the difficulties of identifying any one definition for each of these supernatural entities, or of finding a simple description of their relationships, either with each other or with mortals.

But how do we map out the elements of cultural models, if they comprise, by and large, a body of implicit, unspoken assumptions? One of the richest sources may be cultural discourses – by which I mean simply the written and verbal interactions between members of a culture.[21] As has been amply demonstrated by the investigations conducted within a number of different scholarly disciplines ranging from literary theory to cognitive science to psychotherapy to history, perhaps the richest forms of cultural discourse involve or comprise narrative – which we can loosely define as an account of a sequence of events.[22] Why might this be? Drawing on scholarship from across these disciplines, we find a consensus that crafting a narrative is a process of creating both coherence and significance. It makes sense of otherwise disconnected events by selecting and arranging them in a particular configuration; it allows speaker and audience to create and share their understanding of the world around them, to assert or reinforce their identities.

This creative process does not happen in isolation. First of all, the process of narration itself is a shared one; not only is the narrator active, but so is the reader/listener: 'The process of listening to a story or reading a text is essentially constructive, a filling-in of gaps, a building of fragments into a coherent whole . . .'. Among the Kalapalo of Brazil the 'what-sayers', who accompany story-tellers, help to shape a story as it is being told by means of their interjections – they may make noises indicating the emotional response of the audience, or ask questions to clarify matters, or repeat words or phrases important in the story.[23] This institutionalised method of audience response mirrors a phenomenon that is familiar to most of us from the daily experience of telling and listening to stories.

Second, the process of narration (for narrator and reader/listener) is crucially interrelated to the culture within which it occurs – and to that culture's cultural models or schemas. The process of creating a narrative, the selection and arrangement of events, the negotiation of meaning is one that occurs within the structures of a culture, using that culture's schemas and related discourse.[24] We draw on existing interpretative resources to create our narratives: 'Narratives do not ... spring from the minds of individuals but are social creations. We are born into a culture which has a ready stock of narratives which we appropriate and apply in our everyday social interaction.'[25] These resources may develop from our local context, from friends and family, or from the public sphere, which is filled with forms of information and entertainment, all competing with each other to grab the attention of consumers – often through their use of narrative.[26]

This creation of narrative meaning and identity is not only processual but also relational. The arrangement of events within a story, as well as the weight and meaning we give to those events, will shift and change according to our particular context and the requirements of each new audience.[27] In turn, when individuals are unable to make sense of experiences using the range of available cultural models, the resultant feelings of confusion and helplessness can be very distressing. Those suffering traumatic stress who are unable to recount, or even, in some cases, to remember, their experiences may provide an extreme example of this.

One form of therapy that has been found to be effective in some cases is to enable the individual to tell their story, thus integrating it into their life narrative, and finding a way to make sense of it.[28] Given the opportunity – space to create, with a sympathetic audience – it may be possible to negotiate alternative meanings from existing narrative structures or to create new structures which more closely reflect experiences.[29] However, some traumatic experiences simply resist this approach: for example, the attempts of some holocaust survivors to retell their experiences 'are feeble, stammering, unfinished, incoherent attempts to describe a single moment of being painfully, excruciatingly alive – the closing in of darkness for one particular individual, nothing more and perhaps much less.'[30] In addition to personal pain, there may be social conditions – stigma, disapproval, disbelief – that preclude this process: some holocaust survivors, for example, report that there were few who wanted to hear about what they had experienced; survivors of rape describe how they are unable to reveal this experience to friends or family – and are unable to make sense of it themselves.[31]

As these last examples illustrate, narratives are not simply tools for intellectual cognition; they also encompass emotional data. The stories we tell about ourselves and each other do not just provide us with an account of how things happen, but of how things feel.[32] Not only do we make sense of external events using narrative, we also, crucially, communicate information about ourselves: 'The structure of narrativity demonstrates that it is by trying to put order on our past, by retelling and recounting what has been that we acquire an identity.'[33] The narratives we select will alter in response to new situations and new audiences that demand a reassessment of our storylines.[34]

However, the creation of narrative is not a simple linear process of making meaning, in retrospect, out of what has already occurred. It also helps to shape our expectations of what we can become in the future. The models that we use to structure our narratives provide 'maps' that describe or advise persons on how to think about what is to come, and their place in it: these may bring comfort, or they may problematise and challenge.[35] The therapist Glenn Larner explains how the narratives told by individuals in therapy often express an overriding sense of fate, by which he means the sense of 'what must be' in a person's destiny, recounting 'stories of the past in terms of their meaning for the future'. In response, Larner understands the self as a discursive location or positioning, and therapy as an opportunity for individuals to recognise the narrative they are telling, and change it – not through 'conquering destiny' but through introducing elements of chance, that is, of 'what may be', and so bringing a freedom to choose or act.[36] As this suggests, narratives may offer hope for different possibilities, or a sense of inevitability, insofar as the story structure we appropriate provides a sense of a pre-scripted ending.[37]

In the search for the cognitive structures that underpin and shape ancient ideas of luck, fate and fortune, we are obviously limited in the kind of evidence we can collect.[38] Nevertheless, it is still possible to assemble a variety of discourses, which can be analysed in similar terms for the cultural functions that they may have served. The case studies in the chapters that follow present and explore a variety of different discourses, ranging from lyric poetry of the seventh and sixth centuries BCE, through some of the earliest historical accounts, dating to the fifth century BCE, to rhetorical and philosophical prose from the fourth century BCE. They are not intended to provide a comprehensive overview of either ancient literature or ancient attitudes, but should be read as illustrations of a particular heuristic approach. This investigation will explore these texts for evidence for ancient Greek cultural models of the uncertain future, focusing on deployment of the language of luck, fate and fortune – in particular, use of the terms *moira*, *tuche* and related forms, and *daimon*(*es*). Rather than seeking to isolate precise definitions of these terms, this study will explore the range of meanings they offer, and the models of luck, fate and fortune they suggest. It will explore the different ways in which those models and their meanings are put to use by their ancient writers/speakers: examining, for example, among which social groups models and meanings may have been shared; to what extent these models of luck, fate and fortune are made explicit or left implicit within the narrative – and the intention behind and impact of these different approaches, and finally, the intellectual and emotional significance of the use of these models for their audience.

# CHAPTER V

# THE ARCHAIC POETS: POLITICS OF FORTUNE

(31) Know the fortunate in order to choose them, and the unfortunate in order to flee from them. Bad luck is usually brought on by stupidity, and among outcasts nothing is so contagious. Never open the door to the least of evils, for many other, greater ones lurk outside. The trick is to know what cards to get rid of. The least card in the winning hand in front of you is more important than the best card in the losing hand you just laid down. When in doubt, it is good to draw near the wise and the prudent. Sooner or later they will be fortunate.

(196) Know your lucky star. No one is so helpless as not to have one, and if you're unfortunate, it is because you haven't recognised it. Some people have access to princes and the powerful without really knowing how or why, and it is only that luck has favoured them. It remains for them only to nurture their luck with effort . . . Luck shuffles the cards the way she wants to. Let each person know his own luck, and his own talents; losing and winning depend on it.

(17) Keep changing your style of doing things. Vary your methods. This will confuse people, especially your rivals, and awaken their curiosity and attention. . . . Malice is ready to pounce on you; you need a good deal of subtlety to outwit it. The consummate player never moves the piece his opponent expects him to, and less still, the piece he wants him to move.

Precepts from *The Art of Worldly Wisdom: a Pocket Oracle*[1]

# THE ARCHAIC POETS: POLITICS OF FORTUNE

In 1992 a surprising book spent a year on the bestseller lists: written over 2000 years after the ancient Greek poetry that will be the main focus of this chapter – it offers some intriguing similarities. Its popularity in 1992 was surprising because it was originally published in 1647. The work of a learned Jesuit theologian and philosopher, Baltasar de Gracián y Morales, the *Pocket Oracle* (*oráculo manual y arte de prudencia*) or 'Art of Worldly Wisdom' was a tour de force of the pithy, witty style of *conceptismo*, presenting around 300 apothegms concerned with living in a world in which 'Good people seem to belong to the good old days . . . when virtue is rare and malice is common'.[2]

The professed aim of the *Pocket Oracle* is the perfection of the human spirit, but mention of God is rare: instead, as we see from the few examples gathered here, the *Oracle* provides sound practical advice about strategies for navigating other people's behaviour and harnessing the vagaries of luck, often using metaphors that refer to pastimes involving chance or skill, such as gambling, shooting, cards and board games. With his unblinking view of the subtle conflicts of daily life, the Jesuit author of this publication clearly struck a lasting nerve: not only was the book a bestseller 300 years later, but a website and mailing list (new aphorisms posted and sent out daily by email) are in operation.[3]

I start with these quotations from the *Pocket Oracle* because of the ways in which their subject matter bridges ancient and modern concerns. Startlingly similar to the modern genre of self-help publications, the advice of the *Pocket Oracle* also closely resembles, in its aims and imagery, many of the sentiments found in the ancient poetry that comprises the focus of this chapter. In all three types of publication we find the discourse of luck, fate and fortune being used to make sense of – even to generate lessons about – the changing fortunes of daily life. In particular, the *Pocket Oracle* focuses on the dangers that accrue to the pursuit of power in public life and politics – a particular theme of the ancient poems to be discussed in this chapter – and this may be a significant reason for its enduring popularity.

In this section, we consider the ways in which the language of luck, fate and fortune, and associated rhetoric of responsibility, develops in lyric poetry composed in the archaic period (the seventh–sixth centuries), across the

Mediterranean.[4] These lyric poems throw back the curtain on a Greek stage where multiple characters jostle for our attention. They take us into a world of passionate individuals and troubled communities, revealing the language of fate and fortune in action, to different ends, within a variety of social and performative contexts. Granted, the evidence this material provides is scarcely straightforward: the circumstances of each poem's creation and performance is often hard to identify, the sentiments expressed are cast in a specific idiom, the existing fragments are hard to piece together or set in context. Nevertheless, these poems, their content and characteristics, provide crucial evidence for a period of Greek history and culture for which there is otherwise relatively little data.

## Performance and Politics

Archaic Greece was a performance culture, and it is likely that all these texts were composed for a public presentation of some kind – from choral compositions for community celebrations, to songs for sympotic carousing.[5] It is tempting to find in these poems a relatively straightforward narrative of emerging (usually elite) group identity and community values. The shared references and underlying social values found across this body of poetry frequently suggest an aristocratic milieu, and many of these poems appear preoccupied with the concerns of a wealthy and socially dominant elite, be they hymning festival victors, singing the praises of a beautiful boy or girl, revelling in the alcoholic pleasures of the *symposium*, or urging on the martial spirit.[6]

However, this is not to argue that this material can be categorised simply as 'elite'. Many of these poems evoke fairly common experiences (falling in love, the dangers of sea travel, the effects of and desire for drink). Moreover, some of the poets, or their personae, certainly appear to hail from non-elite backgrounds. There is also the question of the context of their performance, and how this may have influenced the sentiments they express – especially if, as some think likely, these poets would tailor the content and attitudes of particular poems to their different audiences.[7] Recent analyses have argued for a more complex reading that examines how these poems, performed in different contexts, can be seen to express different, even contested, ideologies within communities.

Particularly relevant to this aspect are those poems that appear to be concerned with situations of conflict. In some cases, these are connected to political events and resulting changes, sometimes violent, in civic and community structures. Although we often know very little about their lives, it seems likely that many of these poets were inspired by their observations and/or experiences of conflict. The surviving fragments of both Callinus of Ephesus and Mimnermus of Smyrna include calls to arms to defend a city, and similar concerns characterise most of the extant work of Tyrtaeus of Sparta. Other poems give us other kinds of clashes: factional politics is the context for the poetry of Alcaeus of Mytilene who seems to be writing to encourage support in the struggle against the tyrant, Pittacus. The poetry of Theognis appears to describe the suffering undergone by a member of the elite class as his community undergoes profound political upheaval. In contrast, much of Solon's poetry justifies his reasons for, and approaches to, tackling the sociopolitical turbulence in Athens. There are further fragmentary intimations of conflict across the corpus – perhaps more than at first appear.[8]

In such troubled contexts, it is likely that, as the ancients themselves realised, such poetry could be an effective political instrument.[9] Exactly what kind of instrument is, of course, still up for debate, and the answer is highly dependent on the presumed context of each poem's performance. The meanings and impact of these poems, with their fervent exploration of current events and their ardent articulation of personal feelings, would vary with the particular setting and nature of their performance – recent events, shared experiences, the identity of the performer, the composition of the audience. Should we imagine a gathering of community-minded citizens or a small group of elite symposiasts – and how does that change our reading of the poem? In certain circumstances, poems that laud or ridicule particular individuals should perhaps be read as more than harmless entertainment, and instead suggest an aggressive assertion of power or values by one particular group.[10] The poetic adulation of a beautiful boy or extolling of the joys of wine may have worked to promote feelings of cohesion in a particular political group. When we play with these different configurations, we can sense the contemporary power of these texts – and they emerge as rich, but multi-layered clues not only to the events and attitudes of the time, but also the perception of particular concepts. Examination of the language of luck, fate and fortune and the way it is deployed to further the particular rhetorical stance of each poem, can offer insight into shared cultural models of the uncertain future. In this chapter, I offer a brief overview of how the lyric poets of the seventh and sixth centuries used this language, followed by a particular discussion of luck, fate, and fortune in the poetry of Solon and Theognis.

## Personnel and Personifications

Across the corpus of poetry, the vocabulary of concepts of luck, fate and fortune is similar to that found in Homeric epic, but with some significant differences. Above all, the supernatural personnel involved is much reduced, so, for example, among these poems we find only three significant appearances by *aisa*: two in poetry by Theognis, and one in a poem by Solon.[11] However, these references, and their rarity, in themselves may be significant. These Homeric echoes need to be read with care: as we will see, invocation of the monolithic Homeric model of fate can be used to elicit a variety of effects.[12]

Both uses of *aisa* by Theognis emphasise the individual's impersonally allocated lot in life – already familiar to us from Homer. Theognis lived in Megara during a time of political upheaval, and his poetry concerns the betrayals experienced, and lessons learned as a result, by a man caught up in social and political conflict: his uses of *aisa* fit within this discourse. In one example, *aisa* seems to describe how long one has been given to live: the poet describes how a man might be thrifty if he had the power to see the end of his life, and expected to live longer, but since he cannot, he must choose between living well and saving money. The speaker of the poem opts to emphasise the latter, counselling his audience to be careful with money and live within one's means. His explanation provides a reflection on the values of his community, continuing: 'in such a generation as this it's best to have money. For if you are wealthy many are your friends, but few if you are poor, and you are no longer the same worthy man you once were.'[13]

The meaning of apportionment also appears in the second example of *aisa* in Theognis' work, but with a more ambiguous nuance. The speaker is praying to Zeus for some pleasure to balance his suffering.[14] Specifically, he asks for vengeance against those who have robbed him of his possessions, and then he states 'for thus, it is my due'.[15] In a recent translation, this phrase follows on from his request for revenge: 'May I give pain in return for pain; for that is my due'. But it is also possible that the phrase precedes the observation that follows; that is, 'there is no retribution in sight for me against the men who have my possessions'. If this is the case, then mention of *aisa* seems more to indicate a state of resignation than of expectation – even a consolatory insight. The different impact of these two possible emphases reminds us of the useful fluidity of these terms, and the range of associations they draw upon.

In each of these passages by Theognis, the appearance of *aisa* lends a particular dignity to the sentiments expressed: in one, a call to thrift is set against a gracious consideration of the brevity of life and the question of what it means to live it well; in the other, a cry for vengeance (or encouragement to endure) evokes a far more expansive vision of cosmic justice. Moreover, this epic echo favours the speaker of the poem, implicitly setting him and his audience among a company of heroes, while his experiences acquire a certain timeless nobility by association.

The reference to *aisa* at the beginning of Solon's poem reveals a different nuance, its Homeric echo drawing the audience's attention to the gravity of the situation facing Athens – and Solon. Probably elected archon (chief magistrate) of Athens in 594 BCE, Solon came into office at a time of great sociopolitical discontent – and famously instituted a series of laws aimed at promoting harmony. His poetry, preserved in fragments in later writers, appears to give us a first-hand account of his intentions, allowing readers to glimpse something of the period in which he lived – both the turbulent times evoked by his poems, and the elite environment in which they would have been performed. This combination is a reminder of the role and status of the man himself, and the background for his reforms. His laws were not intended to create a revolution, but to rein in the behaviour and political infighting of the wealthy elite, and institute social stability.[16]

The passage containing *aisa* reads: 'Our state will never perish by the dispensation (*aisa*) of Zeus or the intentions of the blessed immortal gods; for such a stout-hearted guardian, Pallas Athena, born of a mighty father, holds her hands over it. But it is the citizens themselves who by their acts of foolishness and subservience to money are willing to destroy a great city.'[17] Mention of Zeus' will emphasises the significant contrasts between the mythical city of Troy, besieged and destroyed by a vast Greek army, and the very real, and very troubled city of sixth-century Athens. Whereas Troy could *only* endure the destruction that had been planned for it by the gods, Athens' future, the poet claims, is protected by Athena (ll. 3–4). One can't help but think that Solon is writing out of a sense of persuasive (and desperate?) optimism here. In turn, whereas Troy was threatened by an invading force, the threat to Athens comes from within, from its own citizens (ll. 5–8). The contrasts continue implicitly, the emotional dial subtly tuned to 'hope': Zeus' will may have doomed Troy irrevocably, but the poet suggests that this need not be the case for Athens, where mortal decisions could make all the difference . . . if only the wealthy would change their behaviour.[18]

*Moira* appears often to be personified in the work of the lyric poets, a sort of melancholy muse, the inspiration and focus of their meditations on the uncertainty of life. A passage from Solon illustrates the generally held understanding of *Moira*, describing how she 'brings good and ill to mortals and the gifts of the gods are inescapable. In all actions there is risk and no one knows when something starts, how it is going to turn out.'[19] The poets place constant emphasis on the hidden nature of future and fated events, either worked out by *moira* or by the Olympians. Theognis emphasises the mysterious nature of divine plans: 'It is very difficult to know how the god is going to bring about the outcome of an action uncompleted. For darkness extends over it, and in advance of what is going to occur mortals cannot comprehend the limits of their helplessness'; and Solon agrees: 'the mind of the immortals is altogether hidden from men'.[20]

But underlying this description is a paradox: for although mortals may experience future outcomes as unpredictable, *Moira*'s role is, in fact, to set firm and unchangeable boundaries to events. *Moira* acts as a centralised force that dictates a rigid, normative structure to mortal experience. Like Solon (above), Theognis describes how it is impossible to escape *moira*, explaining elsewhere that 'No one can pay a ransom and avoid death or heavy misfortune, if fate (*moira*) does not set a limit, nor, although he wish to, can a mortal avoid mental distress through bribery when the god sends pain.'[21]

As in Homeric epic, we see this sense of imposed and unalterable limits reflected particularly in phrases used to describe death, in particular the seemingly ubiquitous phrase: '*moira thanatou*';[22] but also referring to the *Moirai* (Fates) spinning out the course of life: for example, Callinus states that 'death will occur only when the *Moirai* have spun it out'.[23] While Ibycus pictures the gods and *Moirai* working out a dreadful compact: 'the gods give much prosperity to those they wish to have it, but for the others (they destroy it?) by the plans of the *Moirai*'.[24] These examples are all concerned with the fate of individuals, but a poem of the late sixth century, ascribed to Simonides of Ceos, gives the three sisters a larger civic remit, asking them for peace and order on behalf of the city.[25]

The notion of the allotted share reaches beyond the final portion, death, and is also used to describe many aspects of a man's life, in phrases that use the verb 'to allocate'.[26] Examples from the poet Theognis illustrate the wide application of this term: as well as the individual allotment of good fortune ('Who can endure the sight of this, the noble dishonoured and the base honoured [lit. 'allotted 'a share of' honour']), or of bad ('One must endure what the gods give mortal men and calmly bear both lots, neither too sick at heart in bad times nor suddenly rejoicing in good times until the final outcome is seen'), the verb is also used to describe individual characteristics ('If you sir, had been allotted as much judgement as stupidity . . .' and 'success and good looks . . . fortunate the man who is allotted both of these') and the common state of daily life for mortals ('mankind's allotment is anxieties . . .').[27] In contrast to these generally aristocratic views of life and experience,

Hipponax uses the idea of the lot as part of a prayer, to describe a man's station: 'since it is my lot to have a demented master, I beg of you that I not get a beating.'[28]

This idea that events are allotted at every level of life, from individual experience to cosmic arrangement, is found across most of the poets: thus, Solon, in a brief line in his poem on the stages of life, suggests that this idea of allotment applies to the natural changes of growing up.[29] The poet Mimnermus suggests, in turn, that these allotted roles and experiences were not considered to be only a mortal experience, when he announces how 'the sun's lot is toil every day.'[30] Archilochus is of the opinion that this idea of allotment allows us to glimpse a pattern in man's affairs and experiences: 'Do not exult openly in victory and in defeat do not fall down lamenting at home, but let your rejoicing in joyful times and your grief in bad times be moderate. Know what sort of pattern [*rusmos*] governs mankind.'[31] The idea of this allotment as inescapable offers one form of consolation – Archilochus offers this guidance: 'my friend, for incurable woes the gods have set powerful endurance as an antidote', while Theognis exhorts his audience to bear their experiences with equanimity, facing both good and bad times with equal self-control.[32]

Importantly, as noted, there appears to be no clash between the activities of the gods, and those of *moira*. Indeed, in some poems we find an overlap. For example, in the works of Archilochus, the majority of references to fate and the uncertainty of man's experience involve the activities of the gods: from responsibility for the imposition of good and evil[33] and resulting requests for help[34], to knowledge of the future[35] and responsibility for the cycle of the acquisition and reversal of fortune.[36] More specifically, we find Zeus given responsibility for overseeing man's behaviour.[37] Only one brief fragment indicates, tantalisingly, the role of *moira* among these divine activities – and it also provides one of only three references to *tuche* that survive across the lyric poets. It reads: '*Tuche* and *moira*, O Perikles, give a man everything.'[38] Nevertheless, perhaps this does not discount mortal effort, since another fragment reads: 'Hard work and human effort accomplish everything for mortals.'[39] (It is tempting to start to assemble some kind of overview or even philosophy from these brief excerpts, but, of course, we must be wary of connecting fragments, and the sentiments they seem to express.)

*Tuche* makes two other appearances among these lyric poems, in a passage by Theognis and a fragment from what appears to be a theogony by Alcman.[40] Theognis mentions *tuche* as he exhorts his listener Polypaides not to pray for outstanding excellence or wealth, since 'the only thing a man can have is *tuche*'. At first sight this sentiment appears almost exactly to reverse the role Archilochus gives *tuche*, above, where, alongside *moira*, *tuche* is the provider of all. But however we read it, *tuche* is clearly linked in both fragments to the provision of fortune. Some fuller, and perhaps more optimistic sense of that aspect of her role may be garnered from her appearance in the fragment of Alcman, where *Tuche* appears amongst a family of well-meaning personifications: *Eunomia* ('Good Order') and *Peitho* ('Persuasion') are her sisters, while her mother is *Promatheia* ('Foresight'). These relationships and her activities may link *tuche* to the mortal exercise of forethought or prudence.

Meanwhile, good luck (*agathe tuche*) appears in a poem of Solon, but only bearing an impersonal sense of success. According to Plutarch, the beginning of the epic verse that described Solon's laws included an invocation of *agathe tuche*.[41] This creates a parallel with the prayer formulations that began civic business in the fifth and fourth centuries – and may, in fact, indicate a later date of composition for this poem. Some other compounds of *tuche* are also worth mentioning: in another passage by Solon, success given by the gods to the man who acts badly is described with the phrase *suntuchien agathen* (literally, 'good fortune').[42] This phrase is also found in Theognis, who also uses another *tuche* compound, *dustuchie*, to describe the heavy 'misfortune' that ensues if *moira* does not set a limit to a man's suffering.[43]

The language of luck, fate and fortune is an integral aspect of the rhetoric of most of these poems. Common reflections across all these writers include the uncertainty of life, the unpredictability of lived experience, the power of the gods.[44] As well as lamentation and consolation about the human predicament, these poets offer instruction on attitudes appropriate to particular situations of uncertainty and reversal. These share some basic similarities, but, as we have already seen, there are also significant differences between them, depending on their context. Diverse models of luck, fate and fortune emerge from these different emphases: it appears that the particular workings of *moira* were inextricably linked to the socio-political worlds of those who feared her. The poetry of Solon and Theognis illustrate these aspects further, demonstrating how these different cultural models of luck, fate and fortune could be used rhetorically to achieve different effects.

## Solon: Security and Stability

As we might expect of a politician who is trying to keep a number of different and warring groups satisfied, Solon's poetry does not set out clear or simplistic answers to questions of good and evil, responsibility and innocence, let alone prescribe a straightforward dogma about the nature of man's relationship with fate, fortune and the gods. He emphasises the need for rectitude and the inevitability of cosmic punishment, but also impresses upon his audience the terrible unpredictability of fate and fortune.

Unsurprisingly, many of his reflections on luck, fate and fortune are interwoven with his instructions about civic responsibilities. The role played by these supernatural forces varies: sometimes it simply reinforces a threat; at other times, it seems to allow him to temper his message. For example, he carefully qualifies the kinds of wealth that will merit the punishment of Zeus: 'Wealth which the gods give remains with a man, secure from the lowest foundation to the top, whereas wealth which men honour with violence comes in disorder, an unwilling attendant persuaded by unjust actions, and it is quickly mixed with ruin.'[45]

The enforcement mechanisms are supernatural and involve Zeus, the gods and *moira*: Zeus, we are told, finds out the man who has an accursed heart and reveals him eventually;[46] while the punishment of the gods is not just a penalty imposed from above, but *theon moira*, 'the fate of the gods', an allotment that is inescapable. Even if the wicked seem to have got away with it, divine punishment will catch them up eventually, and if not with them directly, then with their innocent children.[47]

The message is repeated slightly more directly later in the poem where

Solon criticises man's subservience to wealth, and how destructive is a limitless appetite for profit.[48] But again the message in this passage is not simple: he observes how it is the gods that give men the profit that leads to ruin, and this note of supernatural intervention seems to lessen the guilt of the wealthy, although it is unclear from the text whether profit, gods or men themselves are to be considered responsible. Even so, yet again, there is no equivocation about the power of the god, Zeus, or the ruin he sends as punishment.[49]

But the emphasis is on responsibility, rather than treating mortals as merely helpless victims. It may be that mortals know nothing of the plans of the gods, and 'neither augury nor sacrifice will ward off what is destined', but there is an inseparable relationship between divine intervention and inescapable fate, and man's own will and action.[50] On the one hand, the plans of the gods are mysterious,[51] but on the other, if we suffer because of something we have done, we cannot simply blame the gods.[52]

The strong pious foundation that underpins Solon's sentiments does not depict fate and fortune as simple cause and effect. There is nothing predictable about the course of luck, fate and fortune: 'the man who tries to act rightly falls unawares into great and harsh calamity, while, to the one who acts badly the god gives success in all things, an escape from folly'.[53] And Solon is not afraid to question fortune's apparent lack of social scruples, pointing out how dangerous it is when great good fortune (*polus olbos*) pursues those men who do not really have 'mature minds'.[54]

The discourse of fate and fortune in these poems does not provide a single straightforward model – but that is surely not their aim. Instead, the multiple and sometimes seemingly contradictory appearances of these supernatural figures may give us some insight into the complex social and political problems that would have confronted their author. So fate, fortune and the gods appear as explanations for not only the causes of inexplicable suffering, but also the reason why some people receive honours they do not deserve.

The intrusion of fate and the gods in mortal affairs plays a slightly different role when it is offered almost as an exoneration of the bad behaviour of some individuals (perhaps the kind of explanation that might allow individuals to back down from a previous position without losing face?). But the same super-natural figures will ensure that those who escape punishment will not do so for long – and this provides some consolation, presumably in situations where civic justice is perceived to have fallen short.

Above all, there is a discourse of admonition throughout Solon's poetry, which underlines the unpredictable and inexplicable nature of fate, accompanied by the terrible certainty of justice and the vulnerability of all men, whatever their earthly status: 'no mortal is blessed but all whom the sun looks down upon are in a sorry state'.[55] This evocation of a terrifying supernatural threat, which all mortals share and should stand together to confront, creates a compelling context for Solon's discourse of cohesion and civic unity.

## Theognis: Status and Suffering

Theognis' work is also set (if not actually composed) in a context of sociopolitical upheaval, but whereas Solon was orchestrating socio-political change, Theognis writes or speaks as one who is on the receiving end of it. Some have argued that he is a member of an elite class, caught up in the throes of a political revolution. Others have argued that the poems depict a far less rigidly stratified, but more threatening society than that would suggest – one more like 'the violent world of the Sicilian and American Mafia'.[56] In a number of ways, we can add, the experiences that Theognis' poetry describes find echoes in the greed and malicious intrigue we glimpse in Gracián's poetry (quoted at the beginning of the chapter): one in which values of loyalty and generosity have disappeared, no one, especially not friends, can be trusted, and everyone is simply out to gain power for themselves.[57]

Theognis' response, however, is far less optimistic than that of the seventeenth-century Jesuit. Although he does offer some advice, his poetry makes much of his own suffering – he has lost friends to deceit, his farmland has been confiscated and he fears civil strife.[58] He does offer advice, however, to one Cyrnus, and here we find references to fate and fortune as part of a discourse that tends towards consolation rather than admonition, and towards instructions for survival rather than, as in Solon's works, an argument for stability. The model of luck, fate and fortune that emerges, which is concerned, as we will see, with ideas of endurance, is linked closely with Theognis' descriptions of his society, and his experiences of social change.

Compared with Solon's careful description of various social roles and their complex connections with supernatural powers, Theognis' picture is drawn with a far blunter instrument, reflecting more directly the archaic concept of social position. In this model, the status of a person's birth, his moral goodness and his honour were seen as linked, able to be evoked with a single descriptive term. Thus, a man who was *agathos* ('good') was likely to be a member of an elite class, while to describe someone as *kakos* ('bad') indicated that he was low-born and, inevitably, a rogue. These categories seem to have extended to and informed, at least in part, models of fortune, such that good fortune and high status were expected to have a relationship. For example, Archilochus states 'I seem to be to you an unhappy (*anolbios*) man' and goes on to explain that this is 'not the sort of man I am and my ancestors were'.[59] *Olbios* is a word that indicates happiness and blessedness, but with a particular link to prosperity and worldly goods.[60]

In Theognis' poetry, a man who is blessed in this way (*olbios*) has a life of luxury, enjoying aristocratic pleasures: 'dear boys, horses of uncloven hoof, hunting dogs, and friends in foreign parts' or 'goes home and engages in amorous exercises, sleeping with a handsome boy all day long' or 'loves a boy and does not know the sea, and is not concerned about the approach of night on the deep.'[61] And yet, as we see in his poetry, the unpredictability of fortune clashes with normative ideas of what is right and wrong within the strictures of his particular society – and these neat categories of good/bad, well-born/base, lucky/unlucky reach their limits in the face of reality. In a world in which the value terms for right and good were used to describe not only a man's status, but also his sense of entitlement, the unpredictability of events (and their fortunes) must have seemed particularly shocking. In turn, however, this seems to have shaped one model of luck, fate and fortune such that this very quality, the unpredictability of fortune (be it the gods or fate), offered an explanation of life's profound lack of justice.

So, Theognis states that, 'No man is prosperous or poor or of low or high estate without divine aid'; a sentiment he repeats. Just who operates that aid varies: Theognis instructs Cyrnus that no individual is responsible on his own for ruin or profit, but it is the gods who give both; a little later, it is *moira* who gives even an utterly wicked man riches, but she follows a *daimon*; and only a few lines later we are told that wealth is allocated by Zeus, with his scale, inclining it now one way and now another; a few lines further, we find that good fortune has become a *daimon*.[62]

As we have already seen, this is not a way of excusing the evil that men do – Theognis is quite clear about that. Instead, his discourse on the supernatural allocation of fortune actually focuses our attention on other men's wrongdoing, from a variety of rhetorical stances, and introducing a number of different models of fate and fortune's operations. So, at one point he laments that 'even a base man is allotted respect', while those who are *agathoi* are humbled, and he even rails at the gods themselves.[63] Elsewhere, he exonerates the gods, in order to emphasise just how bad mortal behaviour must have been ('Everything here has gone to the dogs and to ruin, Cyrnus, and we can't hold any of the blessed immortal gods responsible . . .'[64]).

An alternative approach assumes that the gods may know something mortals do not: for example, there are some famous lines by Solon in which he observes how misfortune ambushes the man who tries to act rightly, while the one who acts badly triumphs.[65] In place of this terrifyingly uncertain and unfair view of events, Theognis sets up a different contrast, swapping the do-gooder of Solon's passage with a man who is only in search of a good reputation, and his wrongdoer with a man who is really trying to act well.[66] This new version tidies up and makes sense of otherwise inexplicable injustice, crediting the gods with sharp insight, while underlining the awfulness of mortal behaviour and motivation.

This consolatory model – that the gods can see beyond the surface to a man's true worth – appears again when Theognis contrasts the temporary, unworthy successes cherished by those who are low-born, with acquisitions and characteristics of more lasting, and noble, value. Thus, he notes in one passage how men may acquire possessions, but the proper share of excellence only comes to a few.[67] He acknowledges a divine force is in operation in both processes. However, whereas it is an anonymous *daimon* that hands over the worthless goods, it is *moira* who distributes virtue, suggesting that this is a far more long-lasting and deserved allocation. In these last two examples, we see how Theognis' discourse of fate and fortune, and the various models of luck, fate and fortune that emerge from it, interact with a particular model of society: the positions and deserts of the low and the nobly born are compared and contrasted – to the advantage of those who are higher up the social scale. We see this interaction occur again in the instructions he gives Cyrnus about showing the right attitude to events, and how this can offer the opportunity to demonstrate superior social merit. So he instructs him to stand firm in the face of misfortune ('Don't let it show too much; it's bad to let it show'[68]) and encourages him not to show his feelings too readily, since this is a sign of a cowardly character.[69] Elsewhere he explains how the noble man puts up with bad luck, and does not reveal his suffering, while it is a sign of a base man that he does not know how to control his emotions and endure misfortune.[70]

Across the archaic poets we find the language of luck, fate and fortune used to reflect on the unpredictable nature of human life, the gap between merits and rewards, the powers that are in control of these events, the unknown nature and plans of those powers – and the right attitude with which to confront them. It may be that these poetic protests reflect a general sense of uncertainty that arose from living in a dangerous world. Looking at these poems as indices of current potential threats, we learn of a range of risks, such as seafaring or falling in love, which provoke the poets to thoughts of the vulnerability of the human condition.[71] In particular, however, there seems to be a concern to reflect on experiences of political, civic or social upheaval, and to use this language of luck, fate and fortune to explore ways to respond to them.

To this end, the poets exhort, console, exonerate, and admonish, as well as instructing their audiences on how to comport themselves in the face of misfortune.[72] The language of luck, fate and fortune is fashioned to fit different contexts and purposes, various moods and motivations; in the process, we see these poets drawing on a number of different cultural models of luck, fate and fortune. The poetry of Theognis and Solon offers two contrasting examples: Theognis speaks with the voice of an individual trying to survive in, and make sense of, a violent society. He speaks to a particular constituency whose members share his social values, and in his descriptions, luck, fate and fortune offer confirmation of his and his fellows' social status and provide some solace in the face of their unfair suffering. The vagaries of fortune offer occasions to demonstrate (elite) virtues, and the outcome may well be right, even if we mortals cannot see it. In contrast, the figures of luck, fate and fortune that emerge from Solon's instructive poetry offer little comfort. Here we find implacable justice-dealers, single-minded and ruthless, focused on administering retribution and correcting wrong action, even down through the generations, while depictions of the unpredictability of fate and fortune draw attention to mortal ignorance and terrible vulnerability in the face of the unknown. In Solon's poetry, luck, fate and fortune become an external force for every man to fear, and, perhaps, a threat against which to stand together.

The conceptions of luck, fate and fortune that these poems reveal seem to have enjoyed a long legacy. As the quotations from Gracián's much later literary work suggests, these exhortatory, consolatory and instructive models of luck, fate and fortune persist: the language of luck, fate and fortune, and the cultural models it summons, have continued to offer powerful support in the face of social and political struggles.

## CHAPTER VI

# HERODOTUS: PATTERNS OF FATE

JONATHAN: *Fate's behind everything?*
SARA: *I think so.*
JONATHAN: *Everything's predestined? We don't have any choice at all?*
SARA: *I think we make our own decisions. I just think that fate sends us little signs, and it's how we read the signs that determines whether we're happy or not.*
JONATHAN: *Little signals. Yeah.*
SARA: *Yeah.*
JONATHAN: *Fortunate accidents. Lucky discoveries. Columbus in America.*
SARA: *Yeah, or Fleming discovering penicillin.*

From *Serendipity*[1]

Before we plunge into fifth-century Greece and the turmoil that surrounded the invasions of the Persians, we pause for a moment on the snowy streets of twentieth-century New York. In *Serendipity*, a popular romantic comedy, two characters, Jonathan and Sara (played by John Cusack and Kate Beckinsale), meet in a crowded bookstore in New York city, just before Christmas, and more or less instantly know they are made for each other. They part, but not before deciding to let fate rule on whether or not they should be together, writing their details on items that they will release into the world (he on a $5 note he uses to buy a paper; she in a book she sells to a second-hand bookshop). If either of them finds the information of the other, then they know that fate means them to be a couple. Oh go on, guess what happens...

Perhaps because of its unquestioningly romantic approach, the film has proved startlingly popular (one reviewer noted 'About a quarter of the audience I saw *Serendipity* with (evidently a fair national sample) wolfed it down and clamored for more') although others have found it less to their taste (the same reviewer called it 'rotten cotton candy' while Jane Campion's film *In the Cut* provides a devastating criticism of the gender stereotypes and cultural values that *Serendipity* promotes).[2] I reproduce this extract from the film's script here because of its clear exposition of a certain current cultural model of fate and its workings: the idea that a power has mapped out the future, and, if we are only listening to its cues, it will somehow let its recipients know what will happen. As the *Histories* of Herodotus shows us, it turns out to be a model with a long history.

Herodotus' *Histories* was written, as the author states at the beginning of the work, to preserve the cause (*aitie*) of hostilities between Greeks and non-Greeks – a quest, we could argue, that marks him and his work as a product of the intellectual milieu of his time. The work is a *historie*, a term used in the fifth century to indicate an enquiry about the nature of the world, and the account includes methods of argument, and terms found among the philosophical and scientific writing of the late fifth century.[3] Yet against this seemingly rational background, the explanatory position that he takes, the basis for his exploration of events is, to modern eyes, confusing. Rather than a scientific premise of causes and effects, the overwhelming themes of his work reflect the power of fate, and the inevitability of alternating fortunes.

Herodotus' *Histories* marks an intellectual crossroads: the intellectual ambitions of developing scientific inquiry are coupled here with close attention to more traditional sources of times gone by. The *Histories* provides us with stories from a wide range of cultures, local stories rich in local significance, captured at one particular moment by our writer and then carefully placed in his larger account. This seemingly 'rational', even scientific written enquiry, is expressed as, and rooted in, multiple oral accounts, an amalgam of different perspectives on the past, each of which may assign authority for events differently.[4]

## HERODOTUS: PATTERNS OF FATE

Nevertheless, the *Histories* is far from simply a transcription of traditional tales. Instead, as scholars have come to realise, this is a careful weaving of multiple narratives that are intertwined with precise and careful artistry: 'The knots and burrs in the growth of Herodotus' narrative grain are not defects, but intrinsic to the attraction of the timber's polished surface.'[5] The overall effect is, in some ways, kaleidoscopic: the content of the *Histories* comprises a wealth of different stories from a vast range of cultures and communities; this is then reflected through Herodotus' diverse intellectual approaches and narrative styles. The result is multi-dimensional: not only many stories, but also multiple registers, as the author marshals his material into a single, coherent account.

Herodotus' presentation of the natural world provides an example of how implicit assumptions about the world inform, and structure, his apparently sprawling narrative. Scholars have reassembled his conception of the natural world and describe a model that, as Gould put it, is based on a 'projection on to the spatial plane of the fundamental assumption of reciprocity'.[6] This model sets normality at its centre, gradually moving out towards extremities that are increasingly exotic. The topography and nations of the north and south reflect each other: Scythians and Egyptians, Nile and Danube, and, if they exist, the lands and peoples of the Hyperboreans, and Hypernoteans.[7] This may seem at first like a simplistic physical mirroring of countries and cultures. But through Herodotus' careful narrative, it serves several purposes, providing an index of the links between peoples, their landscapes and their politics. It can be read, in turn, as providing the basis for a more complex analysis of national characteristics, one that challenges the very categories it has set up. And it is far from static, prompting a more profound reflection on how and why peoples move from one category to another – for example, from being conquerors to being conquered; from having 'hard' attributes to being a soft and vulnerable nation – in what ways they interact, and with what results, and what this means for an understanding of identity.[8]

Moreover, these physical and spatial patterns are, in some ways, part of Herodotus' conceptual model of causation, as it emerges implicitly from across the narrative(s) of the *Histories*. Overlapping and interacting with these physical/spatial factors are more abstract elements, in particular, the pervading presence and operations of the divine, and of fate and fortune. Herodotus does provide some straightforward authorial statements about these elements, but a second, more complex data set also comes gradually to light, in and across the many stories he tells. These bristle with intra- and inter-narrative clues which slowly reveal the operations of luck, fate and fortune in mortal lives, and the diverse supernatural powers involved in orchestrating them.[9]

## Fate, Fated, Fateful

Among these powers, the more archaic concepts of fate appear very rarely. *Moros* turns up where we might expect it, in the language of an oracle, a prophecy by the mythical seer Bacis to be exact, where it describes the day of doom of an ill-fated army of Median archers.[10] *Morsimos* 'fated' describes the expectation of a noble Persian, Zopyrus, that the rebel city Babylon will fall – he has, after all, seen a mule give birth, which was the condition given by an oracle.[11] However, *moira* does make some significant appearances: the first at the very beginning of Herodotus' work, in the story of Croesus, the sixth-century BCE King of Lydia, and his egregious, but apparently unavoidable, misunderstanding of an oracle from Delphi, which announced that if he invaded Persia he would destroy a great empire. Unfortunately, this famously foretold not his victory over the Persians (as he thought), but his defeat at their hands. The programmatic nature of this story is hard to doubt, but where we might expect it then to introduce a single model of luck, fate and fortune to run throughout the narrative, it actually ushers in a series of different, overlapping models, which vary with the context and characters of their telling.[12]

The first of these is voiced by Solon, who, pictured here as having set Athens up with her new constitution, is on his travels, ostensibly seeing the world, but really avoiding any pressure from the Athenians to repeal the laws that he has established at their request. In his literary guise as a great sage, he visits King Croesus in Sardis, where he stays with him as a guest in his palace. Croesus takes it as an opportunity to display his tremendous wealth, and presses his well-travelled house guest to tell him how happy he seems compared with anyone else. However, far from playing along with his host, in reply, Solon regales Croesus with a lecture that starts with the comforting insight that 'Human life is entirely a matter of chance'; goes on to explain that although Croesus is extremely rich and rules over vast populations he cannot be pronounced fortunate until he dies well; digresses into a meditation on the importance of luck; before ending, cheerfully, with the thought that 'the god often offers prosperity to men, but then destroys them utterly and completely.'[13] Unfortunately, Croesus does not understand the significance of Solon's instruction, or what we might call this 'reversal' model of fortune, and through his own behaviour provides us with another model – that of inescapable fate.

After misunderstanding the oracle, Croesus goes to war and his kingdom falls. Croesus is captured by Cyrus, King of the Persians, and Lydia is absorbed into the Persian Empire. Croesus' protests to the priestess at Delphi that he was treated unfairly by the oracle are met with the simple but unarguable explanation: 'Not even a god can turn aside his allotted fate.'[14] As Apollo explains, it is the *Moirai*, the Fates themselves, who direct events and whom Apollo was unable to divert in Croesus' favour.[15] In this case, Croesus' fate was set many years before when his ancestor Gyges, who had been a favourite bodyguard of the King of Lydia, Candaules, killed his master and took his throne. Croesus is, apparently, paying the penalty for Gyges' actions. This looks rather like a simple 'crime-and-punishment model' of fate – and yet, Herodotus has described earlier how Candaules himself unwittingly manoeuvred Gyges into the situation that resulted in his own death, when he persuaded an unwilling Gyges to view his wife naked. (She sees Gyges and punishes him and her husband by forcing Gyges to choose between Candaules' life and her own.)[16] Throughout the narrative, Herodotus emphasises how Gyges is unable to change or escape events, although he fears the worst: once he has taken the throne, the Delphic oracle confirms his reign – and foretells the punishment of descendant, Croesus. Human life may appear to be a matter of chance, but working alongside, indeed, pulling the strings behind the curtain, is fate in all its inevitability.

*Moira*, in her guise as the allocated portion of a life, may not receive such emphasis again, but she certainly recurs, both explicitly and implicitly, throughout the *Histories*. And although some scholars have seen in her occurrences only a proverbial use,[17] this seems too dismissive of a term that, as we have seen, would have resonated with meaning for its contemporary audience. Explicitly we find *moira* used both by characters and in Herodotus' own narrative, rounding off or explaining the events and outcomes of key narratives. For example, Astyages, King of the Medes, on discovering that his grandson Cyrus, whom he had tried to kill, is still alive, admits to him that 'I saw something in a dream and tried to harm you but it was your *moira* to survive'.[18] Maeandrius, who is ruling over Samos in the absence of the tyrant Polycrates, who has been assassinated, describes to the Samian assembly how his predecessor, Polycrates, whose behaviour as ruler he disapproved of, has now 'met his *moira*'.[19] Both cases echo the familiar meaning of *moira* as the 'lot' or 'apportioned life' of an individual. But we can also see that for the characters themselves, they do more: for Astyages, the reference to *moira* offers a way of explaining (to himself?) his failure to achieve his original murderous goal; for Maeandrius, his careful reference to Polycrates and his *moira* perhaps allows him to suggest to his audience that the tyrant's horrible end was ordained by the gods. (Herodotus has already made this clear to his reader: as we will see, the divinely unavoidable nature of Polycrates' fate has already been heralded with a series of warnings delivered by his friend, King Amasis of Egypt.)

When Herodotus uses *moira* in his authorial voice to describe the end of King Arcesilaus of Cyrene, he introduces a further aspect.[20] Arcesilaus 'fulfilled his *moira*' by burning to death some of his enemies. His actions meant that he inadvertently realised the events of a previous oracle that also foretold his death – and, although he then attempted to avoid the rest of the prophecy, he was murdered. Having observed the care with which Arcesilaus tried to avoid his fate, Herodotus goes on, 'So Arcesilaus, whether with or without meaning to,[21] missed the meaning of the oracle and fulfilled his *moira*.'[22] The basic meaning of *moira* has not changed: it is an allocation, connected with an individual's course of life, and finally his death. But Herodotus' aside adds a further nuance: he seems almost to be suggesting that Arcesilaus might have missed the meaning of this oracle deliberately. The comment may be meant ironically, the author and audience sharing the foolishness of trying to escape *moira*: whether he wanted to or not, Arcesilaus missed the point.[23] But it also highlights the character of Arcesilaus, so capable of great cruelty, so easily realising the actions that led to his death. As with the story of Croesus, this draws our attention again to the curious interconnection of fate and mortal action, and directs our attention to the relationship between fate and character.

Mirroring the story of Croesus and creating a frame for the *Histories*, is another account of a leader and his thwarted military ambitions, in which the role of the gods in ensuring a particular course of events is made explicit. This episode introduces us to some more of the language of fate and fortune in Herodotus. It concerns Xerxes, the leader of the Persians who is on the verge of being persuaded to alter his plans to invade Greece by his advisor and uncle Artabanus. But the King's change of heart is prevented by repeated visits from a 'tall and handsome man' who appears in the night, as a dream, to deliver increasingly threatening messages before flying away. The supernatural fixer also appears to Artabanus, who recognises its origins, referring to it as a '*daimon*ic impulse'.[24] It is clear: Xerxes must invade Greece; he has no choice. King and uncle manage to put a positive spin on it – the gods must want the destruction of Greece, after all! – but it becomes clear later in the narrative that both remain filled with forebodings.[25]

In the case of Croesus, there is at least some idea of the mortal actions that provoke his suffering (even if we do not understand how the connection works); but Xerxes' fate does not even seem to offer that. Some commentators have argued that Xerxes must have committed sacrilege when he 'yoked the Hellespont' in order to cross into Greece, and this is his punishment. However, this crime-and-punishment model of fortune does not (again) really work: there is simply no evidence that this act is one that would have spurred the anger of the gods.[26] Instead, what this action does emphasise is Xerxes' good fortune: he demonstrates a high level of confidence, even arrogance, along with a level of wealth, social standing and ambition (he is the King of the Persian Empire, after all!). It seems that instead we are back to the reversal model of fortune first described by Solon: like Croesus, Polycrates and Arcesilaus, the fate of Xerxes follows that pattern. So are the gods to blame for what happens to Xerxes? The two wise men of the *Histories*, Solon and Artabanus, as they reflect on the cycle of fortune/misfortune, may provide some further guidance.

## Gods and *Daimones*, Dreams and Oracles

Xerxes' own uncle reminds the King of how the gods resent mortal greatness and pride; the reason he gives is that the god is *phthonesas*, 'jealous'; he allows no one but himself to have the pride of ambition (in Greek this is *mega phronein* – a state of mind that may be regarded as admirable among men, even if here it engenders divine jealousy). Solon uses similar terms in his lecture to Croesus: although his mortal subject is nothing more than fortunate, this is enough to gain the unpleasant attention of the gods. As Solon says, before launching into the details of what it means to be lucky or unlucky, 'the god is full of *phthonos* (jealousy) and turbulence towards us', and he ends his lecture reminding Croesus that 'the god promises fortune to many people and then utterly ruins them'.[27]

These are not the only places in the *Histories* that this message occurs: the idea that good fortune brings divine jealousy and then destruction also appears in Amasis' heartfelt advice to Polycrates as he observes, with a sinking heart, his friend's run of good luck: 'I know of no man whom continual good fortune did not bring in the end to evil, and utter destruction', as he explains: 'I know the gods, how jealous they are.'[28] The gods in question in each of these episodes remain unnamed – perhaps because they are behaving badly[29] – but named or not, their role is clear. These three episodes bring another supernatural actor onto the set, alongside mortal action and the cosmic plan of fate, one that is, perhaps, more hands-on in its approach than the others, the *daimon*.

As the story of Xerxes' dream suggested, gods, named or not, are not the only supernatural figures flitting about the storylines of the Histories. Both Greek and non-Greek characters tend to describe events as happening because of *daimones*.[30] *Daimones* appear in dreams giving warnings – as recounted both by characters and by the authorial voice of the narrative.[31] In one example, Herodotus seems to credit a *daimon* with arranging matters to create what we would call a coincidence: following a portentous dream, Astyages, King of the Medes, has ordered his advisor, Harpagus, to expose the child Cyrus. Harpagus takes the child to a cowherd whose wife has, 'by means of divine will' (*kata daimona*), given birth. The child is born dead, and so the cowherd and his wife raise the baby Cyrus as their own, ensuring his survival.[32] *Kata daimona* means literally, 'according to a *daimon*': should we interpret it this way? In English, we can translate it more loosely, with a variety of nuances: so, for example, 'by divine will', which sounds as if any *daimon* is merely a messenger of a god who has been left unnamed, perhaps from piety. Alternatively, 'as chance would have it' rather takes any supernatural personification out of the picture. Both translations are possible, but neither really gives full recognition to the Herodotean context, in which *daimones* are frequently described as, or credited with, manipulating events.

In addition to *daimones*, a number of visions or ghosts (the Greek for this phenomenon is *phasma*, pl. *phasmata*) appear throughout the text. Some of these are supernatural events, for example, when Scyles, King of Scythia, sees his house burning down, struck by a thunderbolt, during the Bacchic initiation that will lead to his death; or the eclipse seen by Xerxes and his army, which results in the horrible death of Pythius the Lydian's eldest son, cut in half and laid out on either side of the road down which Xerxes' army processes out of Sardis; or a divine defence of Delphi (thunderbolts, falling rocks and eerie shouts of triumph), as the Persians attack it. But a number of these *phasmata* are in human form, some offering advice (Aristeas the Proconnesian who returned from the dead to instruct the Metapontians to erect a statue to Apollo), or issuing commands (a mysterious female figure who commanded the Greek ships at Salamis not to retreat); others creating life (the hero Astrabacus appears to the displaced wife of Ariston, King of Sparta, who then gives birth to Demaratus) or killing warriors whose time has come (a mysterious figure seen at the battle of Marathon by the warrior Epizelus who is then struck blind); still others confused with living mortals, are busy fulfilling supernatural plans (see below for the example of Timo, the Parian priestess).[33]

The presence of jealous gods, wilful *daimones* and bossy ghosts seasons the text with a sense of uncertainty; nevertheless, as we found in the lyric poets above, beneath this veneer of unpredictability lurks an unswerving divine plan. With no apparent sense of contradiction, the inescapability of fate is a theme that runs throughout the *Histories*. Stories conveying this message are woven throughout the narrative, forming an image of a world in which, at every turn, the course of events is running according to a divine plan.[34] Various story types recur: those that include the operation of oracles are particularly common.[35] These oracle stories themselves can, in turn, be categorised into various types. One of the most frequently used involves the recipient of an oracle misinterpreting or ignoring the message it conveys and then suffering, usually horribly, if not mortally, in a way he or she had either contrived to avoid or simply disregarded.[36]

Coming as something of a relief are a few stories in which a character does understand the oracle he has received: the Ethiopian King Sabacos is one example. He usurps the Egyptian throne, but gives it up after a dream, which he interprets as having been sent by the gods with the intention of making him commit sacrilege and suffer the consequences. He refuses to do so, instead giving up the throne and returning to Ethiopia, having ruled Egypt for the 50 years ordained by earlier oracles.[37] But although these stories offer some relief, their message is the same: these events must come to pass as ordained, whether mortals choose to co-operate or not.[38] Less overt versions of the same message abound: Herodotus in his own narrative voice frequently uses phrases that stress how events had to turn out the way they did. So for example, as he pursues the course of a story, he mentions 'what had to be', both of events that have happened some time ago and those that have occurred more recently.[39] Nevertheless, this does not mean that human action is immaterial.

## Mortal Intervention?

Fate, the gods, *daimones* and apparitions may be hard at work moving the scenery, but on Herodotus' stage the spotlight is firmly on the mortal actors. Throughout the narrative, the instrument of 'what had to be done' is usually mortal, his or her choice to act, or not, is the crucial mechanism for events. The question of what responsibility these situations hold for their mortal protagonists is a puzzling one for us, and, from the narrative it seems, for the ancients as well, so it is worth examining a few examples in more detail. First, the case of Timo, a Parian priestess, accused by her fellow citizens of revealing to the Athenian general Miltiades how he should go about conquering Paros.[40]

The story goes that Timo gave Miltiades advice (Herodotus does not tell us what she said, only what Miltiades proceeded to do). He then entered the sanctuary of Demeter the Lawgiver by jumping the fence, but was struck by fear, which prompted him to leave. On jumping down again from the sanctuary wall, he hurt his leg – and things started to go very wrong. His failure to annex Paros led him to be prosecuted by his fellow Athenians and fined; his injury eventually caused his death. Herodotus tells us that the Parians wanted to execute Timo for giving away crucial secrets; but they are obviously not sure of their ground because they send to Delphi to find out what to do. The oracle tells them Timo is not guilty, but an apparition had helped to lure Miltiades to the horrible death he was fated to die. Herodotus leaves us with the simple statement: 'that was the Pythia's response to the Parians' question'.

It could be argued that what this means is that Timo is not guilty because she is simply 'an instrument of the god'[41] – she was, in effect, simply acting under orders, and not responsible for her actions. This would provide a pleasingly straightforward analysis, but it would suggest a particularly subservient attitude by the Greeks to supernatural intervention. Such an attitude scarcely fits with the impression of mortal behaviour given in other parts of Herodotus' narrative, especially in light of the ubiquitous struggles by mortals against the supernatural rulings revealed to them via oracles.

It also may not, in fact, give an accurate interpretation of the Delphic ruling. The Greek says literally that Timo is not 'the cause of these things'.[42] The Pythia seems not to be concerned with the guilt (or not) of Timo, but to be taking a larger view of events. The implication is not so much that she is not responsible, as that there were more powerful forces at work. The second part of the Pythia's pronouncement seems to support this. The idea that Timo had 'appeared to Miltiades and led him to evil' implicates her in a divine plan, of which the Pythia has knowledge. The question of Timo's responsibility turns on the larger plan of which her actions were a part. She is to be judged only on the final (and future) results of her actions.[43]

Perhaps the most debated instance of blame and responsibility in Herodotus returns us to King Croesus, famously labelled *aitios* by the Pythia for not checking his interpretation of an oracle that seemed to promise victory.[44] It seems intrinsically unfair, and even more unjust is the idea that his suffering came about, as the Pythia reveals, because he must pay the penalty for his ancestor's wrongdoings.[45] Is this simply evidence for 'an unrationalised collection of attitudes and responses'?[46] Or is it that we, with modern sensibilities, are trying to connect two ideas (guilt and cause), which, for Herodotus at least, only sometimes operated in harmony, and which, crucially, also involved the role of fate?

If, for Herodotus, the key question was not one of guilt, but one of cause, then the explanation of events may be somewhat clearer. Croesus is the cause of his own defeat at the hands of the Persians insofar as he misunderstood the oracle he was given. At another level, the crime of his ancestor is also a cause of his suffering. These are not contradictory statements: they are both legitimate causal explanations – but one describes events on the mortal plane, involving questions of choice and responsibility, while the other provides a glimpse of the supernatural realm, which involves the balance of cosmic justice. If we do start to wonder what might have happened had Croesus *not* misunderstood the oracle, and opted not to invade Persia, but to stay safely at home, then the story of Xerxes, Artabanus and the divine messenger perhaps provides an answer. It is part of the divine plan that Xerxes should invade Greece: his choice to do so is, at one level, simply a cause.[47]

Both Xerxes and Croesus, indeed, most of the individuals who suffer some misfortune in the *Histories*, are of some social and political standing. The disruption of good fortune is a key model of luck, fate and fortune that runs throughout the *Histories*, first expressed by Herodotus himself at the very beginning of this work, and then reinforced by Solon as he discusses mortal happiness.[48] The reasons for such disruptions are plentiful, and overlapping, ranging from fate to whimsical divine jealousy.

However, there is another player that appears in Herodotus' *Histories* as a key contriver of events: *tuche*. The term appears in a range of formulations: *tuche, eutuchie* ('good fortune') and *suntuchie* ('coincidental fortune'). There are no references to *dustuchia* ('bad-fortune' – although see later for the verb

'I suffer misfortune', *dustucheo*). It is worth examining the uses of these terms in some detail, since they offer a different model of luck, fate and fortune, one with a lighter and more surprising touch than the heavy fingers of fate.

## Lady Luck's Lighter Touch

There are three basic uses of *tuche* in Herodotus, each of which offers a different dimension to the meaning of the term. The first two are relatively straightforward; they occur as incidental comments on the main events and each in their way indicates the unpredictable nature of events.

> a) **'Heaven-Inspired or Divine'**: The phrase *theiei tuchei*, 'by a heaven-inspired/divine *tuche*' occurs four times. In the first example, Herodotus uses it to describe the way in which an exiled Samian, Syloson, brother of the tyrant Polycrates, agrees to give his cloak away for free to Darius, at that time a soldier in the bodyguard of the Persian King. When Darius, in turn, becomes King of the Persians, Syloson uses this connection to ask him for help in regaining his country. In this story, we also find the term *eutuchie*, used to introduce the account. In the second example, the hero Heracles is crossing the wilds of Scythia when his horses are spirited away, as Herodotus puts it, *theiei tuchei*. The story told to Herodotus by the Greeks of the Black Sea relates how Heracles' search for the creatures eventually led him to father Scythes, from whom every successful Scythian king is descended. Finally, in the third example the child Cypselus, who will grow up to be a tyrannical ruler of Corinth, escapes death because he smiles at his murderer, *theiei tuchei*.[49] On the one hand, the details of these stories stress the unpredictability of events: the random act of kindness, the uncomprehending smile, the mysterious disappearance that leads to an unguessable outcome. However, all these events, although minor in themselves, lead to extraordinary outcomes: they become marked, in retrospect, by the impact of a greater than mortal power, *tuche*.

b) **'Such a Fate'**: In each of the next four passages, *tuche* carries a basic meaning of 'events that have befallen us', but the imagery is different in each case. In the first two passages, individuals are described as interacting with *tuche* in particularly physical ways and the term seems to describe a quality or property of each individual. The first episode takes place during the Ionian revolt, when some Chians, who have taken refuge in Ephesus, are killed by the men of that town because they wrongly think that their visitors are bandits come to carry off their women. The description of these events concludes with the phrase 'thus they fell into such *tuches*' – not one *tuche*, but several, presumably one for each man who 'fell'. In the second example, the exiled Spartan king Demaratus reaches Asia by 'using/experiencing such a *tuche*'. Here, *tuche* is used to summarise a series of adventures that befall one man.[50]

The next two examples treat *tuche* more simply, involving less imagery and little metaphorical language.[51] In the first of these, we find Achaemenes, brother of Xerxes and commander of the Persian fleet, considering strategy: 'If on top of our present fortunes, when we've just had 400 ships wrecked you send another 300 away from the main body of the fleet . . .' *Tuche*, translated here as 'fortunes', appears in the plural and could simply be translated as 'current events' – although the setting means that it carries definite implications of bad fortune. The second case concerns the behaviour of Artemisia, queen of Halicarnassus and ally of Xerxes, at the battle of Salamis. Finding her ship trapped, she rams an allied vessel, which happens (by means of *tuche*) to be in the way, and sinks it. Herodotus questions whether this was intentional or not, and then goes on to describe how this created a double piece of good fortune for her, insofar as her action meant that her real enemy was deceived into thinking she was on his side – and did not attack her. This second 'good fortune' is unequivocal, but it helps to throw the meaning of the first into some ambiguity, raising the possibility that what happened 'by *tuche*' was somehow intended to happen in her favour.

These are the incidental references to *tuche*. However, in the first book of the *Histories* we find a string of references to *tuche* that draw much more focused attention to this entity, and provide an opportunity to explore Herodotus' understanding of perceptions of *tuche* in more detail. Since they all occur either in the speech or thought of a character, we may gain some idea of current understandings and rhetorical uses of the concept. These references to *tuche* occur in doublets, where the second use of the term builds on, echoing or contradicting, the first. This cluster of appearances may also work to establish the presence and workings of *tuche* before its later, briefer occurrences.

c) **Spotlight on *Tuche*:** The first mention of *tuche* occurs in Solon's lecture to Croesus, king of Lydia. As Herodotus makes clear, Croesus expects to be told that Solon knows no one happier. But Solon will not co-operate. He says: 'For you seem to me to be very wealthy and king of many people. But I still cannot say to you what you ask me until I have learned how well you will end your life. For a very rich man is no happier than a man who lives his life day to day, if *tuche* does not keep up with him and he ends his life still in possession of all the good things.'[52] The great sage's prolix description of the need for *tuche* is the climax of a series of stories about individuals whom he judges to have died in states of good fortune – although they were far from being as wealthy or powerful as Croesus. Throughout this section, the narrative is laced with the expectations, and impatience of Croesus, who longs for the sage to recognise the pre-eminence of his own happiness. But Solon's elaboration creates a pause in the narrative, during which the audience is forced to focus on the important role of *tuche*, and to reflect on her/his/its unpredictable behaviour – but what exactly does *tuche* mean here?

*Tuche* is translated as 'good fortune' in the Oxford World's Classics edition – and that seems to be appropriate. However, the appearance of the same phrase ('*tuche* attends/follows/keeps up with') in the parallel scene between Xerxes and Artabanus suggests a different emphasis.[53] Artabanus says: 'In my experience, nothing is more advantageous than good planning. I mean, even if a setback happens, that doesn't alter the fact that the plan was sound; it's just that the plan was defeated by *tuche*. However, if someone who hasn't laid his plans properly is attended by *tuche*, he may have had a stroke of luck, but that doesn't alter the fact that his plan was unsound.' In this passage *tuche* is responsible for opposing a well-laid plan, suggesting that *tuche* has a more neutral meaning than simply 'good luck': when it attends you, it is on your side, but it can equally well foil things. Solon's turn of phrase in his conversation with Croesus suggests that we all need *tuche*: this power *must* 'attend' a man if he is to end his life well. Together these explanations suggest not only that *tuche* and material wealth are separate, but also that *tuche*'s presence alone does not provide an instant recipe for good fortune either.[54]

The next two references offer another doublet. The scene is the Median court of King Astyages.[55] Frightened by a prophetic dream that foretold that his grandson would take his throne, Astyages ordered his relative Harpagus to kill the baby boy. But Harpagus failed to carry out the task. Many years later Astyages recognises the boy – who will become the great Persian king Cyrus – and confronts Harpagus. When he hears what happened, he pretends to forgive him, saying that his daughter's anger at him had been very upsetting. 'But, seeing as how everything has turned out fine (literally, '*tuche* has changed for the better'), why don't you send your son to meet this young boy and join me for dinner.' When Harpagus' son arrives at the palace, Astyages murders him, dismembers him and then serves him to Harpagus as the main course.

The phrase that Astyages uses literally means '*tuche* has changed for the better' – and the verb is active. The implication is not that any human agent has intervened, but that *tuche* itself has caused these events. The audience/readers, with their privileged viewpoint, may quite rightly suspect that Astyages is lying through his teeth: so is this reference to *tuche* changing simply part of his deceptive rhetoric, or does it have another meaning? We soon find out when he follows this pronouncement with an invitation to what turns out to be a gruesome meal. His discovery of Cyrus means that, in his opinion, *tuche* has indeed shifted in his favour – and he is now back in murderous control. But before this ambiguity is cleared up, there is a second mention of *tuche*.[56] This time we enter the thoughts of Harpagus who, we are told, is encouraged by the fact that his previous disobedience to Astyages has now turned out well, and that in light of good *tuche* he has been invited to dinner at the palace. Astyages' recent reference to *tuche* has already prompted the audience not to take its meaning at face value. Now Harpagus' meditation makes us see this again: Harpagus thinks he has been, and will continue to be, fortunate. The reader/audience will soon know better. Privileged to hear the characters' thoughts as well as their words, we feel the tragic irony of misunderstood *tuche*.

The next two mentions of *tuche* provide another doublet, continuing the story – and the role of *tuche* in these events. Harpagus befriends Cyrus, deciding that he will provide the means for his revenge on Astyages for the murder of his son. He hatches a conspiracy among the most important of the Medes, and then writes to Cyrus to let him know his plan, concealing a letter in the stomach of a hare. The message reads: 'The gods must be watching over you, son of Cambyses, or else you would not have been so lucky' (literally, 'for you would not have arrived at such a great quantity of *tuche*').[57] And, taking us back to divine *tuche* (as above) this receives explicit recognition in the words of Cyrus to the men of Persia, as he encourages them to contemplate revolt against the Medes. He ends his speech: 'for I believe that I was destined by divine *tuche* to undertake this task'.[58] The repeated appearances of *tuche* at key points during this account draw our attention to the pattern or power underpinning these events. The characters themselves may think they know what is happening, but their repeated misunderstandings of how *tuche* is operating in fact reinforce our impression of *tuche* as an autonomous and controlling force.

It has been said that 'with his emphasis on *moira* it seems obvious that Herodotus would give no role to deified fortune'.[59] Yet *moira*, in fact, makes few explicit appearances, while *tuche* is far more common, including two highly significant appearances, introduced by the wise men of the *Histories*, which in many ways provide the causal themes found in the rest of the narrative, and alert the reader/audience to the significance of her less overt activities. Just like the references to oracles, and the authorial comments about 'what must be', etc. these references to *moira* and *tuche* serve a narrative purpose.[60] These terms, phrases and themes – a language of luck, fate and fortune – act as signposts that inform the reader/audience of the nature of the course the protagonist is following – often without his or her being aware of it – and his or her likely end. When the characters themselves use *tuche* terms, especially when they mistakenly believe that *tuche* is on their side and that they are experiencing good luck, these prompt moments of collusion between author and audience, and reinforce the strong sense of fate that suffuses this narrative.

> **d) Good Luck?:** Moments of author/audience collusion also occur around uses of a family of terms indicating 'good luck': the noun, *eutuchie* 'good luck', and the related verb *eutucheo*, 'to be fortunate'. We find these terms used to indicate victories, and the noun *eutuchie* is also used to indicate single moments of unarguable advantage, for example, in the description of Syloson and his meeting with Darius, described above.[61] However, an important part of the essential meaning of these terms is that the good fortune they signify is tenuous and, relatively, momentary. This is established early on in Herodotus' narrative in the accounts of Solon and Croesus. To begin with, as Solon explains to Croesus what it means to be fortunate, he draws a clear contrast between being prosperous but unlucky, and being lucky: the lucky man is more fortunate than the rich man because his luck (*eutuchie*) keeps bad things away. However, Solon then goes on to emphasise the fragility of luck: a man can only be called blessed (*olbios*) if he manages to end his life well. Until that happens, he is only 'lucky' (*eutuchea*).[62] As we know, Croesus rather misses Solon's point, but a little later in the narrative, once he has lost his kingdom and become a captive of the Persian King Cyrus, we find Croesus passing on (and underlining) these insights about luck. He puts the point even more succinctly, describing how men's fortunes are on a wheel, and no man stays well-fortuned for ever.[63]

Following these initial passages, we find members of this family of 'good luck' terms used subtly in a number of episodes in Herodotus' account, helping to draw attention to the difference between material and metaphysical fortune, between temporary advantage or prosperity and long-lasting fortune. For example, in the account of the interactions between Polycrates of Samos, tyrant of Samos, and Amasis, King of Egypt, *eutuchie* is used to describe good fortune in terms of status and wealth, which is susceptible to the jealousy of the gods. Herodotus also uses the verb *eutucheo*, at least once in this episode, to make an ironic observation about Polycrates as 'good-fortuned'; ironic, because we know, Amasis knows and the account makes clear that Polycrates' fortune, however good at the time, is soon to be reversed.[64] A similar ironic use of the verb occurs again – although this time in the mouth of a character, in an interchange between Xerxes and one of his advisers. As the Persian campaign against Greece advances, Achaemenes, a Persian admiral and brother of King Xerxes, tries to persuade the King not to listen to his Greek adviser Demaratus, by reflecting on the nature of Greek character as 'jealous of success and power'. Achaemenes uses the verb *eutucheo* to mean 'success', and rather than intimating any long-lasting achievement, this actually draws our attention to the fragility of fortune – because, of course, Xerxes' invasion of Greece will fail.[65]

Even more subtly, the tentative state of 'good fortune' is communicated in the phrases 'not wholly lucky' (this phrase uses the verb *eutucheo*, and appears twice in the narrative), and 'not wholly unlucky' (this occurs once using the verb *dustucheo*, the only time this verb appears in the *Histories*). The phrase 'not wholly lucky' seems to be used to describe good events that become overshadowed by bad outcomes. In the first example, Herodotus describes how, after the invading Persian fleet had been wrecked in a storm, a man called Ameinocles picked up gold and silver cups that were washed ashore, and became fabulously wealthy. Herodotus observes that although he becomes very rich, he was not wholly fortunate because he would murder his son.[66] The outcome here is quite abruptly presented and no further information is given about this murder. Nevertheless, the effect is powerful: the reader/audience is left to reflect on the meaning of good fortune, and mortal ignorance of what is to come.[67] The second of these two examples involves the surrender of the Thebans to the Persians at Thermopylae. The Thebans pleaded that they had been medisers from the beginning, and had been forced to fight the Persians against their will. Their actions meant that many of them survived, but as Herodotus points out, this was not luck in every respect, because some were killed as they surrendered, while the rest were branded on the orders of the Persian King. Again we find good luck overshadowed by bad outcomes. Herodotus goes on to observe that Eurymachus, the son of the leader of the Thebans, Leontiades, was later killed in the Theban attack on Plataea (431 BCE).[68] This surprising detail smacks of 'just deserts'; it reminds us of how, in some of the archaic poets, punishment for a bad act may be visited on the children of the wrongdoer. Here, it is perhaps a suggestion that in evaluating whether an event indicates good or bad fortune, we need to keep a long view.[69]

The alternative, and unique formulation, of 'not wholly bad luck' is used to describe the fortune of one Hermotimus, who is castrated as a boy by a Chian trader called Panionius and sold to the Persians. Presumably, the emphasis on 'bad' in this formulation arises because of the reversal of good events and bad outcome: here, the course of events goes from an initial event that is bad to an outcome that is better. Herodotus describes how Hermotimus comes to be highly valued by the Persian king, Xerxes, and is clearly allowed to travel on court business. It is while he is on one of these trips that he meets Panionius again, whereupon he wreaks revenge, forcing the trader to castrate his own sons, and them in turn to do the same to their father.[70] The story of vengeance is not a separate episode, but presented by Herodotus as part of his explanation of Hermotimus' eventual 'not wholly bad luck'.

In these episodes we find Solon's model of luck, fate and fortune – the fragility of good fortune coupled with mortal ignorance of the uncertain future – repeatedly reinforced. The implication of these episodes is that no single experience or event can be evaluated on its own – only within the context of a life, or even beyond a life – and that mortals are rarely able to achieve that evaluation for themselves. The narrator occupies a privileged position: each episode emphasises the difference between a character's short-term experience or knowledge of an event, and the narrator's knowledge of the reality of the long-term situation. In turn, we, as reader/audience, are allowed to glimpse events and characters in the story from this lofty position of omniscience. The perspective helps us to see not only the characters' short-comings, but also reminds us of our own ignorance about the consequences of our day-to-day choices.

Not only does Herodotus' model of luck, fate and fortune involve a giddy cycle of reversal, but these swings and roundabouts of luck, fate and fortune are closely managed by a set of supernatural overseers. Can we at least say that there is an element of random chance involved? The term *suntuchie* appears to be used in places where the emphasis of the description is on the coincidental nature of events — and the term has been translated as 'coincidence'. But examination of the use of this term suggests that, for Herodotus, even in apparently random events, there are underlying supernatural forces hard at work.[71]

Herodotus uses the phrase *kata suntuchien* to introduce the sequence of events that occur in the lead-up to Darius' gaining the throne of Persia.[72] Prexaspes was a close friend of Cambyses, the second king of Persia, and, on his instruction, had secretly killed Cambyses' brother Smerdis, because Cambyses had been afraid that Smerdis would make an attempt on the throne. Unfortunately, while Cambyses was away campaigning, his Magian steward realised that no one knew of Smerdis' death: he persuaded his own brother to pretend to be Smerdis and seize the throne. Although, while he lay dying, Cambyses told the Persian nobles what had happened, they refused to believe him. In the end, two parallel events coincided to reveal the truth and allow Darius to take the throne: first, Darius and his supporters decided to attack the steward and his brother, while, at the same time, the steward and his brother persuaded Prexaspes to proclaim to the Persians that they were who they were pretending to be — an opportunity that he used to tell the truth. A coup took place, and Darius reclaimed the throne. In the text, the complex but crucial interweaving of these events is preceded by Herodotus' authorial insertion: 'while they [the conspirators with Darius] were making these plans, the following things took place, *kata suntuchien*, that is, 'by coincidence'.

Other episodes also suggest that this meaning of coincidence is one that excludes mortal intention: thus, in one of the accounts of Polycrates' death, when the tyrant is described as ignoring the messenger of the Persian governor Oroetes — which will result in Oroetes feeling so insulted that he kills Polycrates — Herodotus describes Polycrates' fateful inaction as occurring either 'from forethought', or because 'some such *suntuchie*' engineered it. Similarly, we find *suntuchie* in the story of the birth of the Spartan prince Dorieus to the first wife of King Anaxandrides. This woman had long been thought to be barren, and as a result Anaxandrides has been persuaded to take a second wife. Dorieus, by coincidence, we are told, is born at the same time as this second wife also gives birth to a son, Cleomenes.[73] Dorieus will be the outstanding man of his generation, but his jealousy of Cleomenes drives him out of Sparta, and he dies before he can come to the throne.

If, as these episodes suggest, *suntuchie* does not arise from mortal intention, can we pinpoint a divine cause instead? Clues to the answer may be found scattered through a number of stories across the *Histories* that mention the word *suntuchie* in relation to divine activities: one example is the story of Polycrates and Amasis, where *suntuchie* is the term used to describe the terrible event that Amasis is certain will strike Polycrates because of his good fortune, and which Amasis hopes to avoid by cutting himself off from his friend.[74] Amasis has already explained that this terrible event, whatever it is, will be engineered by a god – who is likely to be jealous of Polycrates' success. With a similar intimation that divine powers are at work, we find Xerxes praying to the gods that no *suntuchie* will disrupt his invasion.[75] A third example that raises the suggestion of supernatural intervention appears in a story near the end of the *Histories*, describing events leading up to the Greek victory over the Persians at Mycale. Ambassadors from Samos come before the Spartan general Leutuchides, who is leading the Greek fleet, and ask him to attack the Persians. If he does so, one of them promises, the Ionians will revolt from the Persians and join with the Greeks. Leutuchides asks the ambassador who has pleaded so eloquently. It is Hegesistratos, which means 'army-leader' and the Spartan leader takes it as a good omen. However, before Herodotus tells us this, he plants a question in our minds. He says that Leutuchides asked this question either because he wanted a portent, or because of the 'coincidence (*suntuchien*) of some god'.[76] The suggestion is that any apparent coincidence has been carefully, and divinely, stage-managed. The idea that this could be the case occurs in one final example, which does not mention the word *suntuchie* explicitly. In Herodotus' description of events leading up to the battle of Mycale he notes a series of coincidental events and rumours that encouraged the troops and sent them into battle with vigour and energy, including news of the Persian defeat at Plataea that same day. In the midst of this account, he notes how there is plenty of evidence for the divine taking a hand in human affairs.[77]

# Conclusion

Herodotus' explanation of the unspooling of events that led to the war between the Greeks and non-Greeks, with its multitude of voices and stories, emphasises that there is no single, simple or overt account: a great chain of motivations and provocations have been involved.[78] Similarly, both characters and author introduce diverse models of luck, fate and fortune: no single model is preferred or made explicit, leaving the reader/audience with material to reflect on and questions to contemplate, rather than a single theory of causation to accept or reject.

In terms of fate, a crime-and-punishment model is apparent in some stories (and is a favourite of modern commentators, as well); so Croesus is punished for his ancestor Gyges' actions, for example. But it is rare to find such a full explanation of fate's machinations. Instead, the two most basic models of fate that emerge from the text or from the characters' own words and actions are the reversal model, in which mortal prosperity is simply overturned (for example, as Solon describes); and the model of inevitable fate (Miltiades, who was doomed, according to the Delphic oracle; Xerxes who cannot be allowed not to invade Greece), in which there is simply no escape from a future outcome. In addition to these two models of fate and fortune, Herodotus introduces the concept of *tuche*, which seems to evoke a further model of luck and fortune, used to describe transient events and states, in various different flavours (good, bad, coincidental, not-so-good, not-so-bad).

At first sight, the reversal model, which is inherently unpredictable, and the model of inevitable fate (which is anything but uncertain), seem contradictory – and they do seem to present the modern mind with the puzzling question of free will in a fated world. Nevertheless, in Herodotus' work they function throughout the text, as we have seen, in perfect harmony. Indeed, we even find the two models operating in combination: for example, in the story of Polycrates, we find both the reversal model and the model of inevitable fate used to explain events, as well as the concept of *tuche* to evoke Polycrates' transient good fortune. This is not to claim that Herodotus' models of luck, fate and fortune are always the same or always straightforward: across the narrative, we find different aspects of these models receiving different emphases, according to the context of the story. Variations may depend on the methods used to manipulate or reveal fate – as we have seen, there is a range of supernatural stage-hands available. Other factors include the combination of models of fate and fortune with other theories of causation that underpin the text, and the responses and expectations of the mortal protagonists.

In terms of the latter, we find that some characters stand out because of their knowledge and understanding of their relationship with fate; others because they do not know or understand this relationship, and yet receive good fortune; still others, because they refuse to understand, although the evidence for their fate is clear. As this suggests, in Herodotus' *Histories*, the language and models of luck, fate and fortune are integrally linked to the process of characterisation – and this introduces another nuance to the models of luck, fate and fortune. Importantly, in many of these models mortal action and supernatural forces are linked, side-by-side, working simultaneously. Indeed, in many of the episodes discussed above, whatever supernatural forces are at work in arranging the fate of a particular individual, they seem to function alongside, and in harmony with, a particular character trait of that individual. For example, Polycrates is portrayed as acquisitive and power-hungry – and it is his constant good fortune and increasing prosperity that will cause the gods to destroy him. Similarly, Croesus is so sure of himself and confident in his power that he goes ahead with his fated war against Persia.

In some ways, this aspect brings to mind the modern debate around the idea of 'constitutive luck', that is, that one form of moral luck we all experience is the kind of character we are born with. This notion of luck has been criticised on the grounds that a person's character cannot be considered a matter of luck, since it is not out of his/her control. Herodotus' work seems to offer a different response, that a person's character is in fact a matter of fate, and *vice versa*: Croesus does not understand the oracle because he cannot, but cannot because he is fated not to do so; Polycrates has unstoppable good fortune because it is his fate to come to a sticky end, and a character that will ensure this happens. This approach can help us to make sense of Herodotus' comments about Arcesilaus, who, Herodotus reminds us, fulfils his oracle, 'with or without meaning to': the oracle is fulfilled because of his character, and his character means he must fulfil the oracle.

These underpinning cultural models of luck, fate and fortune give implicit sense and direction to Herodotus' narrative, allowing him to trace patterns in, and draw meaning from, past events, albeit retrospectively.[79] These models of luck, fate and fortune are models of causation – and they work alongside other models of causation, noted above, which use spatial, social and natural relationships. One famous example is the cycle of victory that runs througout Herodotus' narrative, which depicts how conquerors may be conquered in their turn, as they yield to luxury and grow overconfident.[80] It is easy to see how the reversal pattern of fate and fortune in which the prosperous are cast down, exemplified so often for individuals throughout the text, works alongside this larger narrative pattern, and indeed helps to reinforce it. As this suggests, Herodotus' models of causation are not only a way of talking about the past; they also leave the reader/audience with intimations about the future. The final conquerors in Herodotus' *Histories* are, of course, the Greeks, and, famously, these patterns of causation, the cycle of victory and (I would add) the reversal model of luck, fate and fortune, cast a chill sense of foreboding over their victory at the end of the narrative, with perhaps particular relevance for contemporary Athens and its expanding empire.

But faced with such an admonition about their likely fate, what might an ancient Greek think he could do? We might think that the implication of the *Histories* is that there is nothing mortals can do. Everything is fated, or will be disrupted by the unpredictable working of *tuche* and any experiences of good luck happen by coincidence, or the will of the gods – as the examples of Syloson and Artemisia, discussed above, suggest. Yet this is only part of the story. As Herodotus' description of the great Athenian general, Themistocles, indicates, deliberation is not only useful, but also likely to engender the favour of the gods: 'Men usually succeed when they have reasonable plans. But if their plans are unreasonable, the god does not wish to assent to human intentions'.[81]

What might 'reasonable' mean here (the Greek is *eoikota*)? This could be Herodotus sharing an ironic joke with his reader/audience, since we know that Themistocles' own behaviour may have involved making plans that were deceitful and intended to advance his own self-interest, in addition to strategies that saved the Greeks from Persian domination. But even so, the meaning of 'reasonable' still needs explanation. Looking across the *Histories*, those brought low by the gods are often men with excessive ambition and overweening confidence who stir up the jealousy of the gods. They would have done better to keep their desires in check: is this what 'reasonable' means here? But this analysis depends on the idea that success is necessarily a good thing – and in Herodotus' account, success may result in, indeed, may be an integral part of, an individual's eventual destruction. Think of Polycrates, think of Xerxes, both hideously successful, right up until their death and defeat, respectively.

Perhaps, in Herodotus' discussion of 'reasonable plans', we need to set this term 'reasonable' in a larger context. As we said at the beginning, Herodotus is writing at a time of new scientific inquiry, in which ideas of what is 'reasonable', that is, what seems likely or probable, are gaining increasing significance. Arguments from likelihood abound in contemporary medical writing, and Herodotus himself uses this term, 'reasonable', 40 times throughout the *Histories*, to argue for or against particular events and natural phenomena.[82] In a discussion of character, what would count in this sense as reasonable? We may be tempted to rule out any role for the supernatural, since to our modern minds it does not seem to belong to such an argument. However, bearing in mind the apparent symbiosis of character and fate, outlined above, which plays out throughout the *Histories*, perhaps 'what is reasonable' in terms of mortal plans is integrally involved with the supernatural. Mortal plans will succeed if they further the divine plan for that individual: 'reasonable' here means 'in accordance with fate'. In this picture, the need to be 'reasonable' does not mean that individual actions and intentions are unimportant; far from it. It simply means that in the end, we must all conform to the plans that have been made for us, whether we like it or not, whether we know it or not. As one of the taglines for the film *Serendipity* puts it: 'No name. No address. Just fate.'

# CHAPTER VII

# THUCYDIDES: RHETORICS OF COINCIDENCE

CHIGURH: ... *What's the most you've ever lost on a coin toss?*
PROPRIETOR: *Sir?*
CHIGURH: *The most. You ever lost. On a coin toss.*
PROPRIETOR: *I don't know. I couldn't say.*
CHIGURH: *Call it.*
PROPRIETOR: *Call it?*
CHIGURH: *Yes.*
PROPRIETOR: *For what?*
CHIGURH: *Just call it.*
PROPRIETOR: *Well – we need to know what it is we're callin' for here.*
CHIGURH: *You need to call it. I can't call it for you. It wouldn't be fair. It wouldn't even be right.*

From *No Country for Old Men*[1]

We move from the snowy streets of a New York romcom to the harsher territory of west Texas – and one of the most spine-chilling movie scenes of recent cinema. In the Coen brothers' version of Cormac McCarthy's novel, *No Country for Old Men*, Anton Chigurh, 'a strict, conscientious, self-taught psychopath who vigilantly maintains his mental ill health'[1] stops briefly at a gas station, and is moved to contemplate another murder – that of the gas station owner.[2] But rather than simply doing what he does elsewhere without a qualm (killing), he leaves his decision to the toss of a coin – and in his brief conversation with his puzzled, and wholly unaware victim, he gives the audience a glimpse of his bleak view of luck, fate and fortune.

At the end of the film the coin toss occurs again, but the questions it raises are made more explicit: Chigurh finds Carla Jean, the wife of the man he has pursued throughout the film. Chigurh offers Carla Jean the same opportunity for chance to play a role in her future, again taking out a coin and urging his victim to 'Call it.' Carla Jean refuses to play: whether she lives or dies, she says, is up to Chigurh, not dependent on a game. But Chigurh makes clear that he regards both his own presence, and that of the coin (and the outcome of its toss), as being part of the same unseen, but unavoidable, mechanism, bringing about what must come to pass. And with this final interchange, he shows us again a chilling worldview in which neither individual choice, nor coincidence, is as simple as it seems. Although they may appear to play a significant role in mortal affairs, for Chigurh, both are aspects of the process by which an inevitable sequence of events is brought about. A strikingly similar, largely implicit model of luck, fate and fortune forms the basis for an ancient account of one of the most bloody and long drawn-out wars of the ancient Greek world, Thucydides' *History of the Peloponnesian War*.

As we saw in the last chapter, Herodotus' *Histories* provides plenty of evidence for the operations of luck, fate and fortune. His account offers an explicit, albeit sometimes ambiguous, machinery of luck, fate and fortune chugging along contentedly, just audible, beneath the surface of the narrative, occasionally breaking into plain sight through the operation of oracles, rumoured or overt divine intervention, and authorial commentary concerning 'what must be'. In contrast, Thucydides offers us no such analytical signposts: his description of his own and others' views about the structure of the future, and man's relationship to uncertainty, seems uncompromisingly secular in approach. His account provides a description of the sequence of mortal events, and his own attitudes are largely subsumed within the narrative. In terms of our keywords, *moira*'s appearances are limited to indicating portions or parts, rather than metaphysical allocations of life (although something of this meaning perhaps survives in the idea of the 'part/attribute of a man', a phrase used in Thucydides' description of the changes in behaviour that took place during the violent Corcyrean revolution).[3] Nevertheless, it seems that both the author and his characters are continually aware of the power of *tuche* in the outcome of events.

The most detailed analysis of *tuche* in Thucydides is Lowell Edmunds' *Chance and Intelligence in Thucydides*, which provides a skilful dissection of the role of *tuche* both in the *History* and, according to Thucydides (according to Edmunds) in history itself. On the one hand, Edmunds reports, Thucydides represents history from the point of view of the actors, in which *tuche* is inherently unexpected and disruptive, that which is 'unexpected or contrary to calculation' from a human point of view.[4] On the other, the principles of Thucydides' historiography admit of no such leading role for *tuche*: the historian sought to avoid a reliance on *tuche*, instead using both hindsight and a rigorous method to bring clarity to his account, seeking a clear separation of particular events that were a result of chance, from 'the main trends of a certain period of history', and analysing the relationship between the two.[5] Through this approach, Thucydides depicted the difference between what his characters understood to be the case (using the speeches, in particular), and what actually happened: 'Tyche is then the degree by which the outcome differs from the expectation.'[6] The methodical historian can thus analyse and explain the unexpected, revealing, for example, that chance events originate in men's passions rather than imposing themselves from outside – and these passions 'are not simply random, but work themselves out in an orderly way';[7] or that Nicias' defeat and death in Sicily are not supernaturally imposed but belong to 'a discernible human order of success and failure and in this order is simply a fact'.[8]

In this view, Thucydides keeps in play two separate personae, the Artist who represents, through the words of his characters, their experience of living through events, and the Historian who, with detachment, traces the cycle of greatness and decline, a cycle which, he asserts in the introduction to his work, will be repeated down through time.⁹ For Edmunds this means that Thucydides' work is both theoretical and practical, it is 'both detached and compassionate . . . both rational and tragic' – and it is thus that it will be 'a possession forever', as Thucydides claims at the beginning of his work.[10] This profound analysis is certainly compellingly and thoroughly presented in Edmunds. However, an alternative reading is also possible: that the words of Thucydides' characters intimate their understandings (for they are various) of an ordered and supernatural structure that underpins or directs events, while, in contrast, it is Thucydides' own narrative uses of *tuche* that suggest not only its pervasive influence on events, but also the unpredictable and inexplicable nature of that influence. Granted, Thucydides never explicitly mentions the gods, but he also never denies the supernatural connotations of a set of terms and concepts that are inextricably interwoven throughout his account.

## Luck, Characters, and Characterisation

The significance of *tuche* in Thucydides' *History* is suggested by its frequent appearance and manipulation as a narrative theme. To begin with, different attitudes to *tuche* famously help to flesh out characterisation. One of the most famous examples occurs in the first book of the *History* as the Athenian general, Pericles, and the Spartan king, Archidamus, each contemplate the role of *tuche* in warfare. Pericles' initial remark – that sometimes the course of things is no less arbitrary than the plans of man – does not indicate that he does not appreciate the disruption that *tuche* can wreak, or trivialise its power.[11] His phrasing seems rather to take for granted the dominance of *tuche* (which is why we tend to blame it when things go awry) and the inability of man to completely control his own future. These remarks, addressed to those who are wavering in their support of his strategies, are a reminder that the alternative approach, that is, trusting to *tuche*, may not get them very far either. In light of this, he emphasises the need to maintain one's mindset (*gnome*) despite such disruptions, and not blame *tuche* when things do go wrong. He mentions *gnome* four times as he addresses the Athenians.

The first three appearances cluster in the first section of his speech: it is the first word of his argument, as he announces that his position has not shifted, and he contrasts this with the mindsets of those who waver in the face of events. Then he argues that the question of the moment (whether or not to agree to Spartan demands) is a test for the *gnome* of the Athenians. At the end of his speech, once he has worked through the details of his case, he returns to the role of *gnome*, elevating it almost to a heroic quality by arguing that the Athenians should face the present challenges like their forebears who fought the Persians, and were victorious 'more by their *gnome* than by *tuche*, more by daring than by strength.'[12]

In contrast, as he addresses his people, the Spartan king, Archidamus, shows a more deferential approach towards the inherent unpredictability of *tuche*, noting that it is impervious to reason. The Spartans, in general, approach tuche with caution – indeed, elsewhere in the text they are criticised by others for their rather passive approach to events.[13] This is a reminder to us that different cultural models of luck, fate and fortune (and responses to them) are at play throughout this text: for the Spartans, *tuche* appears to be something that should be endured. We see this in their own words, after the Spartans have been defeated in a sea battle by the Athenians led by Phormio. Afterwards, the Spartan generals try to rouse their men's morale: alongside lack of experience and resources, they emphasise the role of *tuche* in the defeat they have suffered, and they stress the importance of maintaining a steadfast mindset. The meaning of *gnome* here is not wholly dissimilar to that of Pericles' (discussed above), but the emphasis there is more on a considered strategy, whereas here it seems to be referring to a sense of unvanquished morale.[14]

After these first speeches, *tuche* continues to be a frequent rhetorical theme throughout the *History*, appearing in a variety of contexts, introduced by diverse characters in order to plead a range of different cases – and so drawing our attention to a number of different cultural models of luck, fate and fortune. This frequency of *tuche*'s appearance is likely to have reflected at least something of its popularity in the political speechifying of real life: the historian, philosopher and teacher of rhetoric Anaximenes apparently noted that the uncertainty of war was a topos of rhetoric against war.[15] There are examples of this in the *History*: the Spartans use *tuche* to try to dissuade the Athenians from going to war; and, as we will see, the Athenian general Nicias also refers to *tuche* in a similar context, as he tries to argue against the campaign in Sicily.[16] However, in the *History*, *tuche* appears far more frequently in speeches as part of a call to arms: so when the Corinthians are trying to persuade the Spartans to join them in war against Athens, they accuse the Spartans of leaving the growing strength of Athens to *tuche*, rather than taking action.[17] The Syracusan general Hermocrates first introduces the idea of the power of *tuche* as he urges the other Sicilians to stand together against the Athenian invaders. He uses *tuche* to illustrate his understanding of mortal limits and his acknowledgement that man cannot control everything. Later in the text, he uses *tuche* to counter arguments against forming a Sicilian alliance – including those who want to see Syracuse taught a lesson by Athens. Again, he points out that *tuche* cannot be controlled, and that this may mean that the Sicilians get what they want with regard to Syracuse, but may nevertheless still find themselves in desperate circumstances.[18]

*Tuche* also plays a significant role in the 'Melian dialogue'; in this debate representatives from the island of Melos plead with Athenian envoys that Melos be allowed to remain neutral and not be forced to join the Athenian Empire. The Melians mention their hopes for god-given *tuche* as a way of underlining their view of the unjust nature of Athenian power.[19] But this prompts the Athenians to reflect on the natural domination of the weak by the strong, among gods as well as mortals. This view may be uncomfortable for modern sensibilities, but is similarly expressed by a number of other characters in the *History*, not all of them Athenians.[20] The Melian dialogue is often, quite naturally, interpreted as demonstrating Thucydides' concern with Athenian ruthlessness, but it has been suggested that he was rather more concerned with the Melians' almost perverse refusal to save themselves. This is emphasised and may be summarised by the attitudes to *tuche* shown by each party: the final decision of the Melians is to put their faith in *tuche*, which, they say, has saved their city up till now.[21] This encapsulates their determination not to change; their refusal to recognise the extent and seriousness of the mortal threat they face; their dependence on the possibility of an uncertain future. In turn, the Athenian envoys emphasise that the disgrace the Melians are likely to incur is foreseeable, and so is likely to be more shameful than that incurred by *tuche*. They urge them that their choice is to 'regard the future as more certain than what is before your eyes, and what is out of sight . . . as having already come to pass'.[22]

The link between hope and *tuche* is also made in another speech, one concerning a situation of rebellion. This time, the Mytileneans have revolted from the Empire, and the Athenians are debating what to do. The Athenian general Diodotus warns Athens that hope and greed can be more destructive than more visible dangers, and adds to these two the aggravating power of *tuche* – all the more treacherous because she tempts men to have a go although their resources are insufficient.[23] As we will see, other characters, along with Thucydides himself, will echo and reinforce Diodotus' warnings about the temptations posed by *tuche*, especially good *tuche*, in their comments and reflections on *eutuchia*.

These appearances of *tuche* are meant to represent the explicit arguments of individuals, and tend to emphasise the unpredictability of *tuche*. But we also see various other aspects or models of *tuche*. For example, returning to the Melian dialogue, we see that *tuche* may operate differently according to context: in war, *tuche* appears to be a somewhat independent force that, in a conflict, does not necessarily reflect what the numbers on each side would suggest, while the Athenians' parting warning also suggests a *tuche* that causes surprises in terms of the unplanned course of events.[24] There is also an inherent *tuche* belonging to or characterising each side: the Melians discuss the difficulties of confronting the power and the *tuche* of the Athenians; but they also hope that the gods may grant them a *tuche* just as powerful, suggesting that *tuche*, although potent itself, is apportioned by the gods.[25]

Thucydides also includes *tuche* when he is evoking the thoughts of groups and individuals, explaining their actions and reactions in particular contexts – and these again introduce further dimensions or models of *tuche*. So, after suffering a series of defeats, the Spartans are described as disheartened by the many occurrences of *tuche* that have happened contrary to reason or perhaps 'what they expected'. *Tuche* here appears in the singular with a definite article, suggesting that this is a reference to not just simply a curious series of events, and more the multiple manifestations of a powerful force – at least in the minds of the Spartans.[26] A little later, at the siege of Megara, the Spartans, led by Brasidas, show themselves ready to do battle, although they do not actually attack. They do this, we are told, because otherwise they would not have 'been in with a chance (literally, 'in *tuche*'), but would have lost the city, as if they had been defeated.'[27] In this odd phrase, *tuche* almost seems to evoke the understanding of a possibility – an understanding shared by both the Spartans and their enemies. Finally, an example that plays on the opposition we have seen above between *tuche* and mindset (*gnome*), but with a slightly different nuance: Thucydides tells us how, in popular estimation, the Spartans' victory at the battle of Mantinea shook up the widespread criticism of them for being slow or cowardly. Following the battle, they dismiss their allies and return home to celebrate the religious festival of Carneia – and from this behaviour, Thucydides reports, it was generally agreed that although they may have been worsted by *tuche*, they were the same as ever in their mindset (*gnome*).[28] This recalls the use of the term in the speech of Archidamus, where *gnome* meets *tuche* in a spirit of endurance.[29] This, in turn, echoes the use of the term by the Spartans themselves that we have seen before, when, after their defeat at sea by Phormio, their generals sought to raise their morale by discussing the need to remain brave.[30]

The character of the Athenian general Nicias provides perhaps the most detailed opportunity to study the role that *tuche* is understood to play for an individual in the *History*. This is shown both by his own attitude towards *tuche*, and by descriptions of how *tuche* has informed his and others' perceptions of his identity. Thucydides tells us that Nicias is considered most fortunate of the Athenian generals; a quality that the politician Alcibiades puts forward as part of his argument that the Athenians should launch their expedition against Sicily.[31] As one modern commentator observes, this argument only makes sense if this perception of good personal fortune, *eutuchia*, 'is treated as an abiding characteristic'.[32]

Nicias also uses *tuche* himself, in his own rhetoric, exploiting its range of emphases. As the Athenians debate the Sicilian campaign he argues that the *tuche* of the Spartans (here referring to their run of defeats) should encourage the Athenians to concentrate on them as adversaries, rather than launching a new expedition against the Sicilians. The idea here appears to be that *tuche* tends to hang around, offering some kind of persistent personal trait. However, Nicias introduces a contrasting aspect of *tuche* when it becomes apparent that he cannot persuade his fellow countrymen. He explains that he wants to make sufficient preparation that he is 'quite independent of *tuche* before sailing'.[33] It appears that he is worried here about *tuche*'s unpredictable nature. Once in Sicily, the references to *tuche* continue as the campaign slides into catastrophe. When Nicias attempts to rouse his forces he mentions *tuche* twice, first he suggests to the troops that in the course of war, *tuche* cannot always oppose them (indicating a certain cyclical or at least alternating aspect); and later, in a more indirect allusion, he urges them to use their skill against others' well-*tuched* strength.[34] Here we find *tuche* again depicted as a characteristic, although not necessarily a persistent one, and one that empowers other qualities.

As the Athenians sink further towards disaster, and Nicias becomes increasingly sick, his rhetoric, as he addresses the troops, becomes gradually more focused on *tuche*. In his final speech, delivered in a moment of profound personal and political crisis, Nicias suggests something of the nexus of cause and effect that underpins his particular model of *tuche*. Painfully aware of the contrast between his famous good fortune and current predicament, Nicias explains that he can retain some optimism about the future because of his devotion to the gods, and life of justice. The idea that people's *tuche* is linked to their relationship with the gods also seems to motivate his later protestations that their situation might be expected to provoke divine pity rather than jealousy, and that others have attacked their neighbours, 'and done what men will do' without suffering.

In the end, Nicias is executed by his enemies, and Thucydides famously delivers an epitaph that contrasts Nicias' previous good luck with this final state of ill fortune (*dustuchia*), commenting that he, of all men, least deserved it. It could be argued that Thucydides meant to undermine belief in *tuche*, and that the moral of Nicias' story might even be that this supernatural force simply does not exist. However, the repeated references to *tuche* by both characters and narrator throughout this episode tend rather to draw our attention to its implacable, if inexplicable, role in mortal affairs. This is perhaps reinforced by the range of vocabulary that Thucydides uses across his account to refer to *tuche*'s different aspects and activities.

## A Spectrum of Luck

The language of luck used about and by Nicias introduces us to Thucydides' use of a spectrum of *tuche* words, including *eutuchia*, *dustuchia* and *xuntuchia*. Most of the uses of *eutuchia* occur in speeches or in focalisations, that is, in passages that explain characters' motivations for particular actions. As we might expect in such rhetorical circumstances, it rarely seems to be used to mean simply straightforward good fortune, although this meaning does occur with reference to the good fortune that Nicias is said to have enjoyed in his private life, and there is a similar use by Pericles, who uses it to describe the good fortune of those who die gloriously in battle. Both suggest that good luck is a permanent quality – although we learn that this is not the case with Nicias.[35] In contrast, a series of uses show how transitory this kind of luck was considered to be, and how dangerous it was to believe otherwise: so, the Corinthians use it with a sense of foreboding to emphasise how dangerous it is in warfare to become intoxicated by success, and Spartan envoys seeking terms with the Athenians use it to remind their enemy of the transitory nature of success in war.[36] These warnings are played out when Thucydides describes the Athenian point of view following their defeat at Amphipolis: they no longer hold their previous view of the good fortune of success, which had made them reluctant to make peace.[37] The same lesson is brought home when Thucydides discusses the attitude of the Athenian citizens in the aftermath of the first Sicilian campaign (of the 420s) and their over-confidence, whipped up by their temporary good fortune, 'which made them confuse their strength with their hopes'.[38]

Turning to bad luck, or *dustuchia*, we find that, unlike Herodotus,

Thucydides includes several examples of *dustuchia*. Two occur in the narrative, and both describe tragic and violent deaths: one is the death of Nicias, which provides not only a commentary on the unforeseen aspect of his execution (brought about through the influence of a number of his enemies), but also sets up a deliberate contrast to his famed *eutuchia*.[39] The other is the assassination of the Athenian tyrant Hipparchus.[40] The 'bad luck' of the term obviously can be taken to apply to the victim in each case, but it may also have been intended to have resonance for Athens; certainly, it is not the only link between the two episodes. Thucydides finds the confusion and almost wilful ignorance shown by the Athenians who mistakenly view Hipparchus as a tyrant as illustrative of the confusion that they show in the events surrounding the disastrous Sicilian expedition.[41] He uses *dustuchestaton*, the superlative of *dustuches* ('unlucky') to describe this latter catastrophe.[42]

Only once does *dustuchia* get placed in the mouth, or rather the mind of particular characters: during the Sicilian campaign, when the Syracusans are under siege, and facing the loss of their town, they focus, understandably, on how their generals have let them down. There is, we are told, plenty of talk in the town that attributes it to their misfortune (*dustuchia*) or treachery. We can almost hear the spiteful, desperate finger-pointing: with this brief phrase, Thucydides evokes the way in which, especially in a serious crisis, a discussion of responsibility can develop into an accusation of betrayal.[43] The implicit model of *tuche* here shows it belonging to an individual, but working in some ways like a contagion, so that bad luck spreads from the generals (in this case) to the army they lead.

As we have seen so far, the terms *dustuchia* and *eutuchia* seldom appear to signify a purely random event, but appear in contexts that imply a close relationship with associated events or individuals. In contrast, *xuntuchia*, at first sight at least, seems to offer a more neutral description of events than the previous *eu-* or *dus-* types. It appears less frequently in the speeches of characters than in the narrative of the *History*, but when it does appear in a speech, its apparent neutrality is still put to good rhetorical use. For example, the Corcyrean ambassador describes how, if the Athenians are persuaded by the Corcyreans, it will create, in a number of ways, 'a fine *xuntuchia* [literally 'a coincidence of'] our use/service'.[44] He then goes on to list all the ways the alliance will be advantageous for the Athenians – they 'just happen' to be useful to the Athenians, in a war that, he notes, is inevitable. The neutral aspect of the term is important also for the Athenian politician Diodotus in the Mytilene debate, as he discusses the circumstances of, and motivations behind, such insurgencies. He notes how both poverty and plenty can nurture the turbulent emotions that lead men to revolt, as can all the 'chance circumstances' of life (*xuntuchiai* in the plural). The random nature of such circumstances suggests that the Athenians themselves bear no responsibility for such uprisings.[45]

In Thucydides' own voice we find a range of uses for *xuntuchia*, including a number that lay emphasis on the unforeseen aspect of a coincidence, providing vivid evocations of the experiences of those who live through them.[46] Many of them draw attention to this idea that is apparent in Diodotus' speech, that an event may comprise a variety of causes. This is apparent in his comments on the Corcyrean revolution, where he describes how the calamities that occur in Corcyra are 'such as have happened and always will happen while human nature remains the same, but which are more or less severe and differ in form with every new combination of (*xuntuchiai*) circumstances'.[47]

Two further examples occur, and, like the two examples of *dustuchia* described above, one occurs in the description of Hipparchus' assassination, and the other in the account of the Sicilian expedition. In the first, the assassination of Hipparchus is described as occurring because of *erotiken xuntuchian*, literally 'to do with an erotic coincidence'.[48] The second example describes the circumstance that dictates the choice of alliance made by those states that came to fight for or against Sicily, against or with the Athenians.[49] It is opposed here to both expediency and necessity. The repetitive use of these terms across these two passages, especially when coupled with the *dustuchia* doublet described above, seems deliberate – and perhaps lays some further emphasis on the commonalities of these two events, their causes and impacts, their implications, in Thucydides' narrative.

Can we identify *xuntuchia* as the power of random chance, a rational recognition of the role of coincidence? Commentators on the first passage have noted how use of *xuntuchiai* at least provides a 'pioneering scientific statement in itself, with its clear recognition of the importance of differing combinations of circumstances'.[50] However, it has also been noted how, in this episode, the verb used to describe how these *xuntuchiai* bring changes is used elsewhere of attacks by the supernatural death-spirits, the *keres*.[51] Even if we do not accept such a supernatural connection, we can note that here at least it suggests the sudden onset of an ambush (indeed, Thucydides himself uses it in this way), and vividly connects *xuntuchiai* with imagery familiar from elsewhere in Greek literature of *tuche* (or of a *daimon*) falling upon an individual.[52]

## Luck and the Author

Thucydides' use of *tuche* in the words of his characters allows him a way of evoking their personalities, while presumably drawing on themes of fifth-century political rhetoric; but what about his own views? Here I think is where we find a depiction of *tuche* that evokes the unpredictability and randomness of lived experience. There are 11 uses of the term *tuche* in the narrative, and we have already discussed those four that offer some insight into the thoughts of a character or group of characters.[53]

Of the other seven, *tuche* appears three times in the common phrase *kata tuchen*. Two instances offer incidental comments on apparently coincidental weather conditions. However, these, at first sight, casual references, bear closer examination. The first describes the fact that an Athenian ship, on an urgent mission, meets with no contrary wind.[54] This ship has been sent out in pursuit of another craft, dispatched in order to carry out a massacre of the Mytileneans. After the Athenians have second thoughts, they send out this second ship, its occupants charged with the prevention of the mass execution. Thanks to the favourable conditions, it arrives only a little behind that first grim vessel. The second occurrence of *kata tuchen* describes the occurrence of a little squall that carries the Athenian ships into Pylos.[55] This goes against the will of most of the Athenian commanders, but fulfils the (apparently) long-held plans of Demosthenes, who argues that Pylos is the ideal place to fortify and use as a base from which to attack the Spartans. As the events that follow reveal, this is a fortuitous event for the Athenians.

What role is the *tuche* phrase playing in these descriptions? There are other places where weather conditions are mentioned, where they have significant impacts, and this phrase is not introduced.[56] As one scholar noted, the mention of *tuche* in a noun form, rather than as the verb *tunchano*, means that 'the note of accident is clearly sounded'.[57] Nevertheless, the inclusion of the phrase suggests a particular emphasis. In the first episode above (the just-in-timely arrival of the second ship so as to prevent a massacre), we might argue that mention of *tuche* underlines a sense of relief, or even of grim irony on the part of the author; others have suggested this is an example of 'moral luck'.[58] In the second example, Thucydides does tell us that Demosthenes was already urging the other commanders to put in at Pylos and clearly already had knowledge of the terrain. Is it forethought or *tuche* that finally fulfils this plan? As one commentator puts it this episode 'begins a chain of events and actions which Th. represents as accidental or spontaneous even when (it is reasonable to suppose) they were not.'[59]

In each of these examples, we might argue that the phrase is almost being used to provide a measure of focalisation, drawing out the experience of the characters themselves, and a third example of *kata tuchen* also supports this interpretation. In this instance, the phrase appears in a description of a proposal of alliance, made by a couple of mysterious Argives, to the Boeotian ambassadors, who have recently departed from an unsatisfactory meeting at Sparta.[60] Before they left, the Boeotians had already been approached in private by the Spartan hawks (the ephors Cleobulus and Xenares), and urged to make an alliance with Argos, which might then be used to Spartan advantage.[61] These episodes seem to be building to something, and the use of the *tuche* phrase seems to add to this impression. However, curiously, nothing will come of this proposal – so, in fact, it is puzzling that Thucydides should refer to this proposal as 'lucky'. Edmunds explains the use of the term as a whimsy on Thucydides' part, and sees in it a connection to the appearances and absences of ambassadors throughout Book 5.[62] This may be part of it, but it is also possible that *kata tuchen* simply communicates the Boeotians' own point of view: the Argive proposal happens to coincide with that made to them by their Spartan friends. It seems an advantageous situation to them.

As suggested, *tuche* plays a significant role in events at Pylos – and two of the three further occurrences of the term appear in this episode. Thus, *tuche* (given additional narrative force by appearing here with the addition of the definite article) is credited with overturning the usual course of events as the Athenians, famed for their naval prowess, fight on land, while the Spartans, renowned for their infantry, are forced to fight from the sea – with the added poignancy that the Spartans are attempting to enter their own country.[63] The role of *tuche* in this inversion is emphasised again a little later in the battle, when the term occurs as part of the description of the behaviour of the Athenians.[64] Since they are winning, in 'the present *tuche*', we are told, the Athenians are anxious to advance their land invasion from the ships. This not only follows an explicit acknowledgement by Thucydides of the remarkable nature of the battle (with its reversal of the usual roles) but also adds a vivid focalisation – an insight into the Athenians' thought processes, an explanation of their battlefield decisions. From a dominant and organising force, *tuche* might suddenly seem reduced by this cursory reference to merely a description of the current situation. However, the effect of these two references occurring so close together is to remind the reader of *tuche*'s presence, while suggesting that the Athenians themselves are also aware of the role of *tuche* in their current success.[65]

# Luck 'Happens'

In Greek prose, the verb 'to happen', *tunchano*, tends to supply a meaning of general randomness. However, in Thucydides' account of events, random events can, and often do, carry enormous significance. Although sometimes the verb does not really bear translation, Thucydides' use of *tunchano* often introduces significant nuances.[66]

As a first example, use of *tunchano* in descriptions of warfare can lay eloquent emphasis on the unpredictability of events on the battlefield, its appearance helping to evoke the mêlée of battle ('as ship happened to dash against ship').[67] Sometimes this unpredictability may provide a coincidence of objects or circumstances that offers characters a particular opportunity, although not necessarily a happy one: for example, in the besieged city of Corcyra, the beds that 'happen' to be there, supplying cords for those despairing individuals who want to kill themselves; or a fallen wall that provides a means of access to the besieged town of Torone; or the political clubs that 'happen' already to be in existence when Pisander is putting the pieces of the Athenian oligarchic revolution in place.[68] Opportunities also arise from coincidences of relationships, and/or the movements of individuals.[69] The council of 400 'happens' to be in the council chamber when news reaches them of an insurrection in Piraeus, so they are able to act more swiftly. The timing of an event may exacerbate a particular pre-existing situation, for example, the Persian commander Tissaphernes promises to support the Spartan army if the Spartans will join those revolting from the Athenian Empire, and the reason given is that he 'happens' to have had a demand for tax, which he has so far been unable to raise.[70] Finally, the verb may add particular poignancy or horror – for example, when marauding Thracians invade a boys' school, which the pupils 'happen' to have already entered, and the children are massacred.[71]

A slightly different emphasis of coincidence arises in the use of *tunchano* to describe the occurrence of weather conditions and natural events that have a significant impact: for example, the moon's eclipse in Sicily that prevents the Athenian fleet from sailing,[72] or the storm that lowers the spirits of the retreating Athenian army.[73] In these episodes, use of the verb *tunchano* to describe the chance occurrence of these phenomena contrasts with the often profound significance that the characters in the *History* read into them, and the impact they then exert.

Alongside weather, other natural phenomena are also treated with this verb: including disease, and its different manifestations;[74] and the earthquake in Cos ('the greatest in living memory'[75]). Some events are man-made, including the chance movement of a merchant ship that saves an Athenian vessel, causing dismay among the Spartan onlookers; and the appearance of

Sicilian ships under Spartan command near Euboea, which Theramenes uses to strengthen his call to the Athenians to take action.[76] But the verb is also used to indicate the significance of events for which we might expect a certain regularity if not predictability, including: religious festivals (perhaps indicating the coincidence of their appearance with other events rather than the fact that they happen at all);[77] the movement of ambassadors, generals, ships, and troops, suggesting an element of unpredictability about their location;[78] and the taking up or changing of political office.[79]

But this presentation of coincidence acquires a certain sophistication when Thucydides also shows us how one man's coincidence is another man's plan. For example, a meeting of the Chian council is so arranged that it just 'happens' to coincide with a visit from Chalcideus and Alcibiades – who then go on to encourage the Chians to rebel from the Athenian empire.[80] During the Eretrian revolt, the Athenian sailors at Eretria 'happen' not to be in the agora at the crucial time, and Thucydides explains that this is because the Eretrians have schemed to keep them away from the ships.[81] In other places, the verb is used subtly to signal the idea that a strategy may underpin apparently random arrangements: for example, the Corinthians keep as captives those Corcyreans who 'happen' to be the most influential.[82]

Occurrences of *tunchano*, along with appearances of *tuche* are also found clustering around particular themes, for example, around the activities of Themistocles as he makes his escape from Athens. It's possible that these are intended to suggest that this sequence of events was not as coincidental as it may have appeared.[83] There is a cluster of words relating to *tuche* around the events at Pylos and the debate at Melos, both of which we have reviewed above, and each of which gains particular nuances from the appearance of *tuche* terms.[84] In Book 5, a book thick with negotiations, *tuche* terms cluster around the appearance, presence or absence of ambassadors.[85] Finally, and perhaps most tellingly, there is also a cluster of *tunchano* forms and mentions of *tuche* around the description of those events in which Thucydides himself suffered defeat at the hands of Brasidas: we can't help but wonder if Thucydides is implicitly telling his reader something about what happened.[86]

## Rhetorical Luck

Other verbs relating to fortune used by Thucydides include *eutucheo*, *dustucheo* and *xuntunchano* (which mean, respectively (and literally), 'I experience good luck', 'I experience bad luck', and 'I coincidentally happen'). *Eutucheo* appears most frequently (17 times), *dustucheo* far less often (four times), and *xuntunchano* only twice, but only once are any of these verbs used as part of a simple narrative description.[87] Otherwise, all these uses appear in direct or indirect speech, or as part of Thucydides' process of focalising the narrative, giving his reader an idea of the thoughts of his characters. Their particular contexts of use raise again the idea that ideas of luck, fate and fortune (drawing on shared cultural models of these concepts) played a significant role in rhetorical and/or political language; they also bring into play for us the important concept of register.[88]

The verb for experiencing bad luck (*dustucheo*) appears in a number of speeches related to going to war. First, the verb is used by Nicias in an indirect speech in which his argument for peace involves describing the Spartans as being 'in a state of misfortune.'[89] Next, it appears in speeches by the Greek Alcibiades and the Syracusan Hermocrates, as each attempts to persuade his respective audience of his approach to the Athenian invasion of Sicily.[90] In Athens, Alcibiades wants the Athenians to support his right to command the Athenian forces in Sicily. In an attempt to combat his somewhat arrogant reputation, he argues that it is perfectly fair for people like him, who think a lot of themselves, to refuse to be on a level with everyone else: after all, if a man is doing badly, people do not seek to share in his misfortune, and the same principle should be true of good fortune: 'When we are unlucky, we are not spoken to, by the same token we should expect to be looked down on by those who are doing well.' In turn, in Sicily, in the city of Camarina, Hermocrates is trying to persuade the Camarinaeans to support the Syracusans in their coming struggle against the Athenians. He uses the verb as he explains how, unless the Sicilians support each other, misfortune will arrive 'city by city'. The final example describes the Spartans' ruminations about the cycle of fortune/misfortune and their belief that fortune must favour them as they prepare to invade Attica.[91] They explain to themselves their previous experiences of misfortune – they had broken a treaty – and this also explains why they may now experience better luck.

This language of fortune/misfortune is clearly considered appropriate, by Thucydides at least, to this particular (persuasive) register. We have seen already, from their uses in the narrative, that the noun forms of the concepts behind these verbs (*tuche, dustuchia* and *eutuchia*) are concerned with a couple of different models: first, they concern contingent, and often fleeting, events or experiences; but there is also a model in which these qualities attach themselves to people (with more or less justification). Looking at the three examples above, we find that it may be this latter aspect that enables Alcibiades to describe his fortune and others' misfortune as he does, as he tries to argue for the blamelessness of his own good fortune. Even as he discusses shifting patterns of fortune, he seems to take for granted the stability of his own good fortune, while the language of *tuche* seems to shift responsibility away from him, and underlines how unfair it is for others to feel resentment towards him. The Spartans use a similar, but slightly nuanced, model of fortune: they understand that fortune/misfortune is changeable, but still see it as attached to people (individuals or, as in this case, groups). They may have had no luck for a while, but this is not typical: they link their experiences of misfortune to an error in their own (religious) behaviour; they expect their good fortune to return. In contrast, Nicias' use of *dustucheo* picks up on the contingent model of *tuche*. He depicts the *current* state of the Spartans, and his use of the term conveys a warning to the Athenians: their enemy's misfortune may not last, so they must act while the circumstances are favourable to them. Hermocrates' words pick up on a similar model, emphasising *tuche*'s unpredictability to draw attention to the folly of those citizens who assume that their city is immune from misfortune. But his image of how misfortune arrives city by city introduces another aspect – her creeping implacability.

In each of these cases the language is not only appropriate to its persuasive context, but the nuance of its use helps to evoke the character of the speaker: Nicias, renowned for his own *eutuchia* uses the language of *tuche* to persuade the Athenians to pursue a cautious line. Here is reckless, feckless Alcibiades explaining why he is not only not to be blamed for his good fortune, but why no one else may share in it. As for Hermocrates, Thucydides has told the reader that he is intelligent, courageous and experienced, and shown him to be opportunistic and resourceful; he is also a clever and powerful speaker. As we learn, his audience of Camarinaeans are already frightened of Syracuse. His description of the uncontrollable nature of misfortune, especially coupled with his careful description of her relentless progress – reads not only as an explicit warning to the Camarinaeans, but also as a veiled threat.

When we look in turn at *eutucheo*, we find that the same kind of pattern of use emerges. The verb is used 16 times, 11 times in direct speech, and 5 times in Thucydides' descriptions of characters' thought processes.[92] In the former, the verb is used by speakers as one of their weapons of persuasion, drawing attention, in a variety of ways, to various aspects of the nature of good fortune, in order to reinforce a particular argument. We are not surprised to find a cluster of these in Pericles' early speeches, as he tries to persuade the Athenians to stand firm.[93] The first of these appears in his famous funeral speech, where he draws attention to the precariousness of good fortune, highlighting how lucky the old of the city are not to have experienced bereavement until now.[94] The next two come in a single speech, made by Pericles to calm Athenian anger after the second Peloponnesian invasion of Attica. The first of these stresses the contingent nature of good fortune, but sets it firmly in the context of the relationship between a man's fortunes and those of his city, and the implications that this holds for individual action and responsibility.[95] Pericles' argument sets the fortune of the city above that of the individual, emphasising how a ruined city will destroy the fortunes of its citizens despite their personal good fortune, while a flourishing state can always help a suffering individual.[96] His second use of *eutucheo* is part of a description of the ideal life (one of free choice, with good fortune) from which it would be folly to depart – but he quickly explains that the Athenians' present choices are more complicated than that.[97]

As others have observed, Pericles' next assertion that he stands firm ('As for myself, I am the same man and have not shifted my ground') is later echoed by the demagogue Cleon.[98] We can note in addition that Cleon also meditates on the nature of good fortune, providing a series of contrasts to Pericles' use of the term. Where Pericles lays emphasis on the Athenians' own vulnerability to good fortune and their consequent responsibility towards their city, Cleon represents the Athenians as the source, and judge, of Mytilenean good fortune. Where Pericles paints the prolongation of good fortune as desirable, Cleon argues that unexpected good fortune has been bad for the Mytilenean character, prompting unwarranted pride and arrogance – and deserving punishment. A little later, as they try to persuade the Athenians to come to terms, the Spartans make a similar reference to unexpected good fortune and also agree that such an experience is likely to make men arrogant.[99] But in this instance, ironically, the audience for their counsel comprises the Athenians themselves. The Spartans use the language of good fortune to counsel caution: good fortune is one of the outcomes of war that is led by *tuche* – and so remains unpredictable.

Finally, across Books 6 and 7, which relate the planning and fulfilment of the Sicilian campaign, three of the four uses of *eutucheo* appear in the speeches of Nicias, one in a speech by his nemesis, the Sicilian general Gylippos. Nicias is, as we have been told by Alcibiades (later confirmed by himself), a man renowned for his good fortune.[100] But during the course of events described in these books, Nicias' only hold on luck is his use of the verb in his speeches – and he demonstrates a range of its aspects. At first, he tries to put the Athenians off the expedition by emphasising the need for good luck.[101] Later, as we have seen, he tries to raise the morale of his troops, urging them to maintain their fortitude, and to remember that their *episteme* or 'skill', is a match for their opponent's good-fortuned strength.[102] Nicias does not use *gnome* here, which we have seen both Pericles and the Spartans use earlier, to suggest the quality that opposes an enemy's *tuche*.[103] The echo, with its contrast, may be deliberate – intended to suggest that the troops are going to need more than a steadfast mindset, but will need the best of their physical skills. Finally, in a last speech to his soldiers that sounds almost like a prayer, Nicias argues that the enemy have 'had enough good luck'.[104] Here, he seeks an explanation for the Athenians' lack of luck in the possibility that they have somehow offended the gods by making the expedition: this crime-and-punishment model of *tuche* is reminiscent of the Spartan approach, mentioned above. As it does for them, it suggests what we already know about Nicias, that he is used to experiencing, and being seen to experience, good luck. In contrast, Gylippos can scarcely believe the extent of the potential good luck of the Sicilians.[105]

Used in the narrative, *eutucheo* tends to be used to describe success in warfare, although it always suggests a (relatively) fleeting and unpredictable phenomenon. In most of these cases, the verb sometimes seems to be used almost neutrally, merely to describe a set of transitory circumstances.[106] However, in a number of other cases, we meet a new aspect of *tuche* – a more deceptive aspect, as what appears to be good fortune leads to far less positive consequences. So we see the victories of the Athenians generating future problems for them, because they prompt Perdiccas, king of Macedonia (and some of his neighbours) to contact the Spartans and offer them an alliance.[107] Cleon's previous successes, Thucydides seems to suggest, help lead to his misjudged strategy at Amphipolis.[108] In the case of the Spartan general Brasidas and the Athenian politician Alcibiades, Thucydides describes how the fact that good fortune in war brings individual rewards to these two men has bad implications for the cities they represent: Brasidas is unwilling to countenance a peace because of the glory that military success brings.[109] Alcibiades is a slightly more complex case: we know that his hopes for personal gain lie behind his ambitions for fortune in war – and so, it seems, did his fellow Athenians.[110] These desires in turn lead the Athenians to distrust his strategic decisions, turning instead to inferior leaders whose bad judgements, according to Thucydides, will bring the city to ruin.

# Conclusion

Whereas Herodotus' *Histories* reeked of fate, Thucydides' work is riddled with the language and influence of *tuche*: throughout the narrative, *tuche* is involved in every kind of situation at every level of society – be it individual, group or city. But this is far from a single-sided phenomenon: the different uses of *tuche* evoke a variety of cultural models depicting how this force manifested in daily life, shaping events both great and small, and suggesting that Thucydides was drawing on a range of shared cultural models of how *tuche* was perceived to operate in daily life.

Thucydides manipulates these models and the resulting language of *tuche* to different ends, drawing his readers' attention to the 'what might have beens' – what could have happened, but, for various reasons, did not – in the course of events; the differences between the perceptions of his characters and the reality of events and experiences; the contingency of success and failure, all with startling, poignant, and sometimes tragic effect.

As other scholars have observed, in this way, Thucydides may offer the reader something closer to the experience of the action, rather than the privileged vision of history as a series of interweaving, regular, explanatory patterns that Herodotus provides.[111] But Thucydides' presentation of *tuche* is more complex. Characters may suffer the disruption of day-to-day living; nevertheless, they find explanations for their experiences. For Thucydides, the role and force of *tuche* in events is similarly manifest and pervasive. In both cases, while *tuche*'s activities are certainly unpredictable, patterns of activity and particular models of behaviour can still be traced, albeit usually in hindsight.

Is *tuche* a goddess in Thucydides? The question hardly seems to matter: *tuche* is certainly a potent and pervasive supernatural force. Some of the characters in the *History* clearly perceive it as having a supernatural association; even if it is not referred to itself as a deity, its manifestations are described in terms of a gift or punishment of the gods.

Thucydides also preserves some links with earlier notions of fate, in particular some marked similarities with Herodotus' depiction of interaction between luck, fate and fortune, and character. In the previous chapter, a number of episodes were shown to demonstrate how, for Herodotus, a person's fate is interwoven with his character, and vice versa. Something similar may also be apparent in some of *tuche*'s operations in Thucydides: Nicias is the most obvious example of how a person's perceived good luck influences the course of events. In addition, Thucydides' comments about the effects of good luck on Brasidas and Alcibiades, their motivations, and the ways in which their behaviour influences other people and shapes events, for example, draw our attention to the ways in which *tuche* operates across Thucydides' *History* – alongside and in concert with mortal action. But in both these cases, we can see that Thucydides adds a further crucial element to Herodotus' nexus of fate and character: the role of persuasion. In contrast with Herodotus, the machinery of *tuche* plays out more or less smoothly in a context of civic rhetoric. Not only is *tuche* interwoven throughout the narrative, but Thucydides also portrays his characters themselves as using these models and language of *tuche*. Their speeches rarely fail to involve aspects of *tuche*: this force is part of the armoury of rhetoric. This, in turn, becomes, for Thucydides, one of his techniques of characterisation. Thucydides' famous, self-confessed artistry with these speeches raises familiar questions about the trustworthiness of his representations. In the context of this discussion, we should perhaps add a further question; that is, whether or not the emphasis on *tuche* in Thucydides' *History* was a creation of the writer, or accurately conveys the concerns of the original actors described in this text. In the face of such an impossible query, we can perhaps be content to say that, as it stands, the constant appearances of *tuche* in speeches and narrative suggest that both Thucydides, and the politicians of the fifth century and their audiences, understood *tuche*, in all her diverse forms, to be a crucial, shaping force of daily life. The next chapter will suggest that this was also the case in Athens in the fourth century.

# CHAPTER VIII

# THE RESURRECTION OF CHANCE

REP. HENRY WAXMAN: *You had the authority to prevent irresponsible lending practices that led to the subprime mortgage crisis. You were advised to do so by many others. And now our whole economy is paying its price.*

*Do you feel that your ideology pushed you to make decisions that you wish you had not made?*

ALAN GREENSPAN: *Well, remember that what an ideology is, is a conceptual framework with the way people deal with reality. Everyone has one. You have to – to exist, you need an ideology. The question is whether it is accurate or not.*

*And what I'm saying to you is, yes, I found a flaw. I don't know how significant or permanent it is, but I've been very distressed by that fact.*

REP. HENRY WAXMAN: *You found a flaw in the reality...*

ALAN GREENSPAN: *Flaw in the model that I perceived is the critical functioning structure that defines how the world works, so to speak.*

> From testimony at a hearing examining the role of federal regulators in the credit crisis, originally aired October 23, 2008[1]

There is a perfect alignment or echo between our experience in gambling and our experience in the world, and it is in the big win . . . that the echo is most apparent. All the disorder, illogic, injustice, and pointlessness that we have spent our ordinary days ignoring or denying, pretending to see the same world our fellow citizens insist on seeing, trying to go along to get along, trying not to think too much about the implications, all of it flows forth in this confirmation of pointlessness – by luck.

F. and S. Barthelme,
*Double Down: Reflections on Gambling and Loss*[2]

## *Tuche* on Trial

Let's start with a visit to Athens in the year 330 BCE. We are in the lawcourts, before a jury of 500 or so Athenian citizens. The buzz of their conversation hums louder than the bees on Mount Hymettos in July; they have plenty to talk about. These men are here to pronounce judgement on the charges being brought by the Athenian politician Aeschines against one Ctesiphon, an ardent supporter of the Athenian statesman Demosthenes. The charges against Ctesiphon are as follows: he had proposed to crown Demosthenes while he still held an official position in Athens; the proclamation of that crowning had taken place not in the Assembly, but in the Theatre of Dionysus; and finally, that he had introduced false statements into decrees of the Athenian people by describing Demosthenes as having 'by deed and word promoted the people's best interests, and been keen to do whatever good' he could.[3]

The indictment is officially made against Ctesiphon, but, as everyone knows, Aeschines' case is really aimed at Demosthenes himself. Aeschines has bided his time, waiting for the right moment to bring his case, when he reckons he can do the maximum damage to his rival. Ctesiphon made his proposal six years earlier, when Demosthenes was still enjoying great popularity, despite the catastrophic defeat of the Greeks by Philip of Macedon at Chaeronea. Since then, however, Demosthenes' policies have gradually been brought into disrepute: he badly underestimated the competence of Philip's son, Alexander; and was proved wrong again when Alexander chose to show mercy towards the Athenians and pardon their opposition (even forgiving the leaders of the resistance). There were rumours at the time that Demosthenes was in the pay of the Persian king Darius III.[4] Since then Demosthenes seems to have kept a lower profile.[5] As Ctesiphon readies himself to pounce, it may be that Demosthenes' popularity is waning: only a year before (according to a later source) the Athenians had failed to respond to his attempts to mobilise support for King Agis of Sparta in his rebellion against Macedonian rule.[6]

The order of the trial is straightforward: the case against will be made first by Aeschines; in defence, Ctesiphon will make a brief introduction, then Demosthenes will speak, taking on the main charges. His speech, *Peri Tou Stephanou* (known usually in its Latin form as *de Corona* or 'On the Crown'), will become one of the most acclaimed orations of classical literature. In it he observes the usual divisions of a forensic speech: *proemium* (introduction), *prothesis* (the subject of the trial), narrative (a description of the events and characters involved in the case), proof (the argument of the speech) and the epilogue (a conclusion, often containing an emotional summary of the argument).[7] In the narrative, Demosthenes concentrates largely on defending himself against Aeschines' third charge, which concerns his own political career; within this discussion he disposes of charges one and two, against which he has a weaker case, relatively quickly. This larger narrative also encompasses an attack on the character of Aeschines (this was a traditional part of the proof) – which he continues, in one form or another, throughout the rest of the speech. When he comes to the major excursus of his argument (in which he discusses Athens' resources, possible outcomes of other policies, events after Chaeronea, and, finally, the conduct of a dutiful statesman), he introduces the subject of *tuche*. It is on this particular and particularly puzzling aspect of his defence that we will concentrate here.[8]

In most of the speech Demosthenes invokes *tuche* as an unknown, unavoidable force, the mastermind behind events – in this case, the failure of Demosthenes' policies and Athens' subsequent defeat. Reminiscent of the more archaic figure of *moira*, the *tuche* Demosthenes depicts operates alongside gods and *daimones* to create circumstances that are destined and unavoidable.[9] Demosthenes argues that, in the face of such powers, the counsellor can only do his best: even as he makes the wisest and most honourable calculations, he exposes himself to the scrutiny of those to whom he gives counsel, to *tuche*, to the opportunity of the moment, to whomever wishes to speak.[10] The outcome of those decisions, in the end, rests on the will of the gods: Demosthenes illustrates this with the image of a shipowner, who equips his ship as best he can, but cannot prevent the storm that destroys it, and protests, 'and I did not have control over fortune, but she controlled everything'.[11] A little later, he will extend this lesson – of this pure notion of mortal choice – to each of the rest of the Athenians, both alive and long-dead: in a long and heartfelt invocation of the freedom-loving spirit of the Athenians, which includes an appeal to those who fought at Marathon, Plataea, Salamis and Artemisium, he protests that it cannot be wrong for the men of Athens to have chosen to fight, even if, in the end, they lost.[12] Nevertheless, even as he introduces this notion of *tuche*, Demosthenes still manages to emphasise to his audience that he was not actually a general in the battle of Chaeronea, and so cannot bear operational blame for what happened.[13]

But this is only one small part of the story: although Demosthenes has made his own powerful appeal to this model of inevitable fate, in order to argue for his own innocence, he must still deal with Aeschines' more personalised accusations, that it was his own *tuche* at the heart of events. Towards the end of the speech he tackles this more complex, and for him more threatening, idea of *tuche*, devoting fully 23 chapters of his speech to this aspect.[14] Demosthenes' remarks about *tuche* are composed in response to remarks by Aeschines, so let us examine these accusations before we turn to Demosthenes' elaborate defence.

At first sight, we might think that Aeschines is simply accusing Demosthenes of bad policy. As we might expect, Aeschines accuses Demosthenes of being 'responsible for all the ills' that the Athenians, indeed, all the Greeks, have suffered. This seems a familiar accusation from a rival politician, but Aeschines' accusations are more significant.[15] The reason for Demosthenes being at the root of Greece's suffering is not because of his misguided policy, lack of funds, or even corruption (although he does manage to suggest that Demosthenes' opposition to Philip was financed by the Persians), but a far more sinister and inescapable force.

## THE RESURRECTION OF CHANCE

Aeschines vividly describes the disaster at Chaeronea, directing his audience to imagine the extent of Theban suffering: 'But since you were not there yourselves, imagine their disaster; think of the captured city, the levelling of the city walls, homes burned; their women and children led away into slavery; old men, old women, learning to forget their freedom so late in their lives; weeping, beseeching you, angry not with those who were taking their revenge on them, but with those who were responsible' and then he explains how these people viewed Demosthenes, picturing them '... calling on you not to crown, in any way, the accursed man of Hellas, but instead to guard against the *daimon* and the *tuche* that constantly follow him.'[16]

It turns out that Aeschines is not simply describing the results of bad judgment, or a moment of bad luck, but is evoking the presence of an active, personified and supernatural force – one that will not only not allow its target to escape, but also infects those around it. Something of how this might work is revealed in other comments that he makes in other parts of this speech. Earlier in his account, Aeschines has already emphasised how a man's own corrupt character can lead to punishment from the gods – which, in turn, will also fall on those who support him as their political leader.[17] He has also given an example of Demosthenes ignoring divine communication – sending troops to fight despite unfavourable omens – and addressed him as *aliterios* or 'curse' of Greece. The term *aliterios* indicated that a man was of such an unholy state that he offended the gods, and was excluded from entering Greek temples; its use here indicates that Demosthenes should be considered as having offended the gods.[18] With these interjections, with this rhetoric of ill-fortune, Aeschines has compiled a picture of a leader who has not just made bad judgments, but is a liability, not because of his human errors, but because of his toxic supernatural relationships.

Aeschines' accusations are difficult to refute. After all, the events he has described support his case so well; the personalised model of luck, fate and fortune that he appeals to is, as we have seen, shared, well-known and of long standing. Moreover, it seems likely that his charges against Demosthenes drew on and echoed current, popular accusations.[19] In response, Demosthenes attacks, not Aeschines' account of events, but his explanation of them. In the background of his argument, he keeps a firm hold of the model of inevitable fate that he has already established in the earlier part of his speech, but he also nuances Aeschines' model of individual fortune, extending it from people to cities – a model we have seen in operation in earlier writers from Pindar to Thucydides – and draws on other models of luck, fate and fortune, weaving them together in the cause of his defence.[20] This powerful manipulation of the models and language of luck, fate and fortune allows him to focus his audience's attention on the role of mortal decision-making, its interaction with the idea of inevitable fate, and the question of responsibility.

Demosthenes leads into this section of the speech with a summary of the events that followed the defeat, his role in taking measures for defence and the attitude of the Athenians.[21] This is an important introduction for this section on *tuche*, since it allows him to demonstrate how, at that time, he was the recipient of both divine and mortal support. He explains how he was put on trial by his enemies, but 'first, by the gods, and second, by you and the other Athenians' he was acquitted. With this acknowledgement of divine and citizen favour (which he notes, explicitly, shows the Athenians approved of his policies, and suggests, implicitly, that they share responsibility) he begins his excursus on fate.

He opens by stressing again the mysterious nature of *tuche*: no one knows the nature of their own *tuche*, let alone that of another, so it is ridiculous to reproach someone about it, since they have no control over it – and here he invokes the reversal model that we have seen elsewhere.[22] He acknowledges the good *tuche* of Athens, and emphasises this, by drawing attention to a divine pronouncement from Dodona on this subject.[23] To explain recent events, he argues that Athens is only partaking in the present difficult and terrible *tuche* of the world at large. In such circumstances, one must judge each city's fortunes separately, and, compared to other cities, Athens is not suffering so badly. This can be attributed to the decisions she has made; they may not have worked out exactly to plan, but this is because of the general context of misfortune.[24] Similarly, one must judge each individual's fortunes separately, and separately from that of their city. Then, having established this vision of bespoke *tuche*, he goes on to explain the relationship between the *tuche* of a city, and that of its inhabitants: crucially he argues that the fortune of a single individual cannot possibly influence that of a city.²⁵

In support of this, he argues that he himself cannot be thought unlucky, and he picks out in detail the elements of his life that mean he must be counted as fortunate. He is, of course, doing some violence to Aeschines' argument here: this is the introduction of a wholly different meaning of *tuche*, one which refers to temporary prosperity.²⁶ It is a risky ploy, since, as we have seen in previous chapters, and as he himself has acknowledged, the popular reversal model of fortune held that temporary prosperity was likely to result in divine displeasure and ensuing disaster. But Demosthenes takes this rhetorical risk – partly, perhaps, because it means that he can attack Aeschines' family background and social status. But also this account of his own good fortune allows him to tackle Aeschines' charge that he is an evil force within Athens without raising it directly: Demosthenes emphasises how his good fortune has redounded to Athens' benefit, in the form of liturgies. Again, as he did more explicitly above, he links his (good) fortune with that of Athens.²⁷

Demosthenes' final argument brings his audience firmly back to the mortal decision-making context in which he has acted. He points out that if his policies have been wrong, then surely the other politicians of the city, who did not override them, are also culpable. He has done wrong neither voluntarily nor by mistake: he did what was expedient and it simply did not work as planned. In a context of bad fortune, he cannot be held to blame.

Throughout this part of his argument Demosthenes talks explicitly only of *tuche*, the other supernatural figures fall away: this may be a deliberate rhetorical choice, intended to evoke a less anthropomorphic image than mention of a *daimon* or a god. But it would be difficult to argue that Demosthenes intends this discussion to have no divine or religious aspect.²⁸ These passages occur not only in the context of Aeschines' accusations, which are replete with religious associations, but also following Demosthenes' own earlier arguments, which, we have seen, stress divine involvement.²⁹ In this part of his speech, Demosthenes goes on to couple discussions of Athens' fortune with reference to an oracle from Dodona that had proclaimed to the

Athenians that their city would experience good luck, which makes an implicit link between *tuche* and the gods; and he also uses terms that evoke the involvement of *daimones*.[30] Besides, for many, perhaps most, of his audience, such a divine aspect to *tuche* would have been perfectly obvious.

The explanation may be that explicit reference to a *daimon* would remind the audience too explicitly of Aeschines' charge: easier, perhaps, to engage just with the concepts (in all their variety) of *tuche*. Alternatively, it may be a religious scruple (or convention) that prompts Demosthenes not to make explicit reference to the gods here. After all, what is at issue is the allocation of responsibility for Athens' recent bad luck. If the gods were thought to be on Athens' side, and the city's *tuche* is known to be good, and if he needs to absolve himself, then who is Demosthenes to blame for these disasters?[31] Demosthenes' manipulation of these multiple shared models of *tuche* allows an alternative, complex, but plausible explanation of misfortune.

## Models, Metaphors and Motivations

I have started with this interchange between Demosthenes and Aeschines because it illustrates many of the themes of this book. First of all, it draws our attention to the significance of luck, fate and fortune not only for the ancient Greek imagination, but also as part of their discourse of daily life. We have seen – in the lyric poets, in the writings of Herodotus and Thucydides – the language of luck, fate and fortune used in retrospect as part of their narrative account, their explanations of past events. The performative nature of lyric poetry suggests that this language was a part of daily discourse, but, as discussed, the context and nature of its performance is unclear. However, Herodotus and Thucydides offer us examples of characters using the language of luck, fate and fortune – in Thucydides, use of *tuche* in political rhetoric is particularly suggestive. Although the authenticity of those presentations may be debateable, the speeches of Demosthenes and Aeschines build on this aspect: in the midst of a heated political battle, these two politicians devote remarkable time and effort to debating the role of *tuche* in the playing out of events at every level, for all mankind, for the experiences of a city, for the lives of individuals.

In doing so, they invoke a number of models of luck, fate and fortune that we have seen used in earlier writers, ranging from the model of inevitable fate, to the idea of the reversal of prosperity, to the notion of a personalised fortune. These speeches, particularly Demosthenes' skilful handling of these many different available models, demonstrate the ways in which ancient writers and speakers could use the language of luck, fate and fortune to shape and interpret accounts of events, past, present and future. Similar sensitive treatments occur in the other writings we have examined: across genres, and across contexts within those genres, different dimensions of luck, fate and fortune are emphasised for a variety of purposes. In the corpus of lyric poetry there is great emphasis on the rigidity of *moira* and mortal allocation. This is often used as a consolation for troubled experiences, but the different writers use it to different effect. Thus, for Theognis it becomes a vehicle for his shock and distaste at the disturbance of traditional social hierarchies; while Solon draws on it to encourage Athens' citizens to stand together, as an exhortation to individuals to treat each other justly. Herodotus involves a great staff of supernatural personnel to draw attention to the physical and metaphysical structures that underpin and explain all events, past, present and future; while Thucydides, in contrast, is more concerned with the multiple models of *tuche* that manifest in daily life. He also draws our attention to the ways in which individuals, including, and perhaps especially, politicians, used these models to explain events and influence decisions.

Across these various cultural models, the personnel of luck, fate and fortune operate at a range of social levels: from the individual to the group, to the city, to the universe. The level invoked appears to depend less on any widely shared dogma about supernatural structure and far more on the rhetorical stance of the speaker, and the intended effect of his rhetoric in a particular context. So, for example, consolation for, and explanation of, bad experiences may be given through reflection on the operation of luck, fate and fortune at the cosmic level (see for example, Theognis, 1.133–142), but they may also (and especially for a particularly shocking event) be achieved through reference to the personalised fortune of an individual (for example, the *daimon* who jumps on Oedipus and his *dusdaimon moira*, or the reflections of Solon to Croesus in Book 1 of Herodotus' *Histories*).

As this suggests, these terms for luck, fate and fortune can be seen to encompass a number of subordinate senses, which embody 'cultural knowledge' of how the uncertain future is constructed. Moreover, we see that some of these senses reflect powerful metaphorical thinking: so, for example, the imagery of allocation associated with *moira*; the way in which *tuche* or *moira* may ambush their target.[32] Rather than suggesting that this material demonstrates a vagueness about, or lack of understanding of, these terms for fate and fortune, as other scholars have suggested, this analysis rather indicates that speakers and writers, and their audiences, had a deep implicit understanding of these terms and their kaleidoscopic cultural meaning, and were able to work with different senses as they appeared in particular contexts. As has been found by cognitive anthropologists in their analysis of modern speech patterns, it is quite usual for speakers to shift from one sense of a term to another, or place particular emphasis on one sense rather than another.[33]

With the historical perspective that these case studies provide, we can trace the development of some of these meanings, as *moira* was slowly supplanted by *tuche*. This gradual change seems to indicate a shift in the cultural models at play, from a more rigid model of a universe dominated by *moira* (as a force or a personality) and operating, at every level, through a cosmic allocation of justice, to a more fluid, unpredictable and uncertain realm of *tuche*. This shift is not a step-change, but more a modification of emphasis: although references to *moira* may fade, the notion of a universe dominated by a rigid supernatural power of fortune, is, as we have seen most recently in Demosthenes' words above, still retained. As described already in each of the case studies, these shifts in the dominant model of luck, fate and fortune can be linked to changes taking place in social and political contexts. Put very simply, a greater emphasis on *moira*, apparent in discourse from the Archaic period, may reflect a society and culture that comprised more hierarchical social structures; in turn, many scholars have recognised that the rise of *tuche* occurred in an increasingly turbulent social and political context.

Does the rise of *tuche* indicate growing secularisation? Across these analyses, I have kept to a minimum questions about the nature or quality of belief evinced by our subjects – is belief in *tuche* religious or not? Is it 'real' religious belief or not? My belief is that these questions turn on a construction of ancient mentality that is dependent on our own heuristic categories. As I noted above, this tends to happen when we assume that we are seeking to pin down definitions of terms, rather than looking for the cognitive structures that they represent. What I hope these case studies have shown is that these questions might be better constructed if they helped us to explore the many different ways in which ancient Greek discourse reveals, sometimes implicitly, sometimes expressed overtly, the perceived role of luck, fate and fortune across various aspects of daily life. These studies certainly suggest that many people regarded *moira, tuche*, etc. to be strong and active forces shaping events in their lives and others. Underpinning their understanding of these forces were a variety of shared cultural models of how these forces operated, alone, with each other, and in concert with mortal activities. Across a variety of discourses, they used the language of luck, fate and fortune, references to these cultural models to explain, console, exhort, persuade, but also to evaluate behaviour and character, to compete with others for advancement and support. This rhetoric is even used, as we see in Aeschines' and Demosthenes' debate about the nature of each other's fortune, to establish the prevailing understanding of the ideology of luck, fate and fortune itself.[34]

Above all, across all these genres, and with whatever emphasis it receives, it seems to me that the language of luck, fate and fortune is concerned not so much with man's sense of quandary when faced with the unknown future, although this is an aspect of it. More central to its use is the focus it enables on the question of responsibility. This introduces another aspect of cultural models, discussed by cognitive anthropologists, which suggests that part of the implicit knowledge that they transmit between members of a culture is a goal-directed sense of motivation.[35] Again, the particular goal will shift and change according to the sense of the model. We can see this very simply if we return to the term bachelor, which contains within it a world of meanings that describes the cultural expectations about marriage as a life-goal for men of a certain age. Meanwhile, we can note that the word itself nowadays has a slightly old-fashioned feel, probably because the goals and values that it transmits are no longer in step with modern models of relationships.[36] Anthropologists have analysed how particular models may come to have motivational force for individuals, and become a spur to action.

Ancient cultural models of luck, fate and fortune might also be discussed in terms of motivation and goal-directed knowledge. To begin with, the discourse of luck, fate and fortune provides a means of answering that most inexplicable question that has haunted and continues to haunt mortals faced with suffering across cultures and down through time: why me? The different possible answers to this question, and diverse descriptions these will provide of an individual's relationship with the supernatural, are underpinned by, and will result in, a variety of goals and actions. As this suggests, these models of luck, fate and fortune offer a discourse for the discussion of mortal responsibility. This can be seen in Solon's stress on mortal action, Herodotus' search for causes, Thucydides' careful account of the sequence of events, and, powerfully, in the debate between Aeschines and Demosthenes. Although Demosthenes may mention the unpredictable nature of fortune, he places most emphasis on mortal responsibility for action, exploring notions of blame, the limits of human influence and culpability, eliciting a compelling picture of dutiful human action and ideal leadership. And as a language for the allocation of responsibility the language of luck, fate and fortune is, as we have seen, extremely flexible: it provides a range of meanings and emphases that refer to a range of related cultural models, which can be manipulated and generally fitted to a particular purpose. Nor should this identification of a particular use of the discourse of luck, fate and fortune be taken to mean that 'religious belief' in these forces was any the less. If anything, it may help us to see how the cultural models associated with luck, fate and fortune interact with those of other supernatural figures, including the gods.

## Modern Manipulation

The idea of allocating responsibility for the uncertain future to a higher power is not so strange to modern ears, nor is the metaphorical use of terms for, or the manipulation of cultural models of, fate luck and fortune. As we can see in the quotation at the beginning of the chapter, the idea that we operate with a (usually implicit) model of how the world works is not considered surprising. We also find the implicit manipulation of cultural models of luck, fate and fortune alive and well, and potent, in the political rhetoric of our own day – although the terms, and the cultural models they refer to, may be different. Briefly consider, for example, the discourses of luck, fate and fortune at play in the inauguration speeches of, respectively, George Bush and Barack Obama. Both were written at times of crisis, both manipulate the notion of 'The American Dream' – in terms of its historical legacy and its promise for future generations. But the language used, the cultural models evoked, the emphases created in each speech are subtly and powerfully different.[37]

In his speech, delivered in 2005, Bush placed great emphasis on the need to stand together and face the trials of the future. He may have acknowledged that individual decisions carry significance for the outcome of events ('Not because history runs on the wheels of inevitability; it is human choices that move events'). Nevertheless, his rhetoric suggests a sense of unquestioned and unquestioning certainty about what will happen ('We go forward with complete confidence in the eventual triumph of freedom'). The work to be done for the nation will be achieved through the efforts of society as a whole – 'we will bring the highest standards to our schools, and build an ownership society. We will widen the ownership of homes and businesses, retirement savings and health insurance.' And, briefly, he noted that it is this communal identity that will give every citizen 'his or her own destiny', even as he goes on to emphasise how it will also bolster society, giving 'our fellow Americans greater freedom from want and fear' and making 'our society more prosperous and just and equal'. In his speech, Bush linked the powerful contemporary concept of 'freedom' with that sacred term of US political discourse, 'liberty' – each carrying their own powerful set of associations. These, in turn, he used to sanctify a vision of the future as certain, successful, communal and wholly unstoppable: 'History has an ebb and flow of justice, but history also has a visible direction, set by liberty and the Author of Liberty.'

In contrast, Barack Obama's speech evoked a vision of both future and past that turned on the uncertain nature of the future – and emphasised the efforts of individuals. His review of history drew attention to the role of those people who dared to take a chance, to test their luck ('Rather, it has been the risk-takers, the doers, the makers of things – some celebrated but more often men and women obscure in their labor, who have carried us up the long, rugged path towards prosperity and freedom'). And this formed the basis for an exhortation to his listeners for each of them to embrace their responsibility to build America's future, with detailed descriptions of the many different ways Americans might 'pick ourselves up, dust ourselves off, and begin again the work of remaking America.'

In Obama's speech, freedom becomes not the final achievement that will smooth society's path to the future, but part of a context that allows the quest for individual fulfilment. Instead of being carried forward by the twin forces of History and Liberty, as described by Bush, Obama's words stressed responsibility to previous generations of Americans ('We are the keepers of this legacy'), as well as to the future. The unstoppable destiny envisioned by George Bush is here portrayed as highly uncertain – a matter of individual action and immense effort, both moral and physical.

In contrast with Aeschines and Demosthenes, neither modern speaker explicitly mentions the terms luck, fate and fortune: contemporary cultural models of the uncertain future trade in a different discourse. Rather than providing, as the ancients do, explanations of how, why and by whom we are being controlled, both Bush and Obama draw attention to our expectations of control – although for Bush this control is mediated by individual membership of various institutions, from family, to community, to nation. In Bush's rhetoric, 'destiny' appears to tie individuals into a communal future vision that will benefit society as a whole. In contrast, Obama draws attention to the opportunities for individuals to pursue their 'full measure of happiness'. When Obama does finally refer to 'destiny', towards the end of his speech, he almost turns it into an oxymoron: 'This is the source of our confidence – the knowledge that God calls on us to shape an uncertain destiny.' Here is a fate that is not fated – it depends on our efforts – and so, unexpectedly, reinforces Obama's argument for the importance of taking individual responsibility. This aspect is emphasised again through his use of a term that George

Bush's speech omits altogether: Obama uses 'risk-takers' as a term of approbation in a list of those who have laboured for their country, and alongside the more mundane 'doers' and 'makers'. By highlighting these unsung heroes of US history, Obama again directs his listeners to the need to take a chance (on Obama, on ourselves and each other – and on an uncertain future). His language draws on another current discourse about the future – that of 'risk', and, more recently, 'resilience' – that is also used in the fields of strategy and planning.

In our current age, the discourse of luck, fate and fortune clearly conveys a sense of mortal helplessness that – in certain arenas of our post-Enlightenment society – simply cannot be admitted. Modern professional discourse about the future demands a sense of control, conveyed by a new language, with a new set of underlying schemas and associations. This is a discourse that places emphasis on human perceptions, reactions and potential, sometimes conveying – for example, in the notion of 'future-proofing', which has moved from a technical term used of technology products into the literature of management and self-help – extraordinary expectations about man's power over his environment.

And yet, beliefs in the role of luck, fate and fortune (whether we capitalise them as supernatural powers or not) persist, dignifying our lives with an author of some sort, an entity that is controlling the direction of the narrative, whether we call that entity fate, destiny, God, or our inner selves. Indeed, one commentator has suggested that beliefs in fate and attitudes of fatalism maintain their hold on the popular imagination because it is a common experience to feel that we are being directed by some stronger power. Research across a range of fields, from healthcare choices to views on climate change, suggest that these beliefs can have significant impacts on how we live our daily lives, take public and private choices.[38] Moreover, as we have repeatedly observed, the idea that embracing concepts of luck, fate and fortune automatically engender passivity and the relinquishing of all responsibility, as we give up and simply hand over the direction of events to a higher power, is clearly not the case. Concepts of luck, fate and fortune may, in fact, do precisely the opposite, promoting action and the taking of responsibility.[39]

Thus to argue, as Giddens, that the emergence of a new, more assertive attitude to the uncertain future can be traced to Machiavelli's *The Prince*: 'I judge it to be true that *fortuna* is the arbiter of one half of our actions, but that she still leaves the control of the other half or almost that, to us . . .' is to do a disservice to both ancient and modern ideas of fate.

In contrast, the concept of risk, which flourished particularly during the latter part of the twentieth century, although at first sight chiefly concerned with the vagaries of chance, is revealed as a language of control, and faith in that control. It was a world view that replaced Providence with Progress, in particular technological progress. Our economic and technological destiny seemed unavoidable: '. . . two metatrends – fundamental technological change and a new ethos of openness – will transform our world into the beginnings of a global civilization, a new civilization of civilizations, that will blossom through the coming century.'[40]

As Jackson Lears has pointed out in his superlative history of America's relationship with luck, the managerial elite who utilised this rhetoric of risk, chance and progress tended to be 'insulated from the vagaries of chance by economic privilege', while others outside this charmed circle became, if anything, more vulnerable to chance.[41] This division in society is perhaps reflected in the Shell scenarios for 2001, which painted this simultaneous social divide in terms of two possible visions of the future: 'Business Class', a world of 'efficiency, opportunities and high rewards for those who could compete and innovate successfully', and 'Prism', a future of 'conflicts over religion and values, shades of patriotic, populist and nationalist policies'.[42] The discourse of risk has travelled quite comfortably alongside a burgeoning compensation culture: in a world in which we expect to control everything, we naturally demand some kind of recompense when that control falls by the wayside.

A decade later, and a number of terrible events have forced us to recognise our vulnerability, our inability to control the events that shape our lives, our world. From the terrible tragedy of the terrorist attacks on September 11, 2001, to the disastrous consequences of idolising models, calculations and the dream of technological control, as attested by recent financial events.[43]

## THE RESURRECTION OF CHANCE

In this context, there seems to be a rediscovery of contingency. First, there has been a reappraisal of the role of chance in our lives, and growing recognition that we cannot control everything. A recent paper, 'Risk Management Lessons from the Credit Crisis', acknowledges, 'Risk management, even if flawlessly executed, does not guarantee that big losses will not occur. Big losses can occur because of business decisions and bad luck.'[44] The new head of policy at the US Environmental Protection Agency, Lisa Heinzerling, has suggested that 'policy formation based on prediction and calculation of expected harm is no longer relevant; the only coherent response to a situation of chaotically worsening outcomes is a precautionary policy'. Nassim Taleb's *The Black Swan* draws our attention to the importance of making room for chance and the unexpected, for the vagaries of what we might call luck. From the events of the recent economic crisis to discoveries of chaos theory, to research into the role of chance in genetics, there is a growing recognition that we may prepare, but we cannot predict.[45]

And some commentators have argued that recognition of our lack of total control, our exposure to life's lottery, may be salutary. Jackson Lears suggests that there is a crucial relationship between chance and the nature of the human spirit: he observes that the rise of gambling in a society obsessed by control may 'enact a philosophical alternative to dominant managerial ideals of control and accumulation', may indicate an 'appetite for the possibility of grace.' The second quotation at the beginning of this chapter is from a novel by the writer Frederick Barthelme and his brother Steven. In the early 1990s, they gambled away their inheritance (around $250,000) in the gambling boats on the Mississippi. In this passage they offer some thoughts on the emotions that prompted them to keep gambling, even as they continued to lose, and the way in which gambling allowed them the promise that they might rise above a mundane world with its petty rules.[46] Perhaps more concretely, in the 2009 Reith lectures, the political philosopher Michael Sandel warns against attempting to engineer our genetic development and that of our children, because the idea that our fortunes are contingent is probably crucial for the solidarity of society: 'the more alive we are to the chanced nature of our lot, the more reason we have to share our fate with others', and that these efforts to control all aspects of our existence would be likely to 'deaden[s] the impulse to social and political improvement'.[47]

As this book has demonstrated, many of these insights about the crucial role of luck, fate and fortune in our lives, as individuals and communities, have a long legacy. The ancients long ago recognised the impossibility of trying to control and direct everything. They even seem to have understood that this sense of being out of control might offer us significant lessons. For example, we find echoes of Michael Sandell's thoughts on the dangers of seeking genetic control in the writings of both Solon and Demothenes, who each, in their different ways, observed the importance of sticking together in the face of uncertain and violent times. Moreover, we have seen that just as Jackson Lears and the brothers Barthelme have suggested, the ancients believed that there are lessons to be learned from our experiences of luck, fate and fortune, which shape our character, and the nature of the human spirit: think of Sophocles' Oedipus, for example, or Herodotus' story of Croesus.

## Unseen Forces or Individual Autonomy?

We finish with a famous passage from Plato's *Republic* which brings together many of the themes discussed in this book. In this excerpt, Socrates vividly describes how the souls of the dead are gathering, under the management of a prophet, to choose their new 'lots and patterns of lives'.[48] The passage is full of characters and concepts that we have met before. The *Moirai* are running the show: the souls are sent before Lachesis; it is from her lap that the prophet gathers the lots and 'patterns of lives'. The souls are warned: by selecting their new mortal life, their new character, the souls will also choose their 'personal divinity' (*daimon*). And they must understand, 'the blame belongs to he who chooses, god is blameless'. The prophet then flings the lots out among the souls. Each of them picks up the one that lands by his side, and, according to the number they have drawn, steps forward to choose a life pattern from among those laid out before them. There are plenty to choose from: 'They were of every conceivable kind, animal and human. For there were tyrannies among them, some life-long, some falling in mid-career and ending in poverty, exile and beggary; there were lives of men famed for their good looks and strength and athletic prowess, or for their distinguished birth and family connections, there were lives of men with non of these claims to fame. And there was a similar choice of lives for women. There was no choice of quality of character since of necessity each soul must assume a character appropriate to its choice; but wealth and poverty, health and disease were all mixed in varying degrees in the lives to be chosen.'

The prophet pronounces a final instruction, 'Even for the last comer, if he chooses wisely and lives strenuously, there is left a life with which he may be well content. Let him who chooses first look to his choice, and him who chooses last not despair.' And, even as the prophet falls silent, the first soul leaps forward and chooses the greatest tyranny he can find, drawn in by the riches it promised . . . only to find out, on closer examination, that it is his fate to eat his own children, among other horrors. As he realises he has chosen a bad pattern of life he 'does not blame himself, but *tuche*, and the gods, and anything except himself'.

Plato's vision of this allocation of luck, fate and fortune seems at first sight to recognise mortal control. Yet, even as the souls exercise their choices, a sense of cosmic restraint hangs over the whole system: Lachesis is the daughter of Necessity, as the souls are told, and she allocates each soul's *daimon* after they have chosen, while the other *Moirai*, Clotho and Atropos, ensure that each pattern of life is complete, and cannot be undone. So is this a story of control by others? As we might expect, the story is not quite so simple. The souls make their choices based on their previous life experiences, which have educated their tastes, and shaped their appetites. Socrates explains that the soul doomed to feast on his family lived in a well-ordered city before he died. His choices, and his behaviour afterwards, were rooted in this experience, in particular, his lack of suffering. It meant that this soul simply had no understanding of how to navigate through a difficult life. Socrates emphasises the importance of enduring suffering as well as pleasure: any attempt to choose a life that excludes suffering is, in the end, counter-productive. Instead, it is important to learn from experiences, not in order to take control of one's destiny – obviously, that is not possible – but in order to be able to take responsibility for one's choices, whatever the context.

So, should we trust in unseen forces or individual autonomy? Phrased in different terms, in various modern contexts, this is a question that haunts us still, and yet, as we have seen, the choice it presents may well be a false one. Instead, as many of the Greek texts discussed above have indicated, and as current trends also suggest, we may need a cultural model of luck, fate and fortune that embraces, and teaches us to navigate, both.

# NOTES

Thanks are due to a number of people for their encouragement and advice, including John Eidinow, Louise Hickman, Simon Hornblower and Robin Osborne. I am grateful also to Professor Emanuel Voutiras who very kindly passed on a draft of 'Fortune et Infortune', which he and Dr. Charalambos Kritzias have written for *Thesaurus Cultus et Rituum Antiquorum (ThesCRA)* (Los Angeles, CA: John Paul Getty Museum, forthcoming).

## Introduction

1  Spoken by Peter O'Toole as T. E. Lawrence in the film *Lawrence of Arabia* (1962).
2  Later in the film Lawrence will execute Gasim, when he discovers that he has killed one of Auda Abu Tayi's men in a blood feud, potentially endangering the alliance he has established with Auda's Howeitat tribe.
3  Bernstein, Peter L., *Against the Gods: The Remarkable Story of Risk* (New York: John Wiley, 1996), p. 1.
4  Anthony Giddens draws attention to both aspects of risk: see, for example, *The Consequences of Modernity* (Cambridge: Polity, 1990), 'Risk and Responsibility', *The Modern Law Review* 62: 1 (January, 1999), pp. 1–10, *Runaway World: How Globalisation is Shaping Our World* (New York: Routledge, 2000). 'Risk' is a multivalent concept on which a range of analytical approaches have been brought to bear. See, for example, the complex implications for society described by Beck, Ulrich, *Risk Society Towards a New Modernity* (London: Sage, 1992), and Douglas, Mary and Wildavsky, Aaron, *Risk and Culture* (Berkeley: University of California Press, 1982) to name but a few. See Lupton, Deborah, *Risk* (London: Routledge, 1999) for a succinct but detailed overview of approaches to risk.
5  List of actions from *www.colorado.edu/ASEN/SrProjects/Class%20Presentations/PM_Risk.pdf*; linked to from *http://managementhelp.org/risk_mng/risk_mng.htm#anchor1151197*. Professionalisation: see, for example, the Risk Management Association, at *www.rmahq.org/RMA* and the Institute of Risk Management, at *www.theirm.org*.

6   For careful explorations of the differences between luck, fate and fortune see Rescher, Nicholas, *Luck: The Brilliant Randomness of Everyday Life* (New York: Farrar, Straus and Giroux, 2001), pp. 26–30. However, some of his distinctions seem less precise in the light of modern scientific advances in genetics: for example, can we really say that someone is fortunate to be good at mathematics (as he suggests, p. 30), or is it more a matter of luck?
7   See s.v. *Fatum* in Lewis, C., and Short, C., *A Latin Dictionary* (Oxford: Clarendon Press, 1933).
8   All the definitions used in this discussion of terms and their meanings are from the Merriam-Webster *Online Dictionary*, which is based on the *Merriam-Webster's Collegiate Dictionary*, 11th ed. (Springfield Massachusetts: Merriam-Webster 2003); etymologies are from Hoad, Terry, in *The Concise Oxford Dictionary of English Etymology* (Oxford: Oxford University Press, 2003).
9   s.v. 'luck' in Hoad, *Dictionary of English Etymology*.
10  A brief and unscientific survey of news sources online suggests that sports journalism in particular seems to use the imagery of luck, fate and fortune. For an analysis of George Bush's and Barack Obama's rhetorical use of luck, fate and fortune see pp. 155–157 of this book.
11  As Giddens: *The Consequences of Modernity*, pp. 29–31, although in *Modernity and Self-identity: Self and Society in the Late Modern Age* (Cambridge: Polity, 1991), p. 109, he states 'notion of fate and destiny have by no means disappeared in modern societies'.
12  See, for example, Wiseman, Richard, *The Luck Factor: The Scientific Study of the Lucky Mind* (London: Arrow Books Ltd, 2004).
13  For a useful overview of divinatory practices in ancient Greece, see Johnston, Sarah Iles, *Ancient Greek Divination* (Oxford: Wiley Blackwell, 2008); Flower, Michael, *The Seer in Ancient Greece* (University of California Press, 2007) provides a detailed examination of the role of diviners in ancient Greek culture.
14  On binding spells see Eidinow, Esther, *Oracles, Curses, and Risk Among the Ancient Greeks* (Oxford: Oxford University Press, 2007).
15  On the relationship between mortals and heroes, see Kearns, Emily, *Heroes of Attica* (London: University of London Institute of Classical Studies, 1989).
16  The idea that success generated *phthonos*, not just mortal, but also divine, is first found in Aeschylus (see *The Persians*, l. 821 and *Agamemnon*, ll. 1500–1504). Dover, Kenneth, *Greek Popular Morality* (Oxford: Blackwell, 1974), p. 77 ff. suggests that the idea of motiveless hostility on the part of the gods may have been more widespread in the fourth century BCE than our sources suggest.
17  For example, see Homer, *Iliad*, 9.454, 571–2; 19.87, 259, 410; *Odyssey*, 2.135; 15.234.
18  On *karma*, see Keyes, Charles F., and Valentine, Daniel E., eds., *Karma: an Anthropological Inquiry* (London: University of California Press, 1983): the editors stress how concepts of *karma* vary across and within individual cultures, and how important it is to examine them in context. On Chinese concepts of fate see especially Raphals, Lisa, 'Fate, Fortune, Chance, and Luck in Chinese and Greek: A Comparative Semantic History' *Philosophy East and West*, 53: 4, (Oct., 2003), pp. 537–574 and Hatfield, D. J., 'Fate in the Narrativity and

Experience of Selfhood, a Case from Taiwanese *chhiam* Divination' in *American Ethnologist*, 29: 4 (2002), pp. 857–877.

19  As described by Oates, W., *Luck: A Secular Faith* (Louisville, KY: Westminster John Knox Press, 1995), p. 5 and Daniels, I. M., 'Scooping, Raking, beckoning Luck: Luck, Agency and the Interdependence of People and Things in Japan', *Journal of the Royal Anthropological Institute* (n.s.) 9 (2003), pp. 619–638, who also quotes Oates. As Daniels explains, *engimono* do not bring luck by themselves, but work by allowing people to connect to the appropriate gods; further actions (ritual or moral activities) must follow (p. 623).

20  Aristotle, *Physics* II.4.196b6–8 and 196a1–5, respectively (translation by R. P. Hardie and R. K. Gaye, Vol. 2 of Ross, W. D., ed., *The Works of Aristotle*, Vols. 1–12 Oxford: Oxford University Press, 1930, repr. 1952).

21  Studies of ancient Greek attitudes to ideas of destiny include: Greene, William Chase, *Moira: Fate, Good and Evil in Greek Thought* (Cambridge MA: Harvard University Press, 1944); Bianchi, Ugo, *Dios Aisa. Destino, uomini e divinità nell'epos, nelle teogonie e nel culto dei Greci* (Rome: Studi Pubblicati dall'Istituto Italiano per la Storia Antica Fascicolo Undicesimo, Angelo Signorelli, 1953); Dietrich, Bernard C., *Death, Fate and the Gods: The Development of a Religious Idea in Greek Popular Belief and in Homer* (London: The Athlone Press, 1965); Onians, Richard, *The Origins of European Thought: About the Body, the Mind, the Soul, the World, Time, and Fate* (Cambridge: Cambridge University Press, 1951). On *Tuche*, most notably Allègre, Fernand, *Étude sur la déesse grècque Tyché: sa signification religieuse et morale, son culte et ses répresentations figurées* (Paris: Leroux, 1889); Ströhm, Hans, *Tuche: Zur Schicksalsauffassung bei Pindar und den frühgriechischen Dichtern* (Stuttgart: J. G. Cotta, 1944); Buriks, Agatha A., *Peri Tuches* (diss. Leiden, 1948); Dodds, Eric R., *The Greeks and the Irrational* (Boston: Beacon Press, 1957). A rich and fascinating thesis on *Tuche* in Euripides by Vasiliki Giannopoulou has unfortunately not been published. She similarly argues for examining the way in which terms of fate and fortune are used, on the grounds that they reveal 'human uncertainty, ignorance and frailty in the face of the unforeseen future, danger or critical circumstances', calling this 'fortune talk'; I agree, but consider that this discourse goes beyond an expression of uncertainty, to a rhetoric of responsibility, and reveals cultural models and how they change over time. *Tuche* also appears in Kershaw, S. P. (1986), *Personification in the Hellenistic world: Tuche, Kairos, Nemesis*, Ph.D. Thesis, Bristol (*non vidi*).

22  E.g. Dietrich, *Death, Fate*, esp. p. 327; see Greene, *Moira*, especially introduction. On man and fate in Homer, see Vernant, Jean-Pierre, *Myth and Tragedy in Ancient Greece* (New York: Zone Books, 1988), esp. pp. 44 and 50; Williams, Bernard, *Shame and Necessity* (Berkeley and Oxford: University of California Press, 1993, esp. p. 41 for previous scholarship on notions of free will in Homer); Hammer, Dean C., (1988) 'The Cultural Construction of Chance in the *Iliad*' *Arethusa* 31:2, 125–148 redefines the sphere of freedom. On *Tuche*, see further in Chapter III below. Religious significance of *Tuche*, see Mikalson, Jon D., *Honor Thy Gods* (Chapel Hill: University of North Carolina Press, 1991. In contrast, see the collected papers in Matheson, Susan B., ed., *An Obsession with Fortune: Tyche in Greek and Roman Art*, exhibition catalogue, Yale University Art Gallery (New Haven: Yale University Art Gallery, 1994).

23  D'Andrade, Roy G., *The Development of Cognitive Anthropology* (Cambridge: Cambridge University Press, 1995) pp. 122–3; these share some similarities with the schemata described by Sourvinou-Inwood, Christiane, 'Tragedy and Religion: Constructs and Readings', in Pelling, Christopher, ed., *Greek Tragedy and the Historian* (Oxford: Oxford University Press, 1997), pp. 161–186, insofar as those, too, are described as 'a particular type of configuration of assumptions' and 'models of organizing experience'. However, she offers no theoretical basis for them, nor does she relate them to schemas in other disciplines. As described, they 'structure myths, collective representations, and texts' (p. 178) and appear to be separate from, although 'themselves structured by', and thus expressing 'society's beliefs, realities, collective representations, and ideologies, its cultural assumptions'. Her primary interest is in their use to direct the audience (as she says of them: 'the deployment, manipulation, and interaction of which directed in the main line the audience's perception and reception of the tragedy') and does not seem to see the audience as active in this process. A more interactive use of cultural models/schemas is found in the narrative models described by Goff, Barbara, *The Noose of Words: Readings of Desire, Violence and Language in Euripides' Hippolytos* (Cambridge: Cambridge University Press, 1991), pp. 37–9, 59–60 who notes how 'culturally shared narrative models that already assume certain kinds of response in others' are exploited in Euripides' *Hippolytus* as a way of exploring characterisation.
24  Obviously, any violence done in the process to the original approach is entirely my responsibility; but my hope is that those who disagree with the approach or conclusions might offer an alternative.
25  Norman, Donald A., 'Reflections on Cognition and Parallel Distributed Processing' in McLelland, J. L., Rumelhart, D. E. and the PDP Research Group, eds., *Parallel Distributed Processing: Explorations in the Microstructure of Cognition, Vol. 2: Psychological and Biological Models*, (Cambridge: MIT Press, 1986), p. 536, quoted in D'Andrade, *Cognitive Anthropology*, p. 142.
26  Drawing further on the work of cognitive anthropologists in this field, it might even be useful to think about the models being explored in terms of personal semantic networks, that is personal interpretive frameworks shaped by each writer's particular experiences; this does not nullify the approach, since such networks can help to identify sub-cultural differences. See further, Strauss, Claudia, 'Analyzing Discourse for Cultural Complexity' in Quinn, Naomi, ed., *Finding Culture in Talk: A Collection of Methods* (New York; Basingstoke: Palgrave Macmillan, 2005), 203–242, p. 208.

# Chapter I

1  Fenton, Sasha, *The Fortune Teller's Workbook: A practical introduction to the world of divination* (Wellingborough, Northamptonshire: Aquarian, 1998), p. 213.
2  From Wiseman, Richard, *The Luck Factor: The Scientific Study of the Lucky Mind* (London: Arrow Books, 2004), p. 38.

# NOTES

3   Private correspondence with Mary Bryce, editor of *Chat – It's Fate*, 26th March, 2008.
4   'Family of views': Honderich, Ted, *On Determinism and Freedom* (Edinburgh: Edinburgh University Press, 2008), p. 140.
5   Campbell, Joseph, O'Rourke, Michael, Shier, David, *Freedom and Determinism: Topics in Contemporary Philosophy* (Massachusetts: MIT, 2004), p. 2 offers a brief overview of varieties of universal determinism.
6   Zagzebski, Linda T., 'Recent Work on Divine Foreknowledge and Free Will' pp. 45–64, Bernstein, Mark, 'Fatalism', pp. 65–82 and Hasker, William, 'God, Time, Knowledge and Freedom: The Historical Matrix', pp. 264–281, all in Kane, Robert, ed., *The Oxford Handbook of Free Will* (Oxford: Oxford University Press, 2002).
7   Giddens, *Modernity and Self-Identity*, p. 110.
8   *Ibid.*, pleas for the relevance of Fatalism; see also Solomon, Robert C., 'On Fate and Fatalism', *Philosophy East and West* 53: 4 (October 2003), pp. 435–454.
9   On New Age beliefs: Hanegraaf, Wouter J., *New Age Religion and Western Culture: Esotericism in the Mirror of Secular Thought, Studies in the History of Religions, Vol. 72* (Leiden: Brill, 1996).
10  Dolby, Sandra K., *Self-Help Books: Why Americans Keep Reading Them* (Urbana and Chicago: Illinois Press, 2005), pp. 93, 102–104; Dyer, Wayne, *Staying On the Path* (London: Hay House, 2004), p. 16.
11  Dyer, *Staying On the Path*, p. 170; Csikszentmihalyi, Mihaly, *Finding Flow: The Psychology of Engagement with Everyday Life* (New York: Basic Books, 1997), p. 147, cited by Dolby, *Self-Help Books*, p. 100. Of course, there are many variations of New Age beliefs; this is only a very brief and general description of some of the themes that run through some of them.
12  Darke, Peter R., and Freedman, Jonathan L. 'The Belief in Good Luck Scale' *Journal Of Research In Personality* 31 (1997) pp. 486-511. This study revealed few people who believed that they had consistent bad luck; but this could be related to the socio-economic background of the participants, who were visitors to the Ontario Science Centre in Toronto or Introductory Psychology students at the University of Toronto, and New York University (p. 492).
13  See Church, Timothy A., 'Personality Research in Non-Western Culture: The Philippines', *Psychological Bulletin*, 102 (1987), pp. 272–292, on luck as source of hope for success in the Philippines; see also Rothbaum, Fred, Weisz, John R., and Snyder, Sam S. 'Changing the World and Changing the Self: A Two-Process Model of Perceived Control', *Journal of Personality and Social Psychology*, 42 (1982), pp. 5–37; Weisz, John R., Rothbaum, Fred R., and Blackburn, Thomas C., 'Standing Out and Standing In: The Psychology of Control in America and Japan', *American Psychologist*, 39 (1984), pp. 955–969; cited in Darke and Freedman, *Good Luck Scale*. In the study on beliefs in luck, above, those who did think of luck as more like 'chance', that is, as external, unpredictable and uncontrollable did not in fact ignore episodes of good luck as might be expected, but tended instead to behave as if they expected the good luck to be balanced with an episode of bad luck.
14  Huxley, Aldous, *Brave New World Revisited* (London: Chatto and Windus, 1959), pp. 155 and 161.

15  Gleick, James, *Chaos: Making a New Science* (London: Heinemann, 1988) for a useful description of the new scientific uncertainty; it is not clear just what this means for determinism. See also Earman, John, in Campbell *et al.*, *Freedom*, pp. 21–46.
16  See *Genomics and Society* (ESRC Science in Society Programme, 2006) for popular attitudes to genomics. See the wonderfully titled Murphy N. and Brown W. S., eds., *Did My Neurons Make Me Do It? Philosophical and Neurobiological Perspectives on Moral Responsibility and Free Will* (Oxford: Oxford University Press, 2007) for a provocative overview of the role of the neurosciences in helping us to understand human beings as 'rational, free, and morally responsible beings' (p. 3).
17  Useful resources, on which I have drawn extensively here, include Ted Honderich's website, which includes numerous essays by a range of philosophers holding different positions in this debate (*www.ucl.ac.uk/~uctytho/dfwIntroIndex.htm*) and the detailed articles on all aspects of free will and determinism in the *Stanford Encyclopedia of Philosophy* (*http://plato.stanford.edu/contents.html*), as well as Robert Kane's two sets of collected essays Kane, *Handbook* and Kane, Robert, ed., *Free Will* (Oxford: Blackwell, 2002).
18  E.g., van Inwagen, Peter, *An Essay On Free Will* (Oxford: Clarendon Press, 1983); Strawson, Galen, 2002, 'The Bounds of Freedom', in Kane, *Handbook*, pp. 441–460.
19  The terms 'hard determinism' and 'soft determinism' were coined by James, William, *The Will to Believe and Other Essays in Popular Philosophy* (New York: Longmans and Company, 1897); for an example of a hard determinist position see Edwards, Paul, 'Hard and Soft Determinism' in Kane, *Free Will*, pp. 59–67; so-called 'successor' views to this position are discussed below.
20  Traditional libertarian view: Chisholm, Roderick M., 'Human Freedom and the Self', repr. Watson, Gary, *Free Will* (Oxford: Oxford University Press, 2003), pp. 24–35, in which the key aspect was the power of humans. See 'Libertarian Perspectives on Free Agency and Free Will' (part 6 of Kane, *Handbook*, pp. 337–437); more recently, O'Connor, Timothy, ed., *Agents, Causes and Events: Essays on Indeterminism and Free Will* (Oxford: Oxford University Press, 1995).
21  van Inwagen, Peter, 'The Mystery of Metaphysical Freedom' in Kane, *Free Will*, pp. 189–195; Strawson, Galen, 'The Unhelpfulness of Indeterminism', *Philosophy and Phenomenological Research* 60 (2000), pp. 149–56 and Honderich, Ted, *How Free Are You? The Determinism Problem* (Oxford: Oxford University Press, 1993).
22  i) Non-causal; an action is either not caused by anything, or not deterministically caused Ginet, Carl, *On Action* (Cambridge: Cambridge University Press, 1990); ii) an action is caused non-deterministically by an event in which the agent is involved (e.g. Kane, Robert, 'Agency Responsibility and Indeterminism: Reflections on Libertarian Theories of Free Will' in Campbell *et al.*, *Freedom*, pp. 70–88); iii) Agent-cause or agent-causal theories of free will attribute an event or action to an agent and argue that this means that the cause of the event or action cannot be described beyond this point. The causal chain stops with the agent, who is self-determined, see O'Connor, Timothy, *Persons and Causes: The Metaphysics of Free Will*, (New York: Oxford University Press, 2000; and

against, Pereboom, Derk, *Living Without Free Will* (Cambridge: Cambridge University Press). For a detailed overview, on which this summary is based, see Clarke, Randolph, 'Incompatibilist (Nondeterministic) Theories of Free Will', *The Stanford Encyclopedia of Philosophy (Fall 2008 Edition)*, Edward N. Zalta (ed.), http://plato.stanford.edu/archives/fall2008/entries/incompatibilism-theories/; see also Kane, *Handbook*, pp. 23–24.

23  As described by Harry Frankfurt, who argued against it in 'Alternate Possibilities and Moral Responsibility', *Journal of Philosophy* 66 (1969), pp. 829–39.

24  In fact, of Martin Luther and his description of his breaking with the Church of Rome, that '... I can do no other', Dennett argues that this is his moment of greatest responsibility (Dennett, Daniel, *Elbow Room* (Cambridge: Cambridge University Press, 1984) discussed in Kane, *Handbook*, pp. 15–16).

25  See Frankfurt, Harry, 'Freedom of the Will and the Concept of a Person', *Journal of Philosophy*, 68 (1971), pp. 5–20 (repr. Watson, *Free Will*). John Fischer has criticised this position and developed explanations that turn on reasons-responsiveness (see further below) 'Recent Work on Moral Responsibility', *Ethics* 110 (1999), pp. 93–139.

26  Frankfurt, Harry, *Necessity, Volition and Love* (Cambridge: Cambridge University Press, 1999).

27  Fischer, John Martin, *The Metaphysics of Free Will* (Oxford: Blackwell, 1994), and subsequently, Fischer, John Martin, and Ravizza, Mark, *Responsibility and Control: An Essay on Moral Responsibility* (Cambridge: Cambridge University Press, 1998) have developed models of behaviour that defend compatibilism on the grounds that individuals are responsive to an appropriate range of reasons for action (reasons-responsive compatibilism): a person may have 'guidance control' (such that someone can bring about her conduct even when there are no alternative courses of action) rather than regulative control (providing the capacity to regulate between different alternatives). See Fischer, John Martin, and Ravizza, Mark, eds., *Perspectives on Moral Responsibility* (New York and London: Cornell University Press, 1993).

28  E.g., Widerker, David, 'Libertarianism and Frankfurt's Attack on the Principle of Alternative Possibilities', *Philosophical Review* 104 (1995), pp. 247–61.

29  Strawson, Galen, 'Freedom and Resentment', *Proceedings of the British Academy* 48 (1962), pp. 1–25.

30  Originally published in *Proceedings of the Aristotelian Society, Supplementary Volumes*, 50 (1976): Williams, Bernard, 'Moral Luck', pp. 115–135 and Nagel, Thomas, 'Moral Luck', pp. 137–151; reprinted in Williams, Bernard, *Moral Luck* (Cambridge: Cambridge University Press, 1981), and Nagel, Thomas, *Mortal Questions* (Cambridge: Cambridge University Press, 1979). These were then reprinted in Statman, Daniel, ed., *Moral Luck* (New York: State University of New York Press, 1993), on which this chapter draws.

31  Williams, 'Moral Luck', p. 251.

32  Immunity: Statman in Statman, *Moral Luck*, p. 2; Solace: Williams in Statman, *Moral Luck*, p. 36.

33  Nagel, 'Moral Luck', p. 59.

34  Rescher, Nicholas, 'Moral Luck', *American Philosophical Association Proceedings* 64 (1990), pp. 5–20, reprinted in Statman 1993, pp. 140–166 and see also

Rescher, Nicholas, *Luck: The Brilliant Randomness of Everyday Life* (New York: Farrar, Straus and Giroux, 1995).

35  E.g., Thomson, Judith Jarvis, 'Morality and Bad Luck' in Statman, *Moral Luck*, pp. 195–216.

36  For example, Rescher, 'Moral Luck', pp. 154–55 and Zimmerman, Michael J., 'Luck and Moral Responsibility' in Statman, *Moral Luck*, pp. 217–234, esp. pp. 226–9 (Zimmerman attempts to deny the relevance of all forms of moral luck to moral evaluations), and 'Taking Luck Seriously', *The Journal of Philosophy* 99 (2002) pp. 553–576.

37  Fischer, John Martin, and Ravizza, Mark, 1998, *Responsibility and Control: A Theory of Moral Responsibility* (Cambridge: Cambridge University Press); Wolf, S., *Freedom Within Reason* (Oxford: Oxford University Press, 1990); Nelkin, Dana K., 'Moral Luck', *The Stanford Encyclopedia of Philosophy (Fall 2008 Edition)*, Edward N. Zalta, ed., (*http://plato.stanford.edu/archives/fall2008/entries/moral-luck/*).

38  Williams, Bernard, 'Postscript' in Statman, *Moral Luck*, pp. 251–258.

39  As Bobzien, Susanne, 'Stoic Conceptions of Freedom' in Sorabji, Richard, ed., *Aristotle and After* (London, 1997), pp. 71–90, 73–73, points out, we need to be careful of simply assuming that ancient concerns and terms were the same as ours. In the case of the Stoics, they had no term for 'free will' and no term for 'moral responsibility', casting these ideas in terms of the attributability of praise and blame, punishment and reward instead. She describes how the notions of freedom and affiliated concepts changed over time, and how the problem of the free will of decision only occurred quite late in Stoic philosophy. My account draws heavily on hers. See also Long, Antony A., and Sedley, David, *The Hellenistic Philosophers*, 2 Vols. (Cambridge: Cambridge University Press, 1987) Vol. 1, p. 466; O'Keefe, Tim, *Epicurus on Freedom* (Cambridge: Cambridge University Press, 2005), p. 11.

40  See Nussbaum, Martha, *The Fragility of Goodness* and see also 'Luck and Ethics', a summation of her analysis in Statman, *Moral Luck*, pp. 73–108.

41  DK 12 A 9 in Diels, Hermann, and Kranz, Walther, ed., *Die Fragmente der Vorsokratiker*, 10th edn, i-iii (Berlin, 1964–6). This is part of the one original sentence, taken from an account by Theophrastus. Kahn, Charles, 'Anaximander's Fragment: The Universe Governed by Law' in Mourelatos, Alexander, ed., *The Pre-Socratics: A Collection of Critical Essays* (Princeton, NJ: Princeton University Press, 1993), p. 101 calls it 'the most impersonal Greek formula for Fate'. The sentence runs on 'for they pay penalty and retribution to each other for their injustice according to the assessment of Time' (trans. Kirk, Geoffrey S., and Raven John E., Schofield, Malcolm, *The Presocratic Philosophers: A Critical History with a Selection of Texts*, Cambridge, 1983), p. 107.

42  DK 22 B 80; the complete fragment reads: 'It is necessary to know that war is common and right is strife and that all things happen by strife and necessity.'

43  Barnes, Jonathan, *The Presocratic Philosophers* (London: Routledge, 1982), p. 130.

44  Justice: DK 28 B 8, ll.13–15; Necessity: DK 28 B 8, ll. 30–31 (Simplicius Phys. 145, 27); Moira: DK 28 B 8, ll. 37–38 (Simplicius Phys. 146, 7).

45  DK 22 B 14 (trans. Barnes, *The Presocratic Philosophers*, p. 132).

# NOTES

46 DK 22 B 94: Sun will not overstep his measure; otherwise the *Erinyes*, ministers of Justice, will find him out (trans. Kirk, Raven, Schofield, *The Presocratic Philosophers*, p. 203); DK 22 B 28a (trans. Barnes, *The Presocratic Philosophers*, p. 133).
47 DK 22 B 102 (trans. Barnes, *The Presocratic Philosophers*, p. 131).
48 DK 22 B 119 (trans. and discussion, Kirk, Raven, Schofield, *The Presocratic Philosophers*, p. 211).
49 *Ibid.*
50 The atomists apparently accepted the idea of an underlying unchanging 'being', describing the changes that we perceive in the world as the result of the movements of atoms (DK 68 A 37). The idea of 'what must be' in nature was translated into the laws of necessity that govern those movements (DK 67 B 2: 'Leucippus says that everything happens by necessity, and that necessity is the same as fate. For he says in *On Mind*: "Nothing happens at random, but everything happens for a reason and by necessity" ', in Irwin, Terence, *Classical Philosophy* (Oxford: Oxford University Press, 1999), pp. 228–30).

This obviously raises questions about freedom of action, and some commentators have argued that Epicurus argued against the idea of causal determinism suggested by the theory of atoms, because it prevents individuals from exercising the kind of free will that allows for moral responsibility, although lack of clear evidence makes it difficult to identify the exact problem that Epicurus was confronting, let alone the answer he gave. Whatever the exact nature of the problem, Epicurus seems to have posited the idea that atoms did occasionally 'swerve' (Arrian 34.26–30, Diogenes of Oenoanda 32.1.14–3.14, Lucretius, *De Rerum Natura*, 2.251–93). He seems to have rejected determinism, apparently seeing it as more limiting of human freedom than belief in the gods (Diogenes Laertius 10.134): see O'Keefe, Tim, *Epicurus on Freedom* (Cambridge: Cambridge University Press), pp. 65 ff., esp. pp. 87–93 and *Epicureanism* (Durham: Acumen), pp. 73–83. Irwin, *Classical Philosophy*, p. 238.

The later Stoic philosophers provide the first explicit discussion of the themes of free will and determinism. The Stoics believed in fate (*heimarmene*, see Sellars, John, *Stoicism*, [Berkeley: University of California Press, 2006], p. 100) and were criticised (e.g., Cicero, *On Fate*, p. 40) for their determinism. But they also believed in god, who arranges fate in a providential way (god and fate may have been the same thing). In defence, they undertook a variety of compatibilist views of its relationship with what we might call free will. The content of these arguments – in terms, for example, of the causation of events, the nature of freedom, the ways in which actions can be said to depend on actors – changed over time; see further Reesor, Margaret R., 'Necessity and Fate in Stoic Philosophy' in Rist, John M., ed., *The Stoics* (Berkeley: University of California Press, 1978), pp. 200 ff.
51 Barnes, *The Presocratic Philosophers*, pp. 122 ff. Empedocles was concerned with shedding blood, avoiding sacrifice and not eating meat.
52 de Romilly, Jacqueline, *The Great Sophists in Periclean Athens*, trans. by Janet Lloyd (Oxford: Clarendon Press), 1998, p. 80; Allen, William, *The Andromache and Euripidean Tragedy* (Oxford: Oxford University Press, 2003), p. 123.

53 Plato, *Phaedo*, 96A–99D; Irwin, *Classical Philosophy*, pp. 57–60.
54 Enlightenment: Lloyd, Geoffrey E. R., *Revolutions of Wisdom* (Berkeley: University of California Press, 1987).

## Chapter II

1 'Luck Be a Lady Tonight' from the musical *Guys and Dolls*, words and music by Frank Loesser, based on a story by Damon Runyon, 'The Idyll of Miss Sarah Brown'.
2 For the debate about what the original *Tuche* of Antioch was holding, and how this may have changed in images of her over time, see Stansbury-O'Donnell, Mark, 'Reflections of the Tyche of Antioch in Literary Sources and on Coins', pp. 50–63, in Matheson, *Obsession*, pp. 58–5 (See Chapter I, n. 22).
3 Pausanias 6.2.6–7 gives us the name of the artist. He does not suggest that the artist's name is connected to the image – and we know that Eutuchides is known for other sculptures, including a Dionysus (*Liber pater*) (Pliny 36.34) and the river Eurotas (Pliny 34.51, 34.78). The form of the original statue survives in a number of copies, and the written accounts of Pausanias the travel-writer and John Malalas who wrote about the city of Antioch in the sixth-century CE; see Stansbury-O' Donnell 'Reflections' for further information.
4 As part of a polytheistic cult: bronze figurine, 1st century BCE–1st century CE (Museum of Fine Arts, Boston, 67.1036); Cybele from Formia plus mural crown: marble statue, 1st century BCE–1st century CE (Copenhagen, Ny Carlberg Glyptotek 480); Atargatis with mural crown from Dura-Europos, limestone relief, 1st century CE (Yale University Art Gallery, 1935.46). Male figure identified as *Tuche* of Dura on limestone relief from Dura-Europos, 159 CE (Yale University Art Gallery, 1938.5314); see pp. 22–26 of Matheson, Susan B., 'The Goddess Tyche', pp. 18–33, in Matheson, *Obsession*.
5 Broucke, Pieter B. F., 'Tyche and the Fortune of Cities in the Greek and Roman World' pp. 34–49, in Matheson, *Obsession*, p. 40.
6 See Stansbury-O'Donnell, 'Reflections' for a fascinating and detailed examination of the evidence for the influence of this image.
7 Numismatic evidence: Dohrn, Tobias, *Die Tuche von Antiocheia* (Berlin, 1960), pp. 26–28, discussed in Stansbury-O'Donnell, 'Reflections', p. 55. See Palagia, Olga, 'Tyche at Sparta', pp. 64–75 in Matheson, *Obsession*, pp. 22–26, p. 65 on other statuary types used to model *Tuche* figures.
8 See Stansbury-O'Donnell, 'Reflections', p. 60; and, as an example, see the bronze statuette (Roman, 1st–2nd century CE, H. 15.8 cm) Yale University Art Gallery, Leonard C. Hanna Jr., B.A., 1913, Fund. 1986.65.1 and the mould-blown glass bottle, Roman 2nd–3rd century CE, H. 15.8 cm, Yale University Art Gallery, The Hobart and Edward Small Moore Memorial Collection 1955.6.81, *ibid*. p. 54, fig. 31. For examples of carved gemstones see *ibid*. cat. nos. 46 and 47.
9 The sisters are found, for example, in Disney's cartoon *Hercules*, where they were designed by Gerald Scarfe, and in the PlayStation game *God of War II*, in

## NOTES

which the protagonist, a titan called Kratos, must do battle with each of the sisters in order to change his future and gain victory over the Greek gods.

10   Stafford, Emma, *Worshipping Virtues: Personification and the Divine in Ancient Greece* (London: Duckworth, Classical Press of Wales, 2000) and Richard G. Buxton, *From Myth to Reason? Studies in the Development of Greek Thought* (Oxford: Oxford University Press, 1999).

11   A point also made by Stafford, *Worshipping Virtues*, p. 5.

12   Nilsson, Martin, 'Kultische Personifikation' in *Eranos* 50 (1952) pp. 31–40; Walter Burkert, *Greek Religion* (Oxford: Oxford University Press, 1985); Humphreys, Sally C., 'Dynamics of the Greek Breakthrough' in Eisenstadt, Shmuel N., *The Origins and Diversity of Axial Age Civilisations* (Albany: SUNY Press, 1986), pp. 92–110; see also Parker, Robert, *Athenian Religion: A History* (Oxford: Clarendon Press, 1996), pp. 235–6.

13   For example, Dodds (*Greeks and Irrational*, pp. 242–3), set the development of the cult of *Tuche*, and other similar new cults, against a background of increasing urbanisation, anonymity and loneliness, in which 'the progressive decay of tradition set the religious man free to choose his own gods'. He compared the cult of *Tuche* to ruler-cult and similar practices, which, he observed, are 'primarily ... expressions of helpless dependence'. Buriks (*Peri Tuches*, p. 125) described the cult of *Tuche* as a phenomenon of disintegration ... a symptom of a diminished energy and unhinged morals by the side of a decreasing political power. pp. 128–9: she argued that in the fifth century, the rising Greek *polis* relied heavily on a strong belief in the gods, and the poets charged *tuche* with religious feeling: *tuche* was considered as a factum, that is the expression of the gods interfering with human life. She charts its development as an 'agens', finally ruling supreme in the Hellenistic period (which she regards as a period of degeneration for the Greeks), and managing to conquer ethics almost entirely (save for the Stoic bastion). In examining this phenomenon Kajanto, Iiro, 'Fortuna' in Haase W., ed., *ANRW*, II. 17.1 (Berlin-New York, 1981), pp. 502–558, p. 527 draws a distinction between the beliefs of 'ordinary people' and those of the orators, who must follow their lead.

14   Burkert, *Greek Religion*, p. 186 sees the rise of such personifications as filling the vacuum left by the growing scepticism about the Homeric gods – a gift for the intelligent man who cannot 'dispute the importance of the phenomena and situations designated by abstract terms.'

15   Dover, *Greek Popular Morality*, p.140. As he indicates, this range of meanings elicits a range of responses: *tuche* may be viewed as impossible to pray or sacrifice to, her motivations impossible to explain in terms of human emotions or reasoning (other than malice); *moira* may be regarded in the same way (inexplicable, arbitrary and irrational), although it is possible, through her relationship with the will of Zeus, to think of her as bringing to bear supernatural justice. He emphasises the different implications that these various stances hold for morality: if it is fated that I commit a crime, then it is fated that I chose to commit it and can be punished for it; if some choices are fated and others not, then I am only responsible for some choices.

16   Shapiro, Alan, *Personifications in Greek Art: The Representation of Abstract Concepts 600–400 BCE* (Zurich: Akanthus, 1993).

17 Stafford, *Worshipping Virtues*, pp. 227–33, drawing on Gaétan Thériault, *Le culte d' Homonoia dans les cités grecques: Collection de l' orient Méditerranéen No. 26, Série Épigraphique 3* (Lyon: Maison de l'Orient, 1996), esp. pp. 184–88.
18 Burkert, Walter, 'Abstractions and Divinities in an Aegean-Eastern Koiné', pp. 3–20 in Stafford, Emma, and Herrin, Judith, eds., *Personification in the Greek world: from antiquity to Byzantium* (Aldgate: Ashgate, 2005), pp. 5 and 18.
19 Stafford, *Worshipping Virtues*, p. 229.
20 For example, on the timing of the appearance of the cult of *Kairos*, see Allan, 2005; Gasparro, Giulia Sfameni, 'Daimon and Tyche in the Hellenistic Religious Experience', pp. 67–109 in Bilde, Per, Engberg-Pedersen, Troels, Hannestad, Lise, and Zahle, Jan, eds., *Conventional Values of the Hellenistic Greeks* (Aarhus: Aarhus University Press, 1997), p. 84 has argued for *Tuche*'s development into 'a well-defined divine person' and gradual promotion into the realm of *daimones* (as *Agathe Tuche*), starting from 'a strong sense of the sacred attaching to *Tuche*' from at least the fifth century. A chronological overview of the development of cults of particular personifications, see Stafford, *Worshipping Virtues*.
21 Burton, Diana, 'The Gender of Death', pp. 45–68 in Stafford and Herrin, *Personification*, p. 46 drawing on Vermeule, Emily, *Aspects of Death in Early Greek Art and Poetry* (Berkeley and Los Angeles: University of California Press 1979), p. 37, but also points out that Plutarch (*Kleomenes* 9) and Pausanias (3.18.1) may indicate otherwise. The same seems to be the case for the various personifications of the king of the underworld: as Hades, he appears to have received cult only at Elis (Pausanias 6.25.2 f.), whereas in the form of Pluto, with his bride Persephone, he received cult at locations throughout Greece, see Henrichs, Albert, s.v. 'Hades' in Spawforth, Antony, and Hornblower, Simon, eds., *The Oxford Classical Dictionary* (3rd ed., Oxford, 1999).
22 See Wright, Bradford W., *Comic Book Nation: the transformation of youth culture in America* (Baltimore and London: the Johns Hopkins University Press, 2001), and *The Unofficial Guide to the DC Universe: www.dcuguide.com/who.php?name=doctorfate4*. Dr. Fate soon became a member of the Justice League of America (*All Star Comics*, no. 3, Winter 1940). Although his first run came to an end in 1944, he reappeared in the 1960s and 70s. In the 80s, the helmet passed to a couple (Linda Strauss and her stepson Eric who merged to become Dr. Fate); and in the 90s, a resurrected Kent Nelson and his wife Inza took over, until Kent was unable to continue – and Inza took over Dr. Fate's duties on her own. When the Nelsons perished, one Jared Stevens briefly inherited the helmet, before Dr. Fate's mantle passed to Hector Sanders Hall – although Kent Nelson survives as a force within Dr. Fate's amulet, and can be summoned to provide guidance when needed. The latest Dr. Fate appears to be Kent V. Nelson, the grandnephew of the original – but there appears to be some confusion about his identity and origins – and how he will develop.
23 See Goulart, Ron, *Comic Book Culture: an Illustrated History* (Portland, OR: Collectors Press, Inc., 2000), p. 52; this opacity seems to have proved too much, and a year later he had gained a mortal identity, an explanation of his secret powers (inherited from an ancient Egyptian magician/supernatural being, Nabu), and a girlfriend.

# NOTES

24  s.v. Dr. Fate in Horn, M., *The World Encyclopedia of Comics* (London: New English Library, 1976).
25  In later stories, Dr. Fate does develop an explicit role in the assertion of Order, opposing the forces of Chaos that are attacking the world.
26  *More Fun Comics* #65, 1941, reprinted in *Wanted: The World's Most Dangerous Villains, Vol. 3*, DC (National Periodical Publications, 1972–3).
27  These concepts have been covered in great detail by a number of authors; above all see Dietrich, *Death, Fate and the Gods*. His theory of *Moira*'s origins as an 'early goddess closely concerned with death' has not been widely taken up (see Adkins, Arthur W. H., *Classical Review*, n.s. 18: 2 (June 1968), pp. 19–197), but this book still provides a comprehensive survey of Homer's representations of fate, so I will treat only the most salient points here.
28  Homer, *Odyssey*, 3.457 ff.; *Iliad*, 16.367.
29  The Greek is *moira estin* plus an infinitive of death (or doom) *Iliad*, 7.52, 15.117, 16.434, 17.421, 23.80.
30  *Thanatos kai moira*, 'fate and death': *Iliad*, 3.101.
31  Homer, *Iliad*, 18.119; 19.409 f., and, famously, *Iliad*, 16.849 in which Patroclus blames a combination of fate, god and mortal action for his imminent death.
32  The Greek is *kichanei*: see *Iliad*, 17.478 and 672, and 22.436. In *Iliad*, 22.303, Hector may indeed argue that fate is overtaking him, but he also mentions the gods who have called him, and talks of evil death who is near him.
33  Dietrich, *Death, Fate*, p. 198; and *Iliad*, 5.613 f. and 629.
34  Homer, *Iliad*, 21.82, 22.5.
35  Homer, *Iliad*, 19.74–113.
36  *Moira* leads an individual to death at Homer, *Odyssey*, 2.100, 17.326, 19.145, 24.235 and 3.238 (see Dietrich, *Death, Fate*, p. 213).
37  Odysseus' journey home: Homer, *Odyssey*, 5.40 and 19.20.
38  '*kata moiran*', used to describe, for example, the allocation of portions, Homer, *Odyssey*, 3.66, fitting of oars, 8.54; division of spoils, 16.385. Cyclops: 9.352.
39  Homer, *Odyssey*, 19.591–97.
40  Eustathius p. 1686 (Greene, *Moira*, p. 15) described the will of Zeus and fate as synonymous. Greene, *ibid.* provides a range of references, including: all things lie on the knees of the gods, *Odyssey*, 1.267; Oedipus suffered through the destructive plan of the gods, *Odyssey*, 11.276; the death of Patroclus, sufferings of Odysseus and struggles of Greeks and Romans all came to pass by will of the gods, *Iliad*, 19.9, *Odyssey*, 7.214, 12.190 = 17.119; Zeus' plan, *Iliad*, 1.5; *Odyssey*, 11.297; Zeus plans outcome of wanderings of Odysseus and attributes to *Moira*, *Odyssey*, 5.41; 114; Odysseus attributes his suffering to Zeus, *Odyssey*, 9.38, 67, 12.405; or to Zeus' evil *Aisa*, *Odyssey*, 9.52; or to a *daimon*, *Odyssey*, 12.295; gods of heaven, *Odyssey*, 7.242; Zeus plans how to destroy Odysseus and his comrades, *Odyssey*, 9.554–5; see also 4.472 f.
41  Subject to *moira*: Homer, *Iliad*, 16.439–50; *Odyssey*, 3.236–8; 9.528–535. Appealing to fate: Homer, *Iliad*, 17.321; 20.301–2; 20.336; *Odyssey*, 5.41–114, and 5.345. At *Odyssey*, 5.114–115. Hermes tells Calypso to let Odysseus go, because it is his *moira* to go home, but this is simultaneously the message that no one, not even a god can disobey Zeus' will (5.137–139).
42  For example, the idea that gods spin man's destiny appears in the *Iliad* once, at

24.525 – and is immediately followed by the famous image of the urns and the lots – and in the *Odyssey* seven times: *Odyssey*, 1.17, 3.208, 8.579, 11.139, 20.196. Specific gods: in the *Odyssey*, 4.208 (Zeus), 16.64 (a *daimon*).

43  The phrase is *moira theou* ('*moira* of the god') found in the *Odyssey*, 11.292, or *theon* ('of the gods'), *Odyssey*, 3.269 and 22.413.

44  Berry, Edmund G., *The History and Development of the Concept of Theia Moira and Theia Tuche Down to and Including Plato* (Chicago, 1940), p. 5. *Moira* as part of the gods in Leitzke, E., *Moira und Gottheit im alten Griechischen Epos: Sprachliche Untersuchungen* (Diss. Gottingen, 1930) cited in Dietrich, *Death, Fate*, p. 185.

45  Zeus, *Iliad*, 16.252, 647, 800; the purpose of Zeus, *Iliad*, 16.688; the gods, *Iliad*, 16.693; Apollo, *Iliad*, 16. 791, 804, 816; Zeus and Apollo, *Iliad*, 16.844; and *Moira*, Apollo, Euphorbus and Hector, *Iliad*, 16.849 f. See Greene, *Moira*, p. 15.

46  Discussion of *Iliad*, 16.426–61 in Gould, *Herodotus,* pp. 68–69: see also Homer, *Iliad*, 22.179 f.

47  Greeks and Trojans pray, *Iliad*, 3.320 ff.; Hector and Paris, *Iliad*, 6.280–5, 325–330.

48  *Iliad*, 16.644–56.

49  Commentators have argued that Homeric characters do not enjoy the kind of autonomy we value; others have said that they do, and that we must regard the gods as a literary device or a sort of shorthand. Edwards, Mark W., *Homer, Poet of the Iliad* (Baltimore: The Johns Hopkins University Press, 1987), p. 134; Redfield, James M., *Nature and Culture in the Iliad: The Tragedy of Hector* (Durham, NC: Duke University Press, 1994); see Hammer, *Cultural Construction of Chance*, p. 135; also gods are a way of calling attention to the victor. See Schein, Seth, *The Mortal Hero: an Introduction to Homer's Iliad* (Berkeley: University of California Press, 1985), p. 58, and Williams, *Shame and Necessity*, p 41.

50  Griffin, Jasper, 'The Epic Cycle and the Uniqueness of Homer', *Journal of Hellenic Studies*, 97 (1977), p. 39–53, esp. p. 48.

51  Apollo chides, *Iliad* 24.33–63; Achilles instructs, *Iliad* 24.549–551; endurance, *Odyssey* 6.188–190 and 18.134–137.

52  Achilles comforts Priam at *Iliad*, 24.518–533; *Odyssey*, 18.130–142, Odysseus seems to be suggesting that man's own attitude aggravates whatever the gods give.

53  Nock, Arthur Darby, 'Orphism or Popular Philosophy', *Harvard Theological Review* 33 (1940), p. 309 (cited Greene, *Moira*, p. 27).

54  See Gould, Thomas, 'The Innocence of Oedipus: The Philosophers on Oedipus the King', pp. 49–63 in Bloom Harold, ed., *Sophocles' Oedipus Rex* (New York: Chelsea House Publishing, 1988), p. 54.

55  *Iliad*, 3.65.

56  *Iliad*, 3.164 ff.

57  *Iliad*, 6.485 ff.

58  Irwin, *Classical Philosophy*, p. 225: through the gods' influence on our thoughts, beliefs and plans 'Homer shows how we might extend the area we do not control until it includes many actions that we might have thought we did control'. As

# NOTES

Irwin notes, Agamemnon's excuse is neither clearly accepted nor rejected by his audience, and the radical world view it suggests – where every action originates in the will of the gods – is not played out in the rest of the poem.

59 *Iliad*, 9.115.
60 *Iliad*, 2.1–40 and 4.70–72.
61 Spinning, *Iliad*, 24.209; binding, *Iliad*, 4.517, 22.5.
62 Pindar, *Olympian Odes*, 1.40; Ovid. *ad Liv.* 164, *Fasti.* 6.757, *Ex Pont.* 4.15. 36.
63 The idea of fate as a force that binds its victims is elaborated on in Onians, *The Origins of European Thought*, who connects it to images of binding across Greek literature and to *katadesmoi* or binding spells, pp. 363–375.
64 Eidinow, *Oracles, Curses, and Risk*.
65 Homer, *Iliad*, 24.49.
66 Hesiod, *Theogony* 217 and 904.
67 Misery, *Iliad*, 20.30, *Odyssey*, 1.34; Death, *Iliad*, 18.465, 19.421; in Herodotus always of a violent death, see Liddel, Henry George, and Scott, Robert, *A Greek-English Lexicon* (Oxford: Clarendon Press, 1940) *LSJ*, s.v. *moros*.
68 Friedrich Solmsen in his review of Greene's *Fate, Good and Evil* (*Classical Philology* 40:2 [1945], pp. 123–8 notes how this relationship develops over time, such that whereas in Homer Zeus weighs the fates of men to find out what *Moira* has decreed (*Iliad* 8.81, 22.249), by the fifth century, the scales belong to *Dike*, see Aeschylus, *Choephori* 61.
69 As described by Eduard, Fraenkel, *Agamemnon*, 3 vols, (Oxford: Clarendon Press, 1950) Vol. iii, pp. 728–30, who sees Aeschylus' development of this connection in Homer *Iliad*, 19.86 f. in which Agamemnon blames Zeus, *Moira* and *Erinyes* for the *Ate* that caused him to insult Achilles.
70 See Aeschylus, *Prometheus Bound*, 511–525. Further examples: Hesiod, *Theogony* 373–392; Pindar, *Pythian Odes* 4.286–289; Sophocles, *Oedipus at Colonus* 603–5, *Electra* 48, *Ajax* 485 and 803, *Antigone* 1106; Euripides, *Hecuba* 640, 1295. *Ananke* in combination with *tuche*: Sophocles, *Philoctetes*, 1326 (*anankaion*, 'it is necessary to bear *tuche*'); or sending *tuche* *Ajax*. 485 and 803.
71 *To chreon* or *chren* ('necessity' or 'it is necessary') is another phrase that intimates the inescapable demand of fate: e.g., Euripides, *Hecuba* 629.
72 Pausanias, 8.21.2; Plato, *Symposium* 206d.; Pindar, *Olympian Odes* 6.70, *Nemean Odes* 7.1.
73 Euripides, *Iphigenia at Tauris* 205–7; Pingiatoglou, S., *Eileithyia* (cited in Parker *Polytheism* 442n.).
74 Pollux 3.38, but the *Etym. Magn.* 220.54–7 says the Graces of marriage rather than the *Moirai*.
75 Nilsson, Martin, 'Kultische Personifikation' *Eranos* I (1952), pp. 31–40, 38 f. Cited and discussed by Dietrich, *Death, Fate*, p. 60.
76 Dietrich, *Death, Fate*, pp. 61–62.
77 Pausanias, 2.11.4.
78 Bremmer, Jan, 'The Sacrifice of Pregnant Animals', in Hägg, Robin, ed., *Greek Sacrificial Ritual: Olympian and Chthonian* (Stockholm: Paul Forlag Astroms, 2005), pp. 155–65: Athenian sacrifices to the Eumenides: Aeschylus *Eumenides* 108–9; Apollodorus *FGrH* 244 F101; Scholion to Sophocles, *Oedipus at Colonus* 489.

79  Pausanias, 3.11.10.
80  Pausanias, 9.25.4.
81  Pausanias, 2.4.7; Bookidis, Nancy, and Stroud, Ron S., *Demeter and Persephone in Ancient Corinth* (ACSA, 1987), f. 20.
82  Olympia: Pausanias, 5.15.5; Delphi: Pausanias, 10.24, also Plutarch, *On the E at Delphi*, 385c.
83  Pausanias, 8.37.1.
84  Pausanias, 1.40.4.
85  Pausanias, 3.19.4.
86  Pausanias, 1.19.
87  DK 19 (Scholion to Sophocles, *Oedipus at Colonus* 42).
88  Alexiou, Margaret, Yatromanolakis, Dimitrios, Roilos, Panagiotis, *The Ritual Lament in Greek Tradition* (Michigan, 2002), p.114, who cites Mayer, August, *Moira in griechischen Inschriften* (Diss. Giessen, 1927).
89  Alexiou *et al.*, *Ritual Lament*, p. 110 ff.; tracing the origins of the traditional *moirologi* or lament for the dead.
90  A useful and detailed overview of ancient Greek mystery cults in all their variety can be found in the articles in Cosmopoulos, Michael B., ed., *Greek Mysteries: The Archaeology and Ritual of Ancient Greek Secret Cults* (London: Routledge, 2003), and in Bowden, Hugh, *Mystery Cults of the Ancient World*, (Princeton: Princeton University Press, 2010).
91  See in particular Robertson, Noel, 'Orphic Mysteries and Dionysiac Ritual' in Cosmopoulos *Greek Mysteries* and Gordon, Richard, 'Mysteries' and F. Graf 'Orphic Literature' and 'Orphism' in Hornblower and Spawforth, *The Oxford Classical Dictionary*.
92  Col. 18: translation Gábor, Betegh, *The Derveni Papyrus: Cosmology, Theology and Interpretation* (Cambridge: Cambridge University Press, 2004), p. 39. On the presumed genealogy of *Moira*, see *ibid.* p. 159.
93  Most, Glenn, 'The Fire Next Time. Cosmology, Allegoresis and Salvation in the Derveni Papyrus' *Journal of Hellenic Studies* 117 (1997), pp. 117–35 argues that the commentator appears to believe that the poet chose conventional and familiar terms so as to make his message less intimidating: 'Instead of using rebarbative scientific terminology, he used the words of the people' (p. 123). However, this ploy was in danger of backfiring, since initiates risked taking these conventional terms at their face value.
94  Betegh, *The Derveni Papyrus*, p. 202 argues against Walter Burkert ('La genèse des choses et des mots: le papyrus de Derveni entre Anaxagoras et Cratyle' *Études Philosophiques* 25 (1970), pp. 443–55) and Pierre Boyancé ('Remarques sur le Papyrus de Derveni' *Revue des Etudes Grecques* 87 (1974), pp. 90–110) that the identification between Zeus and *Moira* is not total, but *Moira* is 'the active, executive, practical aspect of the god'.
95  Tablet C (Zuntz, G., *Persephone: Three Essays on Religion and Thought in Magna Graecia* Oxford, 1971), l. 3: there are difficulties in reading this text, which is, at first sight, only a jumble of letters. It has been reconstructed several times. Betegh, *The Derveni Papyrus*, p. 336 takes the reading *pammestoi* or *pammestori* and appears to read the *Moira* as singular (in the dative); Bernabé/Jimenez San Cristobal and Graf/Johnson read *pamnestoi Moirai* and read *Moirai* in the plural

## NOTES

(see Bernabé, Alberto, and Jimenez San Cristóbal, Ana Isabel, *Instructions for the Netherworld: The Orphic Gold Tablets* (Leiden: Brill, 2008) where the text is published as L12, and Graf, Fritz, and Johnston, Sarah Iles, *Ritual Texts for the Afterlife* (Routledge: 2007) where the text is published as 4 *Thurii* 2). Bernabé/Jimenez San Cristobal read *Tuche* at the beginning of this line and note that in Orphic literature, *Tuche* is identified with Artemis (p. 143).

96  Bernabé/Jimenez San Cristobal: *Instructions for the Netherworld*, p. 144.
97  Zuntz A1, l.4, (Graf/Johnston 5 *Thurii* 3, who offer a possible alternative reading, in which the epithet of Zeus is translated as 'star-flinger'). There is debate among scholars as to the likelihood that the people with whom this text was buried actually died being struck by lightning, see discussions in Betegh, *The Derveni Papyrus*, p. 337 ff. and Graf/Johnston, *Ritual Texts*, p. 125 ff. Bernabé and Jimenez San Cristóbal, pp. 110–114, provide a detailed analysis of the symbolism that may have been inherent in the reference to Zeus' lightning.
98  See Bernabé and Jimenez San Cristóbal, p. 110.
99  Homeric hero, Graf/Johnston, p. 125.
100 Sourvinou-Inwood, Christiane, 'The Boston Relief and the Religion of Locri Epizephyrii' *Journal of Hellenistic Studies* 94 (1974), pp. 126–37.
101 A selection: *Crito* 33c; *Meno* 99d and 110b; *Republic* 6.492a5, e5, 493a2; see discussion in Kahn, Charles C., *Plato and the Socratic Dialogue* (Cambridge: CUP, 1998); see further discussion in Berry, *Theia Moira*, chs. 4 and 5.
102 *Fatum* and the *Parcae*: Potscher, Walter, 'Das romische Fatum – Begriff und Verwendung' in *ANRW* II.16.1 (1978), pp. 290–354. *Fortuna*: Kajanto, *'Fortuna'*.
103 As above, see Dietrich, *Death, Fate*, p. 11, Bianchi, *Dios Aisa* and *LSJ* s.v. *moros*, *aisa*: the root verb may be *isasthai* (the Lesbian form of *klerousthai*) with the idea of divisions into equal shares. See Bianchi: *Dios Aisa*, pp. 1–8 for etymological origins of *aisa*; also Dietrich, *Death, Fate*, Appendix 2. Used to mean allocation, *Iliad*, 18.327, 15.209; *Odyssey*, 19.84. Adjectival form of *aisa* used to describe appropriate behaviour that is fair or just: *Iliad*, 6.521, 24.425; esp. in the *Odyssey*,: 14.83, 22.46.
104 *Heimarmene*: In Homer, forms of the original verb are most commonly found describing the honour due to a particular mortal or semi-divine character, e.g., *Iliad*, 1.278 (of Agamemnon's stature), 9.616 (Achilles invites Phoenix to share his honour); although it does appear, in impersonal form, as a way of describing an individual's time to die, *Iliad*, 21.281 (Achilles caught in the River Scamander) and *Odyssey*, 24.34 (the spirit of Achilles to the spirit of Agamemnon).
105 Aeschylus, *Agamemnon*, l. 913.
106 Dietrich, *Death, Fate*, p. 12, who cites Krause, W., 'Die Ausdrücke für das Schicksal' *Glotta* 25 (1936) for the falling body theory.
107 Origins suggest bad luck, see Greene, p. 402, App. 4; Pindar, *Pythian Odes* 5.3, 5, 13, 60, 76, 117 (discussed Greene, *Moira*, p. 69).
108 See Antiphon B59 (DK 357).
109 *Moros*, of death: *Iliad*, 21.133 (Achilles to the recently killed Lycaon); *Odyssey*, 1.166; but of bad events: *Iliad*, 6.357 (Helen to Hector of the fate of Paris) and *Odyssey*, 11.618 (the spirit of Heracles speaks of his labours). *Morsimos*: *Iliad*, 20.302 (Aeneas is destined [*morsimon estin*] to escape death); *Iliad*, 5.674, it was not destined [*morsimon*] for Odysseus to kill Sarpedon.

110 *Iliad*, 17.321 (of the plan of Zeus); with an individual association: *Iliad*, 5.209 (of an arrow); 16.707 (Apollo tells Patroclus it is not his *aisa* to sack Troy); 24.224 (Priam thinks his *aisa* may be to die retrieving his son's body); *Iliad*, 20.127 (Hera describes Achilles' future to the gods); *Odyssey*, 5.206 (Calypso to Odysseus); 14.359 (Odysseus, in disguise, telling his own story). Alongside *moira*, *Odyssey*, 5.113 (Hermes instructing Calypso on Odysseus' future).

111 *Odyssey*, 11.61 see Dietrich, *Death, Fate*, p. 257.

112 See Roberts, Deborah, 'Blood or Fate: A Note on Choephori 927' in *Classical Quarterly* n. s. 34: 2 (1984), pp. 255–59. This line appears to personify *aisa* and Roberts argues in support of an emendation that *aisa* should be replaced by *haima*.

113 Socrates in Plato, *Phaedo* 115a personifies *heimarmene* and refers to it self-consciously as a tragic term as he talks about his own death, and Plato himself appears to be deliberately archaising when he uses it in the myth of the *Protagoras*, e.g., 320d1–2 and 321c6 (see Greene, *Moira*, App. 34).

114 For example, *he heimarmene* appears personified or at least as an independent force of fate in: *Phaedo* 115a (to call a man to the end of his life); *Laws* 873c (with *moira* to emphasise the difference between taking one's own life and the course of life ordained by fate); *Laws* 10.904c (the ordering principle that governs the changes of any soul); *Republic* 10.619c (the fated horrors that remain unnoticed by a soul choosing his new life). Other forms of the verb *meiromai*: *heimartai*, 'it is fated', *Republic* 566a (of the inevitable end – exile or tyranny – of a man who advocates the end of private property); *Phaedr.* 255b, (*eiper heimarmenon eie* 'if it is fated that'; *Menexenus* 243e (of the inevitability of civil war). As adjective 'fated/cosmically arranged': *Statesman* 272e (to describe cosmic change); *Phaedo* 113a (the amount of time the souls of the dead stay at the Acherousian lake); *Timaeus* 41e (referring to laws); *Menexenus* 236d (of the journey to come of dead heroes); *Laws* 918e (along with *ananke*, necessity, to persuade women to follow a particular course of life).

115 There is not room here to examine other terms for luck, fate and fortune in Plato: see for example, Berry, *Theia Moira*, chs. 4 and 5, for discussion of *moira* and *tuche* in some of Plato's works.

116 Demosthenes 18.195 and 205; 60.19 (discussed in ch. 8); Isocrates 15.176 (*heimarmenon*) of a court case he cannot avoid.

117 See above p. 21.

118 ca. 430 BCE; Shapiro, Alan H., 'The Judgement of Helen in Athenian Art' in Barringer, J. J. M., Hurwitt, J. M., and Pollitt J. J., eds., *Periklean Athens and its Legacy: Problems and Perspectives* (Austin, TX, 2005), pp. 47–62, 50.

119 Plato, *Symposium*, 202b-d: Diotima is talking about *Eros*; see Dover, *Greek Personal Morality*, pp. 138–141. As an example, see Demosthenes 18.192. See Nock, Arthur, Darby, *Essays on Religion and the Ancient World* I (Oxford: Oxford University Press, 1972), p. 60 for the interchangeability of the terms *theos, theoi, daimon*, Zeus, and words for Fate; and Versnel, Henk, *Self-Sacrifice, Compensation and the Anonymous Gods* in Rudhardt, J., and Reverdin, O., eds., *Le Sacrifice dans L'Antiquite* Fondation Hardt pour L'étude de L'Antiquite Classique, Entretiens, Tome 27 (Geneva: Vandoeuvres, 1981), pp. 135–185, 175 who notes that 'down to late antiquity these different terms are not used in exclusive

*aut-aut* disjunctions, but in a *vel-vel* choice of equally possible or even identical predicates . . .'
120 For example, Demosthenes 14.36, 48.24, Lysias 13.63. See Gasparro, 'Daimon and Tyche' for a useful and thorough overview of the development of the nature of the *daimon*.
121 See Gasparro, 'Daimon and Tyche', p. 77; and on binding spells, see Eidinow, *Oracles, Curses, and Risk*, pp. 148–50.
122 Gasparro, 'Daimon and Tyche', pp. 88 ff. for the close link between *daimon* and *tuche* and the cult relationship between *Agathos Daimon* and *Agathe Tuche*.
123 See discussions of Menander and Demosthenes below; the idea is elaborated into a notion of the nature of one's fortune, for example, Andocides 2.5–7 in which the speaker explains his crimes with reference to *dusdaimonia* ('bad luck'). Eduard Fraenkel, (ed. and comm.) *Aeschylus: Agamemnon*, vol. iii, pp. 632, *ad* 1341, that the *daimon* of this verse 'has lost a good deal of its personal character and is on the way to what we should call an abstract idea' but the examples that he cites in support of his statement beg the question. (F.'s view is cited and elaborated in Finglass, Patrick, (ed. and comm.) *Sophocles: Electra* (Cambridge: Cambridge University Press, 2007) and Garvie, Alex, (ed. and comm.) *Aeschylus: Choephori* (Oxford: Oxford University Press, 1986) p. 184, l. 513: '*daimon* in fifth-century poetry, is almost an abstraction, virtually equivalent to *tuche* or *potmos*, one's fortune good or bad').
124 Greene (*Moira*, p. 12–13) finds 14 in the *Iliad*, 20 in the *Odyssey*; examples include *Iliad*, 9.600, *Odyssey*, 3.166; 7.248; 12.295. Mikalson, *Athenian Popular Religion*, pp. 58–62 (ch. 8) argues that in popular religion the gods were deemed to grant victories, while writers and speakers tended to blame disasters and losses on *Tuche*. This is one of the ways in which, he argues, popular religious attitudes contrasted with the attitudes towards the gods shown by characters in Greek tragedy: 'the religion found in Greek tragedy . . . probably never did and probably never could exist or survive in real life', Mikalson 1991: ix. Some of his arguments on the latter front have been addressed by other scholars, in particular C. Sourvinou-Inwood, who has argued that the gods of Greek tragedy were not the literary constructs he proposes, nor were the attitudes of the characters on stage so far removed from the attitudes of those in the audience; and Robert Parker, who has explored the discourses of public oratory and Greek tragedy, noting the 'theological opacity' of the former, and the 'transparency' of the latter, and noted how both offer insights into 'what it was like to believe in Greek gods' (Christiane Sourvinou-Inwood 'Tragedy and Religion' in Pelling, Christopher, ed., *Greek Tragedy and the Historian* (Oxford: Oxford University Press, 1997) pp. 161–186; Robert Parker 'Gods Cruel and Kind: Tragic and Civic Theology' *ibid.*, pp. 143–160).
125 See *Odyssey*, 5.396; Demosthenes, see discussion in final chapter of this book; not a solution to evil, see Greene, *Moira*, p. 13.
126 See Ackerman, Hans C., and Gisler, Jean-Robert, *Lexicon Iconographicum Mythologiae Classicae* [*LIMC*] (Zurich: Artemis, 1981–) 8.1, 115–125; 8.11, 85–88.
127 Pausanias, 4.30.5; *Homeric Hymn (II) to Demeter*. 420.
128 Hesiod, *Theogony*, 360; Shapiro, *Personifications*, p. 227, suggests that the *Homeric Hymn* draws on Hesiod. Also discussed by Matheson, 'Tyche', p. 31, n. 11.

129 Alcman fr. 64 (Davies); see also Archilochus 8D below.
130 Pindar, fr. 41 (Snell-Maehler).
131 Pindar, fr. 40 (Snell-Maehler). See discussion Hornblower, Simon, *Thucydides and Pindar* (Oxford: Oxford University Press, 2004), p. 195.
132 *Pherepolis* Pindar, fr. 39 (Snell-Maehler); the term may be a pun on *polos/polis* and indicate that she is wearing a mural crown (Matheson, 'Tyche', p. 21).
133 Pausanias, 4.30.6; because of its rarity, it has been suggested that this was a Hellenistic sculpture created in an archaising style (see Heidenreich, R., 'Bupalos und Pergamon' *Archäologischer Anzeiger* (50), 1935, cols. 668–701, but compare Shapiro, 1993, pp. 227–8; ancient *Tuche* at Pharai (but how old is 'ancient'?) 4.30.3.
134 See discussion Matheson, 'Tyche', p. 20, n. 8.
135 Diodorus Siculus 11.68; Cicero *In Verrem* 2.4.117–9; see discussion Broucke, 'Fortune of Cities', p. 36 with n. 9.
136 Nilsson, Martin, *History of Greek Religion*, 2nd ed. (New York, 1964), p. 285, cited by Broucke, 'Fortune of Cities' p. 37.
137 Shapiro, *Personifications*, p. 106, n. 224. (*Tuche* was identified by Körte, Alfred, 'Eichelförmige Lekythos mit Goldschmuck aus Attika', *Archäologische Zeitung* 37 (1879), 93–96.
138 Stafford, *Worshipping Virtues*, p. 14.
139 Although, as Stafford, *Worshipping Virtues*, p. 16 points out, this may be the work of one particular workshop.
140 Stafford, *Worshipping Virtues*, pp. 12–13.
141 See Matheson, *Tuche*, pp. 25–30 for a useful summary of the history and development of *Tuche* in the Hellenistic and Roman periods. Hamdorf, Friedrich, Willem, *Griechische Kultpersonifikationen der vorhellenistischen Zeit* (Mainz, 1964) s.v. *Tuche* for cult evidence. *Orphic Hymn* 72 appears to see her as combined with Artemis.
142 Didrachm of Euagoras II: *Tuche* on reverse wearing mural crown. 361–351 BCE (British Museum BMC 67 c.144.10); see Broucke, 'Fortune of Cities', p. 36, fig. 17: but could it represent another goddess of eastern origin, since, as Broucke points out 47n.), these are also depicted as wearing mural crowns?
143 Pausanias, 1.43.6.
144 Pausanias, 9.16.2.
145 Aelian, *Varia Historia* 9.39; Pliny, *Natural History* 36.23.
146 Cornucopia alone: marble relief, 38–370 BCE, from the Asclepieion at Athens, Athens Nat. Mus. 1343 (*LIMC* s.v., no. 5).
147 Earliest surviving image of *Tuche* with a rudder on a *proxenos* decree from Tegea (IG$^2$ V 2, 1), dating to the fourth century, but earlier in literature: Pindar, fr. 40 (Snell-Maehler); Aeschylus, *Agamemnon* 663–4 and *EpGr* 491.5 (*LIMC* s.v. p. 116); Herzog-Hauser, Gertrud, 'Tyche' in Pauly, August, and Wissowa, Georg, *Real-Encyclopädie der classischen Altertumswissenschaft*, 2. R. XIV,1 (Stuttgart: J. B. Metzlersche, 1943), p. 1686, argued that *Tuche* inherited the rudder from Nemesis.
148 See Gasparro, 'Daimon and Tyche', p. 89 for epigraphical evidence.
149 She is closely associated with *Kairos* in literary sources, e.g., Plato, *Laws* 709b

## NOTES

and found with *Nemesis* on the name-vase of the *Heimarmene* painter; *LIMC* s.v., *Nemesis*, p. 735. A clear association has formed by the Imperial period but may date to the Hellenistic period or earlier, see *IG* IV², 1.311 (Epidauros, 5th–4th century BCE). See Shapiro, Alan, 'The Origins of Allegory in Greek Art' *Boreas* 9 (1986), pp. 4–23, esp. 11–14 and Edwards, Charles M., 'Tyche at Corinth' *Hesperia* 59: 3 (1990), pp. 530–42 for evidence of the relationship between *Nemesis* and *Tuche*.

150 E.g., *LIMC* s.v. Isis, nos. 303–318.
151 ll. 96–148. Menander uses abstractions to introduce two other plays that we know of: Ignorance for the *Perikeiromene* and Proof in a now unknown play (fr. 717 Körte).
152 Beroutsos, Demetrios C., *A Commentary on the "Aspis" of Menander, Part One: ll.1–298* (Göttingen: Vandenhoeck and Ruprecht, 2005), p. 58, l. 148 and p.15; Vogt-Spira, Gregor, 'Dramaturgie des Zufalls: Tuche und Handeln in der Komödie Menanders' *Zetemata* 80 (Munich, 1992), p. 76 ff.
153 Menander, Fr. 89 K-A (see Vogt-Spira, 'Dramaturgie', pp. 58–59).
154 Menander, Fr. Dubium 67 K-A (trans. Arnott, William, Geoffrey, *Menander*, 3 vols, Cambridge MA: Harvard University Press, 2000).
155 Menander, Fr 417 = 872 K-A, trans. Balme, Maurice, and Brown, Peter, *Menander: The Plays and Fragments* (Oxford, 2002), p. 274, no. 25.
156 The Greek title is the *Gnomai Monostichai* ('Single-liners of Wisdom'); see Pernigotti, Carlo, *Menandri Sententiae* (Florence, 2008). Such gnomic sayings were used in antiquity to embellish speeches, to train in rhetoric, to practise composition. Different theories have been put forward to explain the assembly of these sayings – and the relationship between the Menandrian and non-Menandrian material. See Liapis, Vaios, *Menandrou Gnomai monostichoi. Eisagôgê, metaphrasê, scholia* (Athens: Stigme, 2002).
157 See Lattimore, Richard, *Themes in Greek and Latin Epitaphs* (University of Illinois, 1962), pp. 149–150.
158 On the *Heimarmene* vase (around 420 BCE); *LIMC*, s.v., 1.
159 Villard, Laurence in *LIMC*, s.v. *Tuche*, pp. 115–125; the descriptions that follow draw on this catalogue.
160 Although cf. Galen *Protrepticus*, 2.
161 Villard in *LIMC*, s.v. *Tuche*, p. 117.
162 For example, wings: *Hymn to Tuche,* Page, *PMG* frg. 1019.5; scales: Bacchylides 10.46–47; wheel: *TrGF* II F 700 28–29; dice: Sophocles *TrGF* IV F 947 and Pausanias 2.20.3; lot: Aeschylus, *Agamemnon* 332–3, Aristophanes *Ecclesiazousae* 836-7. See Villard, *LIMC* s.v. *Tuche*, p. 116.
163 See Villard, *LIMC* s.v. *Tuche*, nos. 5–10, 46–48 (cornucopia alone); 15–18, 57, 76–78 (sceptre) and 19–27, 54–56, 79–80a (*phiale*).
164 Villard, *LIMC* s.v. *Tuche*, p. 116. The meaning of the rudder is given different interpretations in different authors: Galen (*ibid.*) describes it as a symbol of instability, Artemidorus (2.37) as a symbol of movement (he also says that to dream of *Tuche* sitting is a good sign, since it suggests that she is stable). Dio Chrysostom (63.7) that it shows she directs the lives of men.
165 See Villard, *LIMC* s.v. *Tuche*, nos. 28–43a, 58–68, 81–86 (cornucopia and rudder).

166 Villard, *LIMC* s.v. *Tuche*, nos. 11–13 (Plutus alone); 14, 49–52 (Plutus and cornucopia); 69–72 (on a globe).
167 Villard, *LIMC* s.v. *Tuche*, nos. 76–93 (plus various combinations of attributes); see also Metzler, Dieter, 'Mural Crowns in the Ancient Near East and Greece' in Matheson, *Obsession*, pp. 77–85.
168 Villard, *LIMC* s.v. *Tuche*, nos. 46–75, combined with various attributes.
169 Villard, *LIMC* s.v. *Tuche*, nos. 53 and 54.
170 Polybius, 29.21.3–6.
171 Pollitt, J. J., 'An Obsession with Fortune', pp. 12–17 in Matheson, *Obsession*, pp. 13–17, p. 14. Broucke, *Fortune of Cities*, p. 37 argues that it was the change in the socio-political environment that occurred with the Greek loss of independence to the Macedonians that is most significant: 'stability and order, hallmarks of the Classical world view (reflected in the art produced during the period), were replaced in the Hellenistic age by feelings of chaos and insignificance, as well as by the acknowledgement of the constant possibility of a reversal of both personal and communal fortunes.'
172 Thériault, *Homonoia*, drawing on Rudhardt, Jean, *Notions fondamentales de la pensee religieuse et actes constitutifs du culte dans la Grece classique* (Geneva, 1958) makes this point about the cult of *Homonoia*.
173 Broucke, 'Fortune of Cities' p. 44 also makes this point.
174 See Toynbee, Jocelyn M. C. *Roman Historical Portraits* (London, 1978) pp. 63–65; cited in Broucke, 'Fortune of Cities', p. 48, n. 44.
175 Smith, Amy C., 'Queens and Empresses as Goddesses: The Public Role of the Personal Tuche in the Graeco-Roman World' in Matheson, *Obsession*, pp. 86–105.
176 Polybius, 18.28.5.
177 E.g. Polybius, 1.35.2–5; Walbank, Frank W., 'Fortune (*tyche*) in Polybius', pp. 349–355 in Marincola, John, ed., *A Companion to Greek Historiography* (Oxford, 2007), p. 352 offers this example, but as an example of Polybius' inconsistency. It is not clear to me why such a double explanation should pose a problem. In this instance in particular, it is the absence of *tuche*'s favour that is said to cause the defeat. This personification is generally reserved for unexpected, catastrophic or astounding events: see Walbank, Frank W., *Historical Commentary on Polybius*, 3 Vols (1957–79) i. 18, noted also by Marincola, John, *Greek Historians* (Cambridge, 2001), p. 143.
178 See Walbank, 'Fortune' for discussion of *tuche* in Polybius and other analyses; particular reversals: 29.21.5–6, 38.21.3; retribution: 4.81.5, 15.20.5, 20.7.2; coincidences: 2.20.7, 4.2.4.
179 Trans. Marincola, *Greek Historians*, 144.
180 Polybius, 38.21.3, see Walbank, 'Fortune', p. 350.
181 Broucke, 'Fortune of Cities', pp. 44–46: she appears in coins, for example, obverse silver coin of Constantine the Great 330 CE, diam. 27 mm. see RIC 7 Constantine and Licinius (London 1966) pl. 18, no. 53 (reproduced in a drawing by Broucke, 'Fortune of Cities', p. 44, fig. 27); also gold solidus of Constantius II, which shows *Tuche* of Constantinople and *Fortuna Romana*, 351–355 CE, diam. 21 mm. American Numismatic Society, 1967.153.68 in Broucke, 'Fortune of Cities', p. 44, fig 28. She also appears as a statuette in the Esquiline Hoard (BM EC 66.12–29.23, in Broucke, 'Fortune of Cities', p. 44, fig. 29). The figure continues

NOTES

to have meaning into the 10th century CE: the *Tuche* of Jericho is found on the so-called Joshua Roll (Vatican cod. Palt. Gr. 431: see Weitzmann, Kurt, *The Joshua Roll: A Work of the Macedonian Renaissance* (Princeton: Princeton University Press, 1948)).

## Chapter III

1. From S. Fenton *The Fortune Teller's Workbook: a fun way to discover your future*, on numerology, p. 27: names provide insight into character by translating the letters into a number system.
2. Different heroic aspects of Sophoclean protagonists explored: e.g., Knox, Bernard, *The Heroic Temper: Studies in Sophoclean Tragedy* (Berkeley: The University of California Press, 1964) and see Whitman, Cedric, *Sophocles: A Study of Heroic Humanism* (Cambridge, MA: Harvard University Press, 1951).
3. In some cases, this reading turns on a misunderstanding of Aristotle's analysis of tragedy in the *Poetics* (13). He describes how those individuals who offer the best kind of tragic hero experience their suffering because of a *hamartia* (demonstrated, according to Aristotle, by Thyestes and Oedipus himself), which has been mistranslated as 'a grave moral flaw'. See Lucas, Donald William, *Aristotle: Poetics* (Oxford: Clarendon Press, 1968), p. 304 for misreadings of this passage dating to the seventeenth century, quoted in Meineck, Peter, and Woodruff, Paul, *The Theban Plays by Sophocles (trans. with introduction and notes)* (Indiana: Hackett Publishing Company, 2003). More modern examples include Boal's analysis of theatre *Theatre of the Oppressed* (London: Pluto Press, 2000); Stinton, Thomas, '*Hamartia* in Aristotle and Greek Tragedy' in *Classical Quarterly* n.s. 25 (1975), in *Collected Papers on Greek Tragedy* (Oxford: Oxford University Press, 1990), pp. 143–85. Dihlman, İlham, *Free Will: an Historical and Philosophical Introduction* (London: Routledge, 1999), ch. 2 gives an overview of the history of free will, which uses Oedipus to discuss the importance of humility in acquiring self-knowledge (although he does not discuss Aristotle's analysis of the tragic hero).
4. In classical scholarship, moralistic readings of the play include Bowra, Maurice, *Sophoclean Tragedy* (Oxford, 1944); Drew, Griffith R., *The Theatre of Apollo: Divine Justice and Sophocles' Oedipus the King* (Montreal and Kingston: McGill-Queen's University Press, 1996). This reading is sometimes supported by interpretation of stasimon 2 of the play as indicating that Oedipus should be seen as bordering on the tyrannical; but that this is not necessarily the obvious way to read this chorus, see Segal, Charles, *Sophocles' Tragic World* (Cambridge, MA: Harvard University Press, 1998), p. 189, with n. 29.
5. Discussion, Winnington-Ingram, Reginald P., *Sophocles: An Interpretation* (Cambridge: Cambridge University Press, 1980) pp. 188–197, 201–204.
6. See also Knox, Bernard, *Oedipus at Thebes: Sophocles' Tragic Hero and His Time* (1957, repr. Yale, 1998), p. 29.
7. Dodds, Eric. R., 'On Misunderstanding the Oedipus Rex' in *Greece & Rome*, Second Series, 13: 1 (Apr., 1966), pp. 37–49 and Winnington-Ingram, *Sophocles: an Interpretation*. Knox, *Oedipus at Thebes*, argued that it was intended as a

rejection of newfangled notions presented by the secular thinkers of the time, who were seeking naturalistic explanations for worldly phenomena. In this interpretation, Oedipus, so sure of his intellectual superiority, represents the city of Athens and her people, confident of their imperial supremacy, and the play becomes a warning to those who are arrogant enough to think that mortal power can somehow supplant divine power.

8   Gould, John, 'The Language of Oedipus' in Bloom, Harold, ed., *Sophocles' Oedipus Rex* (1988), p. 158.
9   Reinhardt, Karl, *Sophocles* (Eng. trans., Oxford: Oxford University Press, 1979), p. 98: 'the essential basis of the play . . . is an actively pursued struggle for escape, self-assertion and defence on the part of a threatened world of illusion . . .'
10  Reinhardt, *Sophocles*, pp. 2–3.
11  Jebb, Richard C., *The Oedipus Tyrannus of Sophocles* (edited with introduction and notes by Sir Richard Jebb, Cambridge: Cambridge University Press, 1887) draws attention to the use of the participle implying that the speaker is continuing, rather than beginning, to be pure; and that the conception of *moira* here is personal.
12  Jebb, *Oedipus* (*ad loc.*); see Isocrates 9.58, Herodotus, 4.203.
13  Segal, *Tragic World*, p. 193, for a good discussion of this song, and its implications (through the contrasts it sets up) for the role of Zeus in the play.
14  See Dawe, Roger D., *Sophocles: Oedipus Rex* (Cambridge: Cambridge University Press, 1982): *Tuche* appears once more (in the plural) in the last words of the play, spoken by the chorus, describing the fortunes that Oedipus temporarily enjoyed. These lines are probably spurious, and they add very little to our understanding of *tuche*.
15  *Tuche* used to mark key events in different ways, see Pucci, Pietro, *Oedipus and the Fabrication of the Father* (Baltimore-London: The Johns Hopkins University Press, 1992), esp. p. 32–33.
16  Segal, *Tragic World*, p. 146: 'it is remarkably sparing of direct supernatural intervention'.
17  Segal, *Tragic World*, pp. 186–198. Note the attribution of Delphic oracular power to Zeus (151) and relationship with Apollo and Delphi (497–9). *Stasimon* 2 in particular emphasises this idea.
18  Commentators have, for example, criticised the fact that the survivor from Laius' retinue turns out to be the same man who first rescued Oedipus, and that the messenger from Corinth is the very person who received the baby Oedipus: Dawe, *Oedipus Rex*, p. 19, rationalises it as being necessary because of the number of available actors.
19  The first (94–97), brought from Delphi by Creon, launches the search for Laius' killer, and starts Oedipus' manhunt; the second (711–23) is the oracle given to Laius and Jocasta (she hesitates to ascribe it to Apollo, since she is determined that it is untrue); the third (787–93) is the oracle that Oedipus received as a young man at Delphi.
20  As Dodds, *On Misunderstanding*, p. 41, points out, the oracles in *Oedipus* are not phrased as conditional statements; they do not offer their recipients a choice. For example, in the *Seven Against Thebes*, the oracle tells Laius (742 ff.): 'Do

not beget a child; for if you do, that child will kill you', whereas, in Sophocles' version, the oracle about Oedipus' future is given to Laius as a prediction of inevitable events.
21  Segal, *Oedipus Tyrannus*, pp. 62–62: the riddle is 'a source of pride and confidence, whereas the oracle is a source of anxiety and helplessness'.
22  The genres of oracle and riddle are close; both contain meanings concealed in metaphors. They are explicitly related in Greek literature: Heraclitus calls Delphi's pronouncements signs (DK frag. 93), while Socrates treats the oracle about him ('no one is wiser than Socrates') as material for interpretation, see Plato, *Apology*, 21 B; see further, Roberts, Deborah, *Apollo and His Oracle in the Oresteia* (Gottingen: Vandenhoeck and Ruprecht, 1984) p. 21.
23  Shultz, Thomas R., 'Development of the Appreciation of Riddles' in *Child Development* 45 (1974), pp. 100–105. The process is well described by Lieber, Michael D., 'Riddles, Cultural Categories, and World View' in *Journal of American Folklore* 89 (1976), pp. 255–265; p. 260; but Kaivola-Bregenhøj, Anniki, 'Riddles and Their Use' in Hasan-Rokem, Galit, Shulman, David Dean, *Untying The Knot: On Riddles And Other Enigmatic Modes* (Oxford: Oxford University Press, 1996), pp. 10–36, esp. p. 31 ff. describes how although narratives including riddles, and indeed the old riddle literature, stress the mental agility needed to solve riddles, fieldwork reveals that riddling is seldom an intellectual exercise, and instead people are expected to know the right answers.
24  Aristotle, *Rhetoric*, 1405b.
25  Research into 'true riddles' has suggested that their structure may parallel the structure of the social situation in which they are said to occur (see Georges, Robert A. and Dundes, Alan, 'Towards a Structueal Definition of the Riddle', *The Journal of American Folklore* 76 (1963), pp. 111–118). It is not clear whether this is generally true of ancient Greek riddling narratives.
26  Apollodoros 3.5.8; Athenaeus (10.456b). Other versions exist, all stressing the contrast between a single voice and a variety of limbs: Rokem, Freddie, 'One Voice and Many Legs: Oedipus and the Riddle of the Sphinx' in Hasan-Rokem and Shulman, *Untying The Knot*, pp. 255–270; esp. p. 257.
27  Apollodoros *ibid.* (trans. Frazer).
28  Köngäs-Maranda, Elli, 'Riddles and Riddling: An Introduction' *Journal of American Folklore* 89 (1976) 127–137.
29  Pagis, Dan, 'Towards a Theory of the Literary Riddle' in Hasan-Rokem and Shulman, *Untying The Knot*, pp. 81–108, esp. pp. 94–95, and Baumann, Richard, ' "I'll Give You Three Guesses": The Dynamics of Genre in the Riddle Tale' in Hasan-Rokem and Shulman, *Untying The Knot*, pp. 62–80; Abrahams, Roger D., 'Between the Living and the Dead' *Folklore Fellows Communications* 225 (1980) pp. 2, 183–6.
30  In narrative contexts a riddle is rarely just a game of referential speech: Lieber, *Riddles, Cultural Categories*; Glazier, Jack, and Glazier, Phyllis Gorfain, 'Ambiguity and Exchange: The Double Dimension of Mbeere Riddles', *The Journal of American Folklore*, 89, no. 352: Riddles and Riddling, (Apr.-Jun., 1976), pp. 189–238; Evans, David, 'Riddling and the Structure of Context', *The Journal of American Folklore*, 89, no. 352: Riddles and Riddling, (Apr.-Jun., 1976), pp.

166–188, Ben-Amos, Dan, 'Solutions to Riddles', *The Journal of American Folklore*, 89, no. 352: Riddles and Riddling, (Apr.-Jun., 1976), pp. 249–254.
   For example, a riddle often carries emotional significance as well. Its use within a story may reveal the status and relative power of persons, or draw attention to particular characteristics. The symbolism of the riddle form – knowledge withheld, concealed, sought – may carry ontological connotations for the story in which it appears, embodying the narrative's dynamic of problem and resolution, suggesting the possibilities of re-perception, revealing connections that are transformative not just of language, but also of experience or even events. See Handelman, Don, 'Traps of Trans-formation: Theoretical Convergences between Riddle and Ritual', in Hasan-Rokem and Shulman, *Untying The Knot*, pp. 37–80.
31 Often the case in riddling competitions: see Kaivola-Bregenhøj, *Riddles and Their Use*, p. 26.
32 Roberts, (*Apollo and his Oracle*, 92 n. 50) notes a pattern in literature of those who receive riddles, may be the answer to riddles or seem riddle-like, then become figures of wisdom who give advice in riddle form.
33 Segal, *Tragic World*, pp.148 ff.: ll. 109, 221, 710, 933, 957, 1050, 1058–9.
34 In this observation, I do not mean only the 'two faces' of king and *pharmakos*, or 'scapegoat', as Vernant, Jean-Pierre, and duBois, Page, 'Ambiguity and reversal: on the enigmatic structure of *Oedipus Rex*', trans. (ed.) *New Literary History*, 9: 3, Rhetoric I: Rhetorical Analyses (Spring, 1978) pp. 475–501, esp. p. 484.
35 Vernant, *Ambiguity and Reversal*, p. 494 suggests that in becoming son and husband, father and brother Oedipus compresses the ages of man described in the Sphinx's riddle – and so embodies the answer to that question.
36 Reinhardt, *Sophocles*, p. 106: '... it is not a confrontation of knowledge and ignorance of a certain fact, but of one mode of existence and another ...'
37 Gould, *Language of Oedipus*, pp. 150–1.
38 ll. 316–18.
39 Bushnell, Rebecca W., *Prophesying Tragedy: Sign and Voice in Sophocles' Theban Plays* (Ithaca, NY: Cornell University Press, 1988), p. 77.
40 Greene, *Moira*, p. 347 and pp. 364–5: Chrysippus (Eusebius *Praeparatio Evangelica* p. 4.3) sees the suffering of Oedipus as fated (because it turned out to be unavoidable); while Carneades (Cicero, *On Fate*, 33) argues against the necessity of events that are not wholly contained in nature.
41 Oedipus famously takes responsibility on himself, even though his crimes were committed without intention. The chorus also notes how he has been found out *akonta* (literally, 'not willing', 1213) and, once all has come to light, the servant coming from the house states how the house is polluted with evils that were done consciously, but unintentionally (*hekonta k'ouk akonta*). Cf. Reinhardt, *Sophocles*, 133–4. Oedipus' innocence is further explored in the *Oedipus at Colonus*, (see 437, 521–3, 547 f. and 693–1002) see Dover, *Greek Popular Morality*, 155. Williams, *Shame and Necessity*, p. 60, n.27 and 69) sees this not as the strained language of a writer struggling to come to terms with the growth of moral consciousness, but with Oedipus' attempts to come to terms with what it has meant for his life to have acted as he did. In the reflection of the old man at Colonus, who finds the sufferings of his younger self excessive, he sees the

acknowledgment (prevalent in Greek tragedy) that 'there is an authority exercised by what one has done, and not merely by what one has intentionally done.'
42  Segal, Charles, *Oedipus Tyrannus: Tragic Heroism and the Limits of Knowledge* (Oxford: Oxford University Press, 2000), p. 64.

## Chapter IV

1  Holland, Dorothy, and Quinn, Naomi, 'Culture and Cognition' in Holland, Dorothy and Quinn, Naomi, *Cultural Models in Language and Thought* (Cambridge: Cambridge University Press, 1987), pp. 3–42, p. 3.
2  From the editorial section 'This week in the *BMJ*', describing an article by Hira, Kenji, Fukui, Tsuguya, Endoh, Akira, Rahman, Mahbubur, Maekawa, Munetaka, 'Influence of superstition on the date of hospital discharge and medical cost in Japan: retrospective and descriptive study', *BMJ* 317 (19–26 December, 1998), pp. 1680–1683.
3  Fillmore, Charles, 'An Alternative to Checklist Theories of Meaning' in Cogen, C., Thompson, H., Thurgood, G., Whistler, K., and Wright, J., eds., *Proceedings of the First Annual Meeting of the Berkeley Linguistics Society*, pp. 121–131 (Berkeley 1975); described by Quinn, Naomi, 'How to Reconstruct Schemas People Share, From What They Say' in Quinn, Naomi, ed., *Finding Culture in Talk: A Collection of Methods* (NY: Palgrave, Macmillan, 2005), pp. 35–82, p. 37. She points out, as Fillmore does not, that there are further 'prototype worlds' within the initial prototype world of 'bachelor', such as 'eligible bachelor' and 'confirmed bachelor'.
4  Fillmore, *Checklist*; described by D'Andrade, *Cognitive Anthropology*, p. 123. See also Fillmore, Charles, J., 'The Case for Case Reopened' in Cole, Peter, and Sadock, Jerrold, eds., *Syntax and Semantics*, 8: Grammatical Relations (New York: Academic Press, 1977), pp. 59–81, and 'Topics for Lexical Semantics', in R.W. Cole, ed., *Current Issues in Linguistic Theory* (Bloomington: Indiana University Press, 1977), pp. 76–138 in which Fillmore describes how the meanings of words or expressions are understood by us 'having or activating in our minds schemes or images or memories of experiences within which the word or expression has a naming or describing or classifying function' (see 'The Case for Case Reopened', p. 74).

Quinn, Naomi, ' "Commitment" in American Marriage: a Cultural Analysis', *American Ethnologist*, 9: 4 (November 1982, special issue, Symbolism and Cognition II), pp. 775–798 analyses the word 'Commitment' from an anthropological perspective for the shared knowledge its usage reveals, and its role as a 'scenario word'.
5  As Quinn, *Finding Culture in Talk*, p. 38.
6  See description of the development of ideas of schemas and cultural models in D'Andrade, *Cognitive Anthropology*; a useful overview also in Holland and Quinn, 'Culture and Cognition', and a further helpful and concise summary in Quinn, 'Commitment'.

7   D'Andrade, *Cognitive Anthropology*, p. 132.
8   D'Andrade, *Cognitive Anthropology*, p. 125; example draws on Fillmore, 'Checklist', pp. 125–6.
9   D'Andrade, *Cognitive Anthropology*, p. 179.
10  Stafford, T. F., and Stafford, M. R., 'The Advantages of Atypical Advertisements for Stereotyped Product Categories' *Journal of Current Issues and Research in Advertising*, 24:1 (Spring 2002), pp. 25–38, example from p. 25.
11  D'Andrade, *Cognitive Anthropology*, p. 132.
12  Strictly speaking, D'Andrade argues, not all cultural models are schemas: schemas fit into short-term memory, cultural models may be too complex to do so (D'Andrade, *Cognitive Anthropology*, p. 152). Strauss, 'Analyzing Discourse', p. 203, describes cultural models as comprising 'the shared, taken for granted assumptions that are at the core of what is meant by culture', and as consisting of 'holistic mental schemas'.
13  Kleinman, A., *Patients and Healers in the Context of Culture: an exploration of the borderland between anthropology, medicine and psychiatry* (Berkeley: University of California Press, 1980).
14  God's wrath: see White, A., *Journal of Biblical Ethics in Medicine* 2: 3 and 4 (no date given: www.bmei.org/jbem/volume2.php); jealousy: Ashforth, Adam, *Witchcraft, Violence and Democracy in South Africa* (Chicago: University of Chicago, 2005).
15  Erickson, Barbra E., 'Toxin or Medicine? Explanatory Models of Radon in Montana Health Mines' *Medical Anthropology Quarterly* 21:1 (2007), pp. 1–21, esp. p. 6 on Roy D'Andrade's 'Schemas and Motivation' in D'Andrade, Roy, and Strauss, Claudia, eds., *Human Motives and Cultural Models* (Cambridge: Cambridge University Press, 1992), pp. 23–44. Erickson notes that other categorisations have been suggested using the particular psychological force of a model (be it affective, evaluative or emotional) as their basis.
16  Matthews, Holly F., 'Uncovering Cultural Models of Gender from Accounts of Folktales' in Quinn, *Finding Culture in Talk*, pp. 105–156; Strauss, 'Analyzing Discourse for Cultural Complexity', pp. 208 ff. calls these 'personal semantic networks'.
17  Stafford and Stafford, 'The Advantages of Atypical Advertisements', p. 26.
18  Dru, Jean-Marie and Business Partners, *Beyond Disruption: Changing the Rules in the Marketplace* (Adweek Books, Wiley and Sons, 2002), p. 23.
19  Further discussion of 'bachelor' in this volume, p. 153. See Strauss, Claudia, 'Models and Motives' in D'Andrade and Strauss, Claudia, *Human Motives and Cultural Models*, pp. 1–20.
20  See for example projects included under the EPA/NSF Partnership for Environmental Research as reported in the *2002 Decision-Making and Valuation for Environmental Policy Workshop*, e.g., Paolisso, M. and Chambers, E., 'Applying Consensus and Cultural Models To Improve Environmental Decision-Making'.
21  As opposed to the social discourses of Foucault's sociolinguistic analysis. See collected essays in Quinn, *Finding Culture in Talk*, esp. Hill, Jane H., 'Finding Culture in Narrative' pp. 157–202, esp. p. 15.
22  Links between the different approaches of these different disciplines are beginning to be made: see Nair, Rukmini Bhaya, *Narrative Gravity: Conversation,*

# NOTES

*Cognition, Culture* (London: Routledge, 2003); Schleifer, Ronald, Davis, Robert C., Mergler, Nancy, *Culture and Cognition: the Boundaries of Literary and Scientific Inquiry* (Ithaca, NY: Cornell University Press, 1992); Donald E. Polkinghorne, *Narrative Knowing and the Human Sciences* (New York: SUNY Press, 1988).

23 Brooks, Peter, *Psychoanalysis and Storytelling* (Oxford: Blackwell, 1994), p. 57. 'What-sayers' described in Basso, Ellen B., *A Musical View of the Universe: Kalapalo Myth and Ritual Performances* (Philadelphia: University of Pennsylvania Press, 1985), pp. 15-18, cited in Hill, 'Finding Culture', p. 186). See also Strauss, 'Analyzing Discourse'.

24 White, Michael, *Reflections on Narrative Practice: Essays and Interviews* (Adelaide, South Australia: Dulwich Centre Publications, 2000), p. 9.

25 Bruner, Jerome S., 'Life As Narrative', *Social Research* 54: 1 (Spring) (1987), pp. 11-32, p. 15; see also Murray, Michael, 'The Storied Nature of Health and Illness' in Murray, Michael, and Chamberlain, Kerry, eds., *Qualitative Health Psychology: Theories and Methods* (Thousand Oaks, CA: Sage, 1999), pp. 47-63, esp. p. 53.

26 Laz, Cheryl, 'Age Embodied' *Journal of Aging Studies* 17 (2003), 503-519, pp. 506-7; Murray, *Health and Illness*, p. 49, citing Plummer, Ken, *Telling Sexual Stories: Power, Change and Social Worlds* (London: Routledge, 1995).

27 Murray, *Health and Illness*, p. 50, citing Leudar, Ivan, and Antaki, Charles, 'Discourse Participation, Reported Speech and Research Practices in Social Psychology', *Theory and Psychology* 6 (1996), pp. 5-29.

28 Somers, Margaret R., 'The Narrative Constitution of Identity: A Relational and Network Approach', *Theory and Society* 23 (1994), pp. 605-649, p. 630; see Ochs, Elinor, and Capps, Lisa, 'Untold Stories' in *Living Narrative* (Cambridge, MA: Harvard University Press, 2002), pp. 251-290.

29 See Herman, Judith L., *Trauma and Recovery: From Domestic Abuse to Political Terror* (London; Pandora, 2001).

30 Wiesel, Elie, 'A Plea for the Survivors' in *A Jew Today* (trans. Marion Wiesel), (New York: Random House, 1978), p. 198, quoted in Greenspan, Henry, 'Lives as Texts: Symptoms as Modes of Recounting in the Life Histories of Holocaust Survivors' in Rosenwald, George, and Ochberg, Richard, eds. *Storied Lives* (New Haven, CN: Yale University Press, 1996), pp. 145-164, p. 149.

31 Greenspan 'Lives as Texts', pp. 150-151. On survivors of rape: personal testimony, Rape Crisis helpline volunteer.

32 Velleman, David, 'Narrative Explanation', *The Philosophical Review* 112: 1 (Jan., 2003) pp. 1-25, esp. pp. 18-19.

33 Ricoeur, Paul, *The Creativity of Language: Interview by Richard Kearney* (Paris, 1981) in Ricoeur, Paul, and Valdes, Mario J., *A Ricoeur Reader: Reflection and Imagination* (University of Toronto, 1984), p. 467.

34 See papers in Briggs, Charles, ed., *Disorderly Discourse: Narrative, conflict and inequality* (New York, Oxford, 1996) and in Rosenwald, George and Ochberg. Richard, eds., *Storied Lives* (New Haven, CN: 1996), Linde, Charlotte, *Life Stories: The creation of coherence* (Oxford/New York: 1993), Ochs, Elinor, and Capps, Lisa, *Living Narrative* (Cambridge MA, 2002); Stromberg, Peter, *Language and Self-Transformation* (Cambridge, 1993); Hill, 'Finding Culture'; Somers, *Identity*, p. 614.

35 Murray, *Health and Illness*, p. 48; Phoenix, Cassandra, and Sparkes, Andrew C., 'Young Athletic Bodies and Narrative Maps of Aging' in *Journal of Aging Studies* 20: 2 (2006), pp. 107–121, esp. pp. 107–109; for a useful description of the processes and techniques involved in such narration see Holstein, James A., and Gubrium, Jaber F., *The Self We Live By: Narrative Identity in a Post-Modern World* (Oxford: OUP, 2000), pp. 103–123; discusses 'narrative maps', pp. 178–179.

36 This sense of fate that Larner alludes to goes beyond that which arises in telling a story for which we already know the end (a straightforward and universal narratological experience). Larner's point is that a sense of destiny can become a self-fulfilling prophecy, closing off other possibilities. Larner, Glen, 'Through a Glass Darkly: Narrative as Destiny' in *Theory and Psychology* 8: 4 (August 1, 1998), pp. 549–572, quotations from pp. 556 and 558.

37 Freeman, Mark Philip, *Rewriting the Self: History, Memory, Narrative* (London and New York: Routledge, 2003) explores what he calls 'the poetics of life history' (p. 222), and the complex relationship between the self and narratives of the self.

38 Quinn, Naomi, 'Introduction' in Quinn, *Finding Culture in Talk*, pp. 26 ff. provides a description of a number of types of discourse obtained in ways that for obvious reasons are not available to an ancient historian.

# Chapter V

1 Gracián Y. Morales, Baltasar, *The Art of Worldly Wisdom: a Pocket Oracle* (trans. Christopher Maurer) (New York: Doubleday, 1992).

2 On *conceptismo* see s.v., Bleiberg, Germán, Ihrie, Maureen, Pérez Janet, eds., *Dictionary of the Literature of the Iberian Peninsula*, Vol. 1, (Westport, CT: Greenwood, 1993). Quotation from Precepts from Gracián Y. Morales, *The Art of Worldly Wisdom: a Pocket Oracle*, p. 120.

3 See www.balthasargracian.com.

4 As Carey, Christopher, 'Genre, Occasion and Performance' in Budelmann, Felix, ed., *The Cambridge Companion to Greek Lyric* (Cambridge, 2009) pp. 21–38, has noted, there is debate around the question of membership of the lyric corpus. In this section, I use this label in its broader sense to include elegy and iambic poetry, but will concentrate on the lyric poets of the Archaic period. For detailed summaries of the biographies of these poets see West, Martin s.v., in Homblower and Spawforth, *Oxford Classical Dictionary*.

5 Carey, 'Genre', p. 23.

6 For the difficulties of identifying, or designing schema for identifying, the social standing of particular poets from their poetry, see Irwin, Elizabeth, *Solon and Early Greek Poetry: The Politics of Exhortation* (Cambridge: Cambridge University Press, 2005), pp. 58–62; Carey, 'Genre', pp. 162–67.

7 See Irwin, *Solon*, pp. 86–87.

8 For example, Archilochus of Paros (frr. 105–6 for political dangers, using a seafaring allegory; frr. 94–98 for the dangers of battle).

# NOTES

9 A point made by Irwin, *Solon*, pp. 1–3: see Heraclitus (on Hesiod) 57 DK; Herodotus, 5.67.1 and Aristotle, *The Constitution of the Athenians*, 5.2.
10 Bowie, Ewen L., 'Sympotic Praise' in *Gaia* 6 (2002), pp. 169–199 discusses the many different types of praising that can be found across the corpus of Archaic poetry – and which probably intimate the subtlety of conversation at the symposium.
11 *Aisa*: Solon, fr. 4.2, Theognis, 1.345, 1.907. There is another mention of *aisa* in a fragment of Stesichorus, but not enough remains of the latter to be informative (*kat' aisan* in Stesichorus S1021.10).
12 As an example consider the epic term *peprotai* found in *Anacreontea* 36.10. The poem bewails man's inability to pay off death, and explains the speaker's reasons for not hoarding wealth: 'If I am fated to die, what use is gold?' The use of this epic term for fate's attentions brings with it implicit reminders of the spirit with which the heroes of the *Iliad* faced their futures. For them it resulted in brave and noble deeds; in comic contrast, here it leads the poet to extol the joys of drink, carousing with friends or enjoying the 'rites of Aphrodite on a soft bed' (trans. Campbell, David, *Greek Lyric II* (Cambridge, MA: Harvard University Press, 2006)). However, this may be a deliberate archaism: this poem is likely to date to the Hellenistic period, rather than, as was believed until the nineteenth century, being composed by Anacreon himself (see West: s.v., in Hornblower and Spawforth, *Oxford Classical Dictionary*).
13 Theognis, 1.907, all Theognis trans. Gerber, Douglas E., *Greek Elegiac Poetry from the Seventh to the Fifth Centuries* (Cambridge, MA: Harvard University Press, 2003).
14 Theognis, 1.341–50.
15 The Greek is *aisa gar outos esti*.
16 See Ober, Josiah, *Mass and Elite in Democratic Athens* (Princeton: Princeton University Press, 1991), pp. 60 ff.; Osborne, Robin, *Greece in the Making 1200–479 BC* (London: Routledge, 2001), pp. 215–225.
17 Solon, fr. 4.
18 The passage goes on to describe how the rich, through their greed and injustice, have brought the city an 'inescapable wound', but Solon's discussion of the benefits of lawfulness indicate that there is hope for change.
19 Solon, fr. 13.63–6, trans. Gerber, *Greek Elegiac Poetry*.
20 Theognis, 1.1075–8; Solon, fr. 17.
21 Theognis, 1.1187–90.
22 Solon, frr. 20.4, 27.18; Theognis, 1.340, 1.820; Callinus, fr. 1.15; Tyrtaeus, fr. 7; (Callinus and Tyrtaeus, trans. Gerber: *Greek Elegiac Poetry*).
23 Callinus, fr. 1.8–9; it continues ll. 12–13 'for it is no way fated (*heimarmenon*). that a man escape death' (trans. Gerber, *Greek Elegiac Poetry*).
24 Ibycus, 282A. 11–14, trans. Campbell David, *Greek Lyric III* (Cambridge MA: Harvard University Press, 2001).
25 Ascribed to Simonides of Ceos by Wilamowitz, Ulrich von, *Isyllos von Epidauros* (Berlin: Weidmann, 1886), p. 16; Bowra Maurice, *Greek Lyric Poetry* (Oxford: Oxford University Press, 1936) pp. 397 ff.
26 The Greek is *lanchanein*.
27 Theognis, 1.1110–1111, 592, 453, 934, 729.

28  Hipponax fr. 40.2; trans. Gerber, Douglas E., *Greek Iambic Poetry from the Seventh to the Fifth Centuries BC* (Cambridge, MA: Harvard University Press, 2006).
29  Solon fr. 27.5–6: the child in his third year of life is 'allotted' down on his cheeks.
30  The Greek is *elachen*, Mimnermus, fr. 12.1 (trans. Gerber: *Greek Elegiac Poetry*).
31  Archilochus fr. 128. 4–7 (trans. Gerber, *Greek Iambic Poetry*).
32  Archilochus fr. 13.6; Theognis, 657–66.
33  Good or evil: Archilochus fr. 12.
34  Archilochus fr. 108.
35  Archilochus fr. 298.
36  Archilochus fr. 130.
37  Explicitly, Archilochus fr. 177 and fr. 122.
38  Archilochus fr. 16, discussed further below.
39  Archilochus fr. 17.
40  Theognis, 1.129–30; Alcman fr. 64.
41  Solon, fr. 31.2; (Plutarch, *Life of Solon*, 3.5) the attribution is doubtful, according to Gerber, since there is no other evidence that Solon wrote poetry in hexameters, the metre in which these lines are composed.
42  Solon, fr. 13.70.
43  *Suntuchien agathen* found also in Theognis, 1.590; *dustuchie* at 1.1188.
44  Mimnermus, fr. 2; Semonides fr. 1.
45  Solon, fr. 13.9–13.
46  The Greek is *alitron thumon* (ll.27–28).
47  Solon, fr. 13.31–2.
48  Solon, frr. 4.5–6 and 13.71–75.
49  The lines read (74) *kerdea toi thnetois opasan athanatoi / ate d'ex auton anaphainetai, hen opote Zeus / pempsei teisomenen allote allos echei*. (Greene: *Moira*, p. 24 agrees with Wehrli 1931: 12, n.1 that *auton* means the men themselves, but does not explain how this fits with Solon's final observation that the ruin is sent by Zeus.)
50  Solon, fr. 13.55–56.
51  Solon, fr. 17.
52  Solon, fr. 11.2 (following Diod. Sic. 9.20.2): if you have suffered because of your wrong action, he instructs his Athenian audience, as he warns them about the tyrant Peisistratus, do not lay blame for this on the gods.
53  'Fortune' is *suntuchien agathen* 13.70.
54  Solon, fr. 6.3–4.
55  Solon, fr. 14.
56  See van Wees, Hans, 'Megara's Mafiosi: Timocracy and Violence in Theognis' in Brock, Roger and Hodkinson, Stephen, eds., *Alternatives to Athens: Varieties of Political Organisation and Community in Ancient Greece* (Oxford: Oxford University Press, 2002).
57  Theognis, the treachery of friends, 1.59 = 1.79–82, 113, 299–300; out for themselves, 1.83–6 and 221–6.
58  Advice: Theognis' advice is far less detailed than that offered by the *Pocket Oracle*. As well as a long diatribe about who is not to be trusted, and recom-

## NOTES

mending fortitude in the face of misfortune (see below), he does offer some insights into the value of planning: (1.1052–54) 'Never made a mistake through haste, but plan in the depths of your heart and with your good sense. The heart and mind of madmen are flighty, but planning leads to benefit and to good sense.' And at (1171–6) he praises the exercise of judgement (*gnome*). In terms of his own suffering: lost friends: 1.811–113; possessions and land confiscated: 1. 346–7 and 1197–1201; fear of civil strife: 1.47–52.

59   Archilochus fr. 23.11.
60   See references s.v. *olbios* in *LSJ*. When, in Herodotus' *Histories* (1.32) Solon contrasts being blessed with having great wealth, he appears to be challenging the prevailing belief that wealth equals blessed. He certainly takes King Croesus by surprise . . .
61   Theognis, 2.1253, 1335, 1375.
62   Theognis, 1.165–6, repeated at 171–2. Gods: 1.133–142; *Moira* and *daimon*: 149–150; Zeus: 157–8; and *daimon*: 161–4.
63   Respect: Theognis 1.666; humbled: 1.111, and railing at the gods: 1.373–400.
64   Theognis, 1.833–36.
65   Solon, 1.65–70.
66   Theognis, 1.585–590; see Greene, *Moira*, p. 34.
67   Theognis, 1.149 f.
68   Theognis, 1.359; see also 591 and 817.
69   Theognis, 1.1029–30.
70   Theognis, 1.441–446, cf. 1162af.
71   Sea faring both literally (Archilochus, frr. 8–13) and as a metaphor for other dangers (frr. 105–6).
72   There may not be evidence for self-conscious rhetorical forms for this period or genre of literature, nevertheless these poems appear to use the language of luck, fate and fortune as what later rhetorical practice would dub *paraenesis* (or moral exhortation).

## Chapter VI

1   Dialogue between Jonathan (John Cusack) and Sara (Kate Beckinsale) in the film *Serendipity* (2001).
2   Apello, Tim, 'A Simple Twist of Fate', *The Nation*, November 5, 2001; see Williams, Bronwyn T., Zenger, Amy A., *Popular Culture and Representations of Literacy* (London: Routledge, 2007), pp. 33–37 for *In the Cut*'s critical relationship to *Serendipity*.
3   Thomas, Rosalind, *Herodotus in Context: Ethnography, Science and the Art of Persuasion* (Cambridge: Cambridge University Press, 2000), esp. p. 166 and ch. 6.
4   On the nature of Herodotus' sources see Luraghi, Nino, *Local Knowledge in Herodotus' Histories* (Oxford: Oxford University Press, 2007), pp. 138–160. Smith, Andrea L., 'Heteroglossia, "Common Sense," and Social Memory' in *American Ethnologist* 31: 2, (May, 2004), pp. 251–269 is an example of current research in anthropology exploring the 'heteroglossia' of collective memory.

5   Griffiths, Alan, 'Stories and Storytelling in the *Histories*', pp. 130–144 in Dewald, Carolyn, and Marincola, John, *The Cambridge Companion to Herodotus* (Cambridge: Cambridge University Press, 2006), p. 134.
6   See Gould, *Herodotus*, ch. 5, pp. 86–109.
7   Herodotus, Bk. 2 (Egyptians), Bk. 4 (Scythians), 2.33 (Danube/Nile), 4.36.1 (Hyperboreans/-noteans).
8   See Hartog, François (trans. Janet Lloyd), *The Mirror of Herodotus: The Representation of the Other in the Writing of Herodotus* (Berkeley, London: University of California Press, 1988) with Pelling, Christopher, 'East is East and West is West – or Are They? National Characteristics in Herodotus' in *Histos* 1 (1997).
9   Harrison, Thomas, *Divinity and History* (Oxford: Oxford University Press, 2000), p. 223, n. 1 for discussions of free will in Herodotus.
10  Herodotus, 9.43.1–2.
11  Herodotus, 3.150–160.
12  See Flower, Harriet I., 'Herodotus and Delphic Traditions About Croesus' in Flower, Michael A. and Toher, Mark, eds., *Georgica: Greek Studies in Honour of George Cawkwell* (London: Institute of Classical Studies, 1991), p. 57 for an overview of these approaches.
13  1.32.3–9; quotations from Herodotus, *The Histories*, Oxford World's Classics (trans. Waterfield, Robin), eds. Waterfield, Robin and Dewald, Carolyn (Oxford: Oxford University Press, 1998). Similar thoughts are also expressed by Artabanus 7.10e and see also 7.46. It has been suggested that this moralising framework is the product of 'a tradition of prose storytelling in Ionia, absent from mainland Greece except Delphi' (Murray, Oswyn, *Early Greece* (Cambridge, MA: Harvard University Press, 1993), p. 27, discussed further in 'Herodotus and Oral History' in Luraghi, Nino, *The Historian's Craft in the Age of Herodotus* (Oxford: Oxford University Press, 2007), pp. 16–44). This seems to raise more questions than it answers, proposing a tradition of prose storytelling for which we have no other evidence, and suggesting that Delphi could preserve a somehow isolated narrative tradition. In contrast, as we have seen, similar sentiments about the inevitability of fate, the bringing down of the proud, the raising of the humble, appear, *passim*, throughout the lyric poetry of earlier writers.
14  Herodotus, 1.91.1: the Greek for 'allotted fate' here is *pepromenen moiran*.
15  Herodotus, 1.91.2.
16  Herodotus, 1.8–1.13.2.
17  Harrison, *Divinity and History*, p. 241.
18  Herodotus, 1.121.
19  Herodotus, 3.142.3.
20  Herodotus, 4.164.4.
21  The Greek is *eite ekon eite aekon*.
22  Gould, *Herodotus*, p. 73, translates this as 'either as a result of his own deliberate act or because he inadvertently failed to grasp the oracle'.
23  See Asheri, David, Lloyd, Alan B., Corcello, Aldo, Murray, Oswyn, Moreno, Alfonso, eds., and trans. Graziosi, Barbara, Rossetti, Matteo, Dus, Carlotta and Cazzato, Vanessa) *A Commentary on Herodotus Books 1-IV* (Oxford: Oxford University Press, 2007), p. 692 (*ad loc.*) 'whether he wanted it or not (= though

## NOTES

he did not wish it, though he had tried to avoid it), having misinterpreted the oracle (cf. 1.71.1; 9.33.2) he fulfilled his destiny'.

24  Herodotus, the vision, 7.12; Artabanus, 7.18.
25  Herodotus, 7.47. Draws on or participates in a tradition of doomed wise advisors (see Pelling, Christopher, 'Thucydides' Archidamus and Herodotus' Artabanus' in Flower and Toher, *Georgica*, pp. 120–121). Artabanus is wiser than he knows – as Pelling points out (p. 137) – when he raises the question of land and sea (7.49).
26  Scullion, Scott, 'Herodotus and Greek Religion' in Dewald and Marincola, *Cambridge Companion to Herodotus*, pp. 192–194.
27  Artabanus at 7.10e and Solon, at 1.32.1 and 9.
28  Herodotus, 3.40.2–3.
29  Herodotus seldom names gods when discussing events in his authorial persona, although there are numerous examples where his characters do so. A selection: 1.44.2 and 174, 5.49.7, 8.129, 9.7a.2.
30  Herodotus, 1.86.2, 1.87.4, 3.65.4, 3.119.6, 6.12.3.
31  Herodotus, 3.65.4 and 1.210.1.
32  Herodotus, 1.111.1.
33  Scyles, King of Scythia at 4.79.1–2 (being struck by lightning may have held great significance for some Mystery rites, see above p. 179, n. 97); the eclipse seen by Xerxes and his army at 7.37–40; the visitation at Delphi at 8.37.2–3. Aristeas at 4.15.2–3; the female commander at 8.84.2; Demaratus' mother at 6.69; the blinding of Epizelus and the death of the warrior standing beside him at Marathon, at 6.117.3.
34  A selection: Amasis at 3.43.1; Cambyses at 3.65.3; unnamed Persian at 9.16.4.
35  There is perhaps some evidence that Herodotus believed in them himself, see 1.91.4, 8.20, 77 and 96; 9.43. It may be that priests at oracles, including Delphi, provided him with information for his work (Flower, Harriet, 'Herodotus and Delphic Traditions about Croesus', in Flower and Toher, *Georgica*, p. 61).
36  Mistaken interpretations: Spartans at 1.66, Siphnians 3.57–58, King Cleomenes 6.80 – madness or arrogance (both closely related). Successful: Liches, 1.67–8; Psammetichus, 2.152; Paionians, 5.1; Cypselus 5.92e; Miltiades son of Cypselus, 6.34–36.
37  Sabacos at 2.139; Aristodicus at 1.158–60; Themistocles at 7.143 ff.
38  Other story types that seem to convey a message about the unavoidability of fate include the intertwining of natural and supernatural aspects that play throughout significant events. For example the various catastrophes that beset Xerxes' invasion of Greece – from the destruction of the Persian fleet by a storm (7.188–93) that may be the result of the Greek prayers to the winds (7.189.3), and the more explicitly divinely prompted storm at 8.12–13: beautifully explored by Pelling, 'Archidamus and Artabanus', pp. 137–139.
39  Distant events: 1.8.2, 2.161.3, 4.79.1, 5.92d, 6.134–5; more recent: Demaratus' deposition, 6.64, and the failure of the Persians to take Naxos, 5.33.2; see also 9.109.2.
40  Herodotus, 6.134 (giving the whole Timo story as the Parian version of events). Adkins, Arthur, *Merit and Responsibility* (Oxford: Clarendon Press, 1960), p. 123 (also cited in) Harrison, *Divinity and History*, pp. 228–9 discusses the Timo example.

41  Harrison, *Divinity and History*, p. 229 compares her to the Pythia.
42  The Greek is that she is not *ten aitien touton*, and *aitia* is used in other parts of the *Histories* in explanations of natural events to mean 'cause'. *Aitios* as part of a causal explanation: 2.26.1, 3.12.2. This interpretation of *aitios* may also help to explain some other rather odd uses of the word in other stories about mortal culpability for particular events: for example, when Herodotus talks in terms of those who are 'most *aitios*' of particular offences: 3.52.7 (Periander sends an army against Procles, because he is most *aitios* for his troubles); 4.200.1 (those guilty of Arcesilaus' murder and H. comments on those who are *metaitioi* 'guilty alongside them'); 6.50.1 (Cleomenes sends an army against those of the Aigenetans who are 'most guilty' of plotting against Greece).
43  How, Walter W., and Wells, Joseph, *A Commentary on Herodotus 2 Vols*. Vol. 2 (1912, repr. Oxford: Oxford University Press, 1990) (*ad loc.*) in their commentary note that Stein suggests that the verb *phanenai* 'to appear' indicates that Timo appeared as a phantom to the general.
44  Herodotus, 1.91.4.
45  Herodotus, 1.91.2.
46  Harrison, *Divinity and History*, p. 228.
47  Various attempts have been made to explain away this change of heart by the king: these are listed in Pelling, 'Archidamus and Artabanus', p. 140.
48  Herodotus, 1.5.4: that the cities that were once great are now small, and *vice versa*, evidence of the reversal of human fortunes.
49  Herodotus, 3.139.3, 4.8.3, 5.92c.3.
50  Herodotus, 6.16.2–17.1, 6.70.3.
51  Herodotus, 7.236.2, 8.87.3.
52  Herodotus, 1.32.5.
53  Herodotus, 7.10d.
54  How and Wells: if H. meant that wealth is not happiness (as Aristotle, in *Eth*. x.8.9–11, where he refers to this passage), he certainly fails to say so; if he means that a man may be unlucky though wealthy, he is elaborately stating the obvious.
55  Herodotus, 1.118.2.
56  Herodotus, 1.119.1.
57  Herodotus, 1.124.1.
58  Herodotus, 1.126.6.
59  Lateiner, Donald, *The Historical Method of Herodotus* (Toronto: University of Toronto Press, 1989), p. 218.
60  Harrison, *Divinity and History*, p. 231; Gould, *Herodotus*, p. 76, who sees a telling Homeric echo in Herodotus' use of such phrases.
61  Victory: 1.65.1, 171.3 and 8.60a; advantage: 3.139.2, and for Artemisia, 8.87.4 and 8.88.3.
62  Herodotus, 1.32.6 and 7.
63  Herodotus, 1.207.2.
64  At 3.44.1, perhaps with irony, although it also appears elsewhere in the passage with a more neutral sense: 3.40.1–3, 3.43.1.
65  Herodotus, 7.236.
66  Herodotus, 7.190.1.

67 See How and Wells for analysis of the phraseology of this passage, indicating that Ameinocles kills his son himself, albeit involuntarily.
68 Herodotus, 7.233.2.
69 Solon, 13.30, see above, ch. 5.
70 Herodotus, 8.105.1.
71 Herodotus, 5.65.1 and 9.21.1.
72 Herodotus, 3.74.1 ff.
73 Herodotus, 3.120–1, 5.41.1.
74 Herodotus, 3.43.2.
75 Herodotus, 7.54.2.
76 Herodotus, 9.91.1. How and Wells (*ad loc.*) say that this is equivalent to *theiei tuchei*, but is a divine *tuche*, the same as the *syntuchie* of a god?
77 Herodotus, 9.100.
78 Pelling, 'Archidamus and Artabanus', p. 139: 'Human and divine elements simply co-exist side by side, and reinforce one another – just, indeed, as they had done in Homer'. Gould (*Herodotus*, pp. 70–71) compares activities and beliefs of the Azande tribe of the southern Sudan to explain how the Greeks could accept 'parallel sets of causation, one human, the other supernatural, neither of which renders the other inoperative' (p. 71).
79 Grethlein, Jonas, *The Greeks and Their Past: Poetry, Oratory and History in the Fifth Century BCE* (Cambridge: Cambridge University Press, 2010) in his examination of the presentation of the past across Greek literature also draws attention to the role of patterns in Herodotus' narrative as part of his examination of the expression of Chance in this text (p. 15). Grethlein focuses in particular on Herodotus' use of *prolepsis* and *analepsis* to 'stress that the characters are liable to miscalculations and subject to forces beyond their reach'. As he notes (p. 5 and n. 29), he chooses an etic over an emic approach, preferring to trace the modern idea of contingency, rather than pursue occurrences or uses of *tuche*.
80 Made explicit by Cyrus at 9.122. See discussion, Pelling, 'East is East', who also cites Greenblatt, Stephen, *Marvelous Possessions: The Wonder of the New World* (Oxford. Oxford University Press, 1991).
81 Herodotus, 8.60c.
82 E.g. Herodotus, 2.22 and 2.25.2; see Thomas, *Herodotus in Context*, p. 168, n. 1 and 190 n. 51 where she notes that *eikos* occurs forty times across the *Histories*; also Flower, 'Herodotus and Delphic Traditions', p. 72 and her conclusion that the word comes from a family of meanings indicating the 'rules of logic governing cause and effect in the universe'; she discusses the phrase 'as seems likely' (*hos eikasai*), in the context of the fate of Croesus' son Atys, which Herodotus attributes to the punishment of the gods (1.34.1).

## Chapter VII

1 Dialogue between Chigurh (Javier Bardem) and the proprietor of the gas station (Gene Jones) in the film *No Country for Old Men* (2007).
2 'Texas Noir' Walter Kirn, *The New York Times*, July 24, 2005.
3 Thucydides, 1.10.2, 74.1, 2.21.3, and 'part/attribute of man': 3.82.4.

4   Lowell, Edmunds, *Chance and Intelligence in Thucydides* (Cambridge, MA: Harvard University Press, 1975), quotation from p. 207.
5   Edmunds, *Chance*, p. 205.
6   *Ibid*. p. 206–7, drawing on de Romilly, Jacqueline, *Histoire et raison chez Thucydide* (Paris: Les Belles Lettres, 1976), p. 176.
7   Edmunds, *Chance*, p. 198.
8   Edmunds, *Chance*, p. 200.
9   Edmunds, *Chance*, p. 5 notes how the truths of history and of historian remain conflated in Thucydides' work. My description builds on, but has a different emphasis from, that of Connor, W. R., 'A Post Modernist Thucydides' *The Classical Journal* 72: 4 (Apr.–May 1977), pp. 289–98, esp. p. 297: 'Thucydides the artist can thus remain a follower of Periclean rationalism as he shapes and presents his material; Thucydides the thinker on the other hand is free to pursue an interpretation and explanation of events that emphasizes the power of the irrational.'
10  Edmunds, *Chance*, p. 6.
11  Pericles' speech: Thucydides, 1.140–44. On the plans of men, see 1.140. 1. See Jahn, Beate, *Classical Theory in International Relations* (Cambridge: Cambridge University Press, 2006); Edmunds, *Chance*, pp. 16–17, argues that Pericles is trivialising chance, by making human planning the criterion by which it is judged.
12  Thucydides, 1.144.3.
13  Archidamus at Thucydides, 1.84.3; Corinthians criticise Spartans: 1.71.1; Edmunds, *Chance*, p. 17.
14  Thucydides, 2.87.2–3.
15  Anaximenes, [Arist.] *Rhet. Ad Alex.* 1425b2–33 (cited by Edmunds: *Chance*, p. 15).
16  Thucydides, 4.18.5; 6.11.6 and 23.3, see later discussion.
17  Thucydides, 1.69.5.
18  Thucydides, 4.64.1–5.
19  Thucydides, 5.104.1.
20  Thucydides, 5.105.1, cf. 4.61.5.
21  Thucydides, 5.112.2–3, and see Bosworth, Brian A., 'The Humanitarian Aspect of the Melian Dialogue' *Journal of Hellenic Studies* 113 (1993), 30–44, p. 40.
22  Thucydides, 5.113.1.
23  Thucydides, 3.45.5–6.
24  Thucydides, 5.102.1; 5.111.3.
25  Thucydides, 5.104.1, and 112.2.
26  Thucydides, 4.55.3.
27  Thucydides, 4.73.3.
28  Thucydides, 5.75.3.
29  Hornblower, Simon, *A Commentary on Thucydides, Vol. III: Books 5.25–8.109* (Oxford: Oxford University Press, 1991) *ad loc.*, p. 194, thinks that reference to bad luck here is 'striking', contrasting it with the explanation of religious offences mentioned at 7.18. Edmunds (*Chance*, pp. 101, 178, 183) thinks this is just a reference to defeat at Sphacteria.
30  Thucydides, 2.87.2–3, see discussion at the beginning of this chapter.

## NOTES

31 Thucydides, 5.16.1, 6.17.1. At 3.97.2 Demosthenes is described as being 'persuaded by his advisers', and 'hoping in his *tuche*' (with a definite article) because no one had opposed him. Sordi, Marta, *La Fortuna Nell'Immagine dell' Uomo Politico Greco tra la Fine del v nel IV secolo a.c.* (Milan: Vita e pensiero, 1991) argues that fortune played an increasingly important role in the imagination of politicians of the fifth and fourth centuries.
32 Dover, Kenneth, (ed. and comm.) *Thucydides Book VI* (Oxford: Clarendon Press, 1965) on Thuc. 6.17; he notes how such a characteristic is 'logically incompatible with its treatment as pure chance'.
33 Thucydides, 6.11.6 and 23.3.
34 Thucydides, 7.63.4.
35 Nicias at Thucydides, 7.77.2 – this and 5.16 discussed above; Pericles at 2.44.2.
36 Corinthians at 1.120.3 and 4; Spartans 4.17.4.
37 Athenians at 5.14.1.
38 See 4.65.4, (trans. Warner, Rex, *Thucydides History of the Peloponnesian War*, London: Penguin, 1972); on *tuche* and hope, see also the speech of Demosthenes, Thucydides, 3.97.2. Thucydides, 8.106.5: a similar connection between hope and *eutuchia* occurs when the Athenians hear of the naval victory at Cynossema: Thucydides, with characteristic stylistic density, describes the Athenians hearing of 'the unhoped-for good-*tuche*' from the arriving ship.
39 Thucydides, 7.86.5. Edmunds (*Chance*, p. 200) argues that Thucydides uses the term because he both agrees with and is detached from the actors' point of view: first the death of Nicias is the 'bad luck' that disrupts the prosperity that Nicias had hoped to continue; second, it is for Thucydides the historian a fact that cannot be explained. Edmunds goes on 'this reversal is not altogether unpredictable and does not "befall" Nicias' from some superhuman realm, as the pious Nicias doubtless believed.' For a start, this discussion seems to me to elide what is clearly a more complex set of beliefs held by Nicias, involving both supernatural and mortal causes; but more fundamentally, as with Edmunds' analysis in general, it begs the question of Thucydides' beliefs, based on his use of terms that carry a supernatural connotation which he never explicitly denies.
40 Thucydides, 6.55.4.
41 Thucydides, 6.54.1.
42 Thucydides, 7.87.5.
43 Thucydides, 6.103.4.
44 Thucydides, 1.33.1.
45 Thucydides, 3.45.4.
46 Thucydides, 3.112.7, fleeing their attackers, the Ambraciots swim out to the Athenian ships that happen to be there; 5.11.2, the battle springs out of a chance event, and a sense of panic.
47 Thucydides, 3.82.2; trans. Hornblower, Simon, *A Commentary on Thucydides, Vol. 1: Books I-III* (Oxford: Oxford University Press, 1991), ad loc., p. 481.
48 6.54.1.
49 7.57.1.
50 *ad loc.*, Hornblower, *Commentary, Vol. 1*.
51 The Greek is *ephistontai*. See *ad loc.* Marchant E. C., *Commentary on Thucydides,*

Book 3 (London: Macmillan, 1891); see *Iliad*, 12.326; Sophocles, *Iphigenia at Tauris*, 776 and Euripides, *Hippolytus*, l. 819. In Thucydides, use of the term to mean suddenly coming upon one as in an ambush (8.69.4), even springing upon one (3.82.2).

52  Contra Edmunds, *Chance*, p. 198 (see discussion above).
53  Edmunds, *Chance*, p. 176, reduces this to seven. He excludes 5.75.3 (discussed above); 4.73.3 and 5.16.1 (indirect discourse) and 4.118.1 (a decretal formula).
54  Thucydides, 3.49.4.
55  Thucydides, 4.3.1.
56  For example, at 4.6.1 where the bad weather has caused hardship in the Spartan army stationed in Attica, and is one of the factors that prompts them to go home.
57  Cornford, Francis, *Thucydides Mythistoricus* (1907, repr., London: Routledge and Kegan Paul, 1965) p. 88, n. 2.
58  'Moral Luck', suggested by Robert Parker, cited Hornblower, Simon. *Thucydides* (London: Duckworth, 1987), p. 192, n. 2. Edmunds (*Chance*, pp. 177–8) argues that the Athenians have committed themselves to *tuche* because of the anger in which their initial decision was made, seeing a contrast between the *gnome* of Pericles and the *gnome* of the people (3.36.2), mastered by passion, 'a prooemium to tyche'; he sees this *kata tuchen* as ironic, an interpretation that seems excessively complicated – and to impose an unnecessarily cynical viewpoint on Thucydides.
59  It is not clear just how long Demosthenes has held these plans for Pylos: Hornblower, Simon, *A Commentary on Thucydides, Vol. II: Books IV-V.24* (Oxford: Oxford University Press, 1996) discusses the arguments for and against the idea that Demosthenes rather than Thucydides makes the comment that D. had come on the campaign for this purpose (4.3.2). Quotation from Hornblower *ibid., ad loc.*, p. 152.
60  Thucydides, 5.37.3.
61  On the unsatisfactory nature of this passage and its contents, see Hornblower, *Commentary, Vol III, ad loc.*, p. 82.
62  Edmunds, *Chance*, p. 179.
63  Thucydides, 4.12.3; Edmunds, *Chance*, p. 177 states that 'Here tyche is the present situation' and the 'neutral sense of tyche so common in Plato'. But if this is so, it seems an elaborate formulation. Commentators have noted a comparison with the reversals that also arise from the Sicilian disaster – although *tuche* makes no explicit appearance there: Macleod, Colin, 'Thucydides and Tragedy' in *Collected Essays* (Oxford: Clarendon Press, 1997), pp. 140–158, pp. 142–3, noted by Hornblower, *Commentary, Vol. II, ad loc.*, pp. 166–167.
64  Thucydides, 4.14.3.
65  Compare Demosthenes' confidence in his *tuche* (3.97.2), discussed above. A similar phrase occurs at 7.33.6, where *tuche* again seems to describe the current or particular circumstances in which the Athenians find themselves. A *stasis* has just occurred at Thourioi, which has expelled the anti-Athenian party from the city. 'In this *tuche*', the Athenians attempt to persuade the remaining Thourians into an alliance. However, the focalisation is a little more questionable here: although it's possible that Thucydides is simply giving us a neutral record of

# NOTES

events, the passage could also be read as including the very proposal made by the Athenians to the Thourians. In this case, how should we translate *tuche*: is she 'favourable' (as she would be for the Athenians) or does she represent a more vulnerable situation (for the Thourians who remain in the city)?

66. Edmunds notes that the verb need not always be translated. For more significant uses, he gives five categories: a) coincidence (p. 190: e.g., 2.49.1, 1.136.3, 4.13.4, 7.50.4, 7.79.3); followed by its use b) to describe the arrival of ships (p. 191: e.g., 1.57.6, 104.2, 116.1 (twice), 2.3.1, 93.2, 3.3.4, 33.1, 105.3, 4.9.1, 104.5, 8.61.2, 79.2, 91.2); c) with the genitive to indicate good luck (*ibid.* 1.137.2, 3.3.4; with notion of good luck, with the genitive: 7.25.2); d) in the vicinity of *pipto* (the verb 'to fall') and compounds (p. 192: e.g., 1.106.1, 2.4.5 and 25.2, 3.30.2 and 98.1, 4.12.2, 7.29 and 70.4, 8.41.2; with a non-human subject 2.91.3); and, finally, e) randomness (e.g., 3.43.5, which illustrates how chance can be reduced to the subjective – and that this is the basis for Pericles' thought on chance (control of people in democracy is possible)). However, in his elaborations on each category, he does note that some of them might be better considered as sub-categories of the first and by far the largest category 'coincidence', and his sub-divisions give some idea of this verb's many uses.
67. Should not be translated, see Edmunds, *Chance*, p.190. In battle: 1.55.1, 1.57.6, 1.103.3, 1.106.1, 2.04.5, 2.05.4, 3.98.1, 3.108.2, 3.111.2, 4.111.2, 4.116.2, 5.12.2, 7.23.2 and 7.70.4.
68. Thucydides, 4.48.3, 4.112.2, 8.54.4; other examples include: 3.20.3.
69. Thucydides, 1.9.2, 1.92.1, 1.135.3, 1.136.3, 1.137.2, 2.13.1, 3.70.5, 3.82.5, 8.12.2.
70. Thucydides, 8.92.6, 8.5.5, see also 8.105.3 where the effects of the disorganisation of the Spartan forces is made worse by the Syracusan force also having given way.
71. Thucydides, 7.29.5.
72. Thucydides, 7.50.4.
73. Thucydides, 7.79.3.
74. Thucydides, 2.49.1 and 51.1.
75. Thucydides, 8.41.2.
76. Thucydides, 2.91 and 8.91.
77. Thucydides, 5.75.2 and 7.73.2.
78. Thucydides, 1.72.1, 1.104.2, 1.116.1, 2.25.2, 2.31.1, 2.91.3, 2.93.2, 2.95.3, 3.3.2 and 4, 3.33.1, 3.90.2, 3.102.3, 3.105.3, 3.112.1, 4.104.5, 4.113.2, 4.129.3, 4.130.3, 4.132.2, 5.22.1, 5.30.5, 5.44.1, 5.46.5, 5.50.5, 5.76.3, 6.61.2, 6.102.2, 7.2.4, 7.4.3, 8.17.3, 8.21.1, 8.31.1, 8.61.2, 8.79.2.
79. Thucydides, 5.36.1, 6.96.3, 8.61, 8.98.1.
80. Thucydides, 8.14.2.
81. Thucydides, 8.95.4.
82. Thucydides, 1.55.1.
83. Thucydides, 1.135.3, 136.3 and 137.2.
84. At Pylos: 4.3.1, 12.3, 14.3; or in reference to Pylos 4.55.3: observed by Edmunds, *Chance*, p. 178. At Melos, see Thucydides, 5.98.1, 5.104.1: the Melians emphasise their trust in divine *tuche*. At 5.111.3 *tuche* and 111.5 *tunchano*: that the Melians risk incurring, through their own folly, worse dishonour than fate would have incurred. At 5.112.2, the Melians reply with one further *tuche*; and at

5.113.1 the Athenians emphasise how the Melians trust in *tuche* and how foolish this is; they summarise the decision of their enemies.
85 Thucydides, 5.22.1, 5.30.5, 5.44.1, 5.46.5, 5.50.5, 5.76.3; also noted by Edmunds, *Chance*, p. 179.
86 Thucydides, 4.104.5, 111.2, 112.2, 113.2, 114.3, 116.2, 118.11, 124.4.
87 *Xuntunchano*, 7.70.6, which describes the clash of two ships.
88 *A communication situation that recurs regularly in a society* (in terms of participants, setting, communicative functions, and so forth) *will tend over time to develop identifying markers of language structure and language use, different from the language of other communication situations* (author's italics), p. 20 in Ferguson, Charles A., *Dialect, Register, and Genre: Working Assumptions about Conventionalization* in Douglas Biber & Edward Finegan (eds.), *Sociolinguistic Perspectives on Register* (Oxford, 1994), pp. 15–30; but compare Paul Simpson's inclusion of register as a 'regular, fixed pattern of vocabulary and grammar' (2004, p.104); in Simpson, Paul, *Stylistics: A resource book for students* (New York, 2004).
89 Thucydides, 5.46.1.
90 Thucydides, 6.16.4 and 6.77.2.
91 Thucydides, 7.18.2.
92 Direct: 2.44.4, 2.60.3, 2.61.1, 3.39.4, 4.17, 4.18.4, 4.62.4, 6.23.3, 7.63.4, 7.68, 7.77.3. Indirect: 4.79.2, 4.117.2, 5.7.3, 5.16.1, 6.15.2.
93 Edmunds notes an 'implicit Periclean doctrine of tyche, according to which the statesman is seriously affected by tyche only in its effect upon the gnomai of the people, which he must know how to control' (*Chance*, p. 193).
94 Thucydides, 2.44.4.
95 Thucydides, 2.60.3.
96 Here he uses the verb *kakotucheo* a strong and rare term suggesting the strength of the case that Pericles is trying to make.
97 Thucydides, 2.61.1.
98 Thucydides, 3.38.1: see Hornblower, *Commentary, Vol. I, ad loc.*, p. 425 for translation and n.
99 Thucydides, 4.17.4 and 4.18.4.
100 Thucydides, 6.17.1; confirmed by himself 7.77.2.
101 Thucydides, 6.23.3.
102 Thucydides, 7.63.4.
103 Pericles at Thucydides, 1.40–44; Spartans at Thucydides, 2.87.2–3.
104 Thucydides, 7.77.3.
105 Thucydides, 7.68.3.
106 For example, Thucydides, 4.117.2.
107 Thucydides, 4.79.2.
108 Thucydides, 5.7.3.
109 Thucydides, 5.16.1.
110 Thucydides, 6.15.2.
111 See Connor 1984: p. 249; I agree with Grethlein, *The Greeks and Their Past*, pp. 254–268, that Thucydides does not offer stable, repeated narrative patterns in the same way as Herodotus.

# NOTES

## Chapter VIII

1. From a transcript of Greenspan's testimony at a hearing examining the role of federal regulators in the credit crisis, originally aired October 23, 2008; *www.pbs.org/newshour/bb/business/july-dec08/crisishearing_10–23.html*
2. Frederick and Steven Barthelme *Double Down: Reflections on Gambling and Loss*, (Houghton Mifflin Harcourt, 1999) p. 96.
3. Demosthenes, *On the Crown* 57, trans. *Greek Orators V: Demosthenes On the Crown* (trans. and comm. S. Usher) (Oxford: Aris and Philips, 1993).
4. See Aeschines 3.156, 173, 209, 239, 250, 259, and discussion G. L. Cawkwell, 'The Crowning of Demosthenes', *Classical Quarterly* 19 (1969), pp. 163–180, esp. pp. 176–7.
5. The sources record little activity for this period, see Cawkwell 'The Crowning of Demosthenes' pp. 173 ff.
6. Plutarch, *Demosthenes*, 24.1 states that Demosthenes tried to raise support for Agis, but gave up in the face of Athenian refusal; contemporary sources say that Demosthenes opposed joining Agis. Cawkwell discusses *ibid*. pp. 178 ff.
7. See discussion of contents of classical guidelines and handbooks for public speaking in Kennedy, G. A., *Classical Rhetoric and its Christian and Secular Tradition from Ancient to Modern Times* (Chapel Hill, NC: UNC Press, 1999), esp. 20–29.
8. Usher, *Demosthenes On the Crown* provides a clear and detailed guide to Demosthenes' speech in the introduction.
9. Demosthenes, *On the Crown*, 189–194; see 193, 195 and 200 for references to gods, and 192 for a *daimon*. Destined: *heimarto* at 195.
10. Demosthenes, *On the Crown*, 189.
11. Demosthenes, *On the Crown*, 194–5.
12. Demosthenes, *On the Crown*, 207–8.
13. Martin, Gunther, *Divine Talk: Religious Argumentation in Demosthenes* (Oxford: Oxford University Press, 2009), p. 95, comes to similar conclusions.
14. Sections 252–275 of Demosthenes, *On the Crown*.
15. Aeschines, 3 (*Against Ctesiphon*), 253.
16. Aeschines, 3.157.
17. Aeschines, 3.134–5.
18. Aeschines, 3.131: compare discussion of *aliterios* Usher *Demosthenes On the Crown*, p. 228. See also Martin, pp. 89–91.
19. See discussion also in Martin, *Divine Talk*, pp. 89–92.
20. See chapters II and VII.
21. Demosthenes, *On the Crown*, 248–50.
22. Demosthenes, *On the Crown*, 252.
23. Demosthenes, *On the Crown*, 253.
24. Demosthenes, *On the Crown*, 253–4.
25. Demosthenes, *On the Crown*, 255 and 270–1.
26. Martin, *Divine Talk*, p. 98, notes the distortion, but sees it as a way for Demosthenes to avoid Aeschines' argument about his evil influence on the city;

27 Demosthenes, *On the Crown*, 257–8.
28 Here I disagree with Martin, *Divine Talk*, who argues (p. 97) that *tuche* is presented here 'as a state of luck without any emphasis on her divine nature, not indicating any influence of the divine on the course of events' and see also p. 207.
29 Including the idea of pollution, which Demosthenes does not address directly, although his comments at 271 do seem to be a way of referring to it; see discussion Martin, *Divine Talk*, pp. 98–100.
30 Oracle: Demosthenes, *On the Crown*, 253; *daimones*: the Greek is *eudaimonia* (254) and *eudaimonizo* (260).
31 Reluctance to suggest that the gods do not support Athens noted as a characteristic across the orators in Parker, 'Gods Cruel and Kind', and discussed again in Martin, *Divine Talk*, p. 205.
32 See Lakoff, George, and Johnson, Mark N., *Metaphors We Live By* (Chicago: Chicago University Press, 1980); see the analysis of metaphorical thinking in the language of 'commitment', discussed in Quinn, 'Commitment', p. 785.
33 Quinn, 'Commitment', p. 794 on shifts between the senses of 'commitment'.
34 Matthews, 'Uncovering Cultural Models', p. 152, finds similar use of variants of cultural models in folklore narratives.
35 A useful discussion of models and motivation in D'Andrade, *Cognitive Anthropology*, pp. 231–241; see Quinn 'Commitment' p. 795.
36 This example given by Quinn 'Schemas People Share', p. 37, although not as part of an explanation of goals.
37 At the time of writing, these speeches could be found: George W. Bush, Second Inaugural Address, http://news.bbc.co.uk/1/hi/world/americas/4192773.stm and Barack Obama. Inauguration speech: http://news.bbc.co.uk/1/hi/world/americas/obama_inauguration/7840646.stm
38 Solomon, 'Fate and Fatalism'; Green, Lee, Lewis, Rhonda K., *et al.*, 'Powerlessness, Destiny, and Control: The Influence on Health Behaviors of African Americans' in *Journal of Community Health* 29: 1, February, 2004. The study conducted a survey of 1,253 African Americans (in churches in Alabama) and discovered a significant link between particular health behaviours and belief in fate or destiny.
39 Ethnographic work on this idea in Hatfield, 'Fate in the Narrativity and Experience of Selfhood'.
40 Schwartz, Peter, and Leyden, Peter, 'The Long Boom: A History of the Future, 1980–2020', *Wired* 5.07 (July 1997).
41 Lears, Jackson T., *Something for Nothing: Luck in America* (London: Penguin, 2003), pp. 322–3.
42 *Shell Global Scenarios to 2025, Executive Summary*, Shell Intl, 2005; www.shell.com/home/content/aboutshell/our_strategy/shell_global_scenarios/previous_scenarios/previous_scenarios_30102006.html.
43 See Jorion, Philippe, 'Risk Management Lessons from the Credit Crisis', *European Financial Management*, 2009 (forthcoming); see also Maggi, Bernardo, and Guida, Marco, 'Modeling Non Performing Loans Probability in the Commercial Banking System: Efficiency and Effectiveness Related to Credit Risk in Italy'

# NOTES

*Dipartimento di Economia Working Papers*, no. 1 (May 10, 2009); Lowenstein, Roger, *When Genius Failed* (New York: Random House, 2000); see also Adams, John, 'Making God Laugh', *Financial World* February 2006 and 'Risk Management: Cutting the CRAP', *Inform, the Journal of the Institute of Risk Management*, March, 2006.

44  Jorion, 'Risk Management', p. 17.
45  Heinzerling, L. and Ackerman, F., 'Law and Economics for a Warming World', *Harvard Law and Policy Review* 1: 2, (2007) pp. 331–362. Taleb, Nassim, *The Black Swan: The Impact of the Highly Improbable* (New York: Random House, 2007).
46  See discussion by Lears, *Something for Nothing*, p. 23, who also quotes this passage from Barthelme.
47  At the time of writing, the Reith Lectures, 2009, could be found at *http://www.bbc.co.uk/programmes/b00729d9*
48  Plato, *Republic*, 617c–621a. (translations from Lee, Desmond, *Plato The Republic* (London: Penguin, 1987).

# INDEX

*Adbusters* 17
Aeschylus 37
  *Agamemnon* 42
  *Prometheus Bound* 37
Aeschines, *Against Ctesiphon* 144–150
*Agathe Tuche* 48, 50, 85
*Agathos Daimon* 48
*Aisa* 27, 41, 80–82
Alcaeus 79
Alcman 45, 85
*Ananke* 37
Anaximander, see Pre-Socratic Philosophers
Antiphon 24
Aphrodite 38–39, 41, 44, 47
Apollo 33, 34, 36, 38, 55, 57, 59–61, 97, 101
Athena 38, 82
Archilochus 84–85, 89
Aristotle 8, 21–22, 62–63
Artemis 37, 38
*Ate* ('Divine madness') 31, 34–35, 44
Atropos, see *Moirai*

Barthelme, Frederick and Steven 144, 159
Binding spells 35
Bush, George, Jr. 155–56

Callinus 79, 83

Callistonicus (sculptor) 48
Chance 3, 4, 8, 12, 18, 45, 74, 134, 158–159
  in Archaic poetry 77
  in Herodotus 97, 101, 113
  in Thucydides 120, 121, 126, 130–131
*Chat—It's Fate!* 14
Clotho, see *Moirai*
Cognitive linguistics 68
Cognitive anthropology 9, 68–69, 152–3
Coincidence,
  in Herodotus 100, 113–115, 117
  in Thucydides 119–142, esp. 129–131, 136
Compatibilism 18–19
  Semi-compatibilism 19
Csikszentmihalyi, Mihaly 16
Cultural discourse 72
Cultural knowledge 69–70, 152
Cultural models 9–11, 67–75, 80, 86, 91–92, 117, 123, 136, 141, 151–156
  Explanatory models 67, 70
Cynicism 21

*Daimon(es)* 23, 44–45, 72, 75
  in Aeschines, *Against Ctesiphon* 147
  in Archaic poetry 83

in Demosthenes, *On the Crown* 150
in Herodotus 99–102
in Sophocles' *Oedipus the King* 59–60
de Gracián y Morales, Baltasar 76–77
Death 29, 31, 33, 35–36, 39–43, 49, 56, 58–60, 83, 97–99, 101, 103, 105, 113, 121, 129
Demetrius of Phaleron 51–52
Demosthenes, *On the Crown* 144–150
Dennett, Daniel 18
Derveni Papyrus 40
Destiny 3, 13–14, 53, 56, 74, 155–158
Determinism 8, 10, 14–23, 41, 64
  Hard and Soft 18
  Epistemic, Logical, and Natural 14–15
*Dike* 36
Dionysus 47, 144
Dolby, Sarah K. 15
Dr. Fate 30
Dreams, in Herodotus 100
*Dustucheo* ('I experience bad luck')
  in Herodotus 111–115
  in Thucydides 136–7
*Dustuchia* ('Bad luck')
  in Thucydides 128–9
Dyer, Wayne 16

Edmunds, Lowell 121
*Engimono* 7
Epicureanism 21
*Erinyes* ('Furies') 6, 22, 31, 34, 35, 36, 37
Eros 41
*Eudaimonia* ('Good luck') 22
*Eumenides/Semnai* ('Kindly Ones', see *Erinyes*)
*Eunomia* ('Good order') 36, 45, 85
*Eutucheo* ('I experience good luck')

in Herodotus 110–115
in Thucydides 136, 138–140
*Eutuchia* ('Good luck')
in Herodotus 110–115
in Thucydides 125, 126, 128–129, 137–138

Fate 2–5, 13–16, 22, 27, 30–45, 53–56, 61–65, 67, 72, 74, 151, 156, 157–158, 159 and *passim*
  (see also *Aisa, Fatum, Heimarmene, Potmos, Moros, Moira*)
  in Archaic poetry 80, 83–84, 86–87
  in Demosthenes, *On the Crown* 146
  in Herodotus 93–94, 96–99, 100–101, 103–104, 110, 115–118
  in Thucydides 141–142
Fatalism 15, 157
*Fate Magazine* 14
*Fatum* 3, 41
Fenton, Sasha 12, 53
Fischer, John Martin 19
Foreknowledge, divine 15
*Fortuna* ('Fortune') 3, 41, 52, 158
Fortune (see *Moira, Tuche*) 3–5, 7, 8, 41, 44, 45, 46, 48, 51, 67, 76, 151, 152, 153, 154 and *passim*
  in Aeschines, *Against Ctesiphon* 148
  in Archaic poetry 83, 84, 85, 86, 87, 88, 89, 90, 91
  in Demosthenes, *On the Crown* 146, 148–150
  in Herodotus 97, 99, 100, 104, 106, 107–108, 110–115, 116–118
  in Sophocles' *Oedipus the King* 58–60
  in Thucydides 126–127, 128, 136–140
Frankfurt, Harry 19
Free will 8, 10, 13–14, 17–23, 28, 41, 62, 66–67, 115

210

# INDEX

Freud, Sigmund 55
Funerary inscriptions 39

Genomics 17, 159–160
Gods 6, 24, 29, 33, 44, 51, 67
    (and see under names of individual gods)
    gifts of 34, 82
    and *moira* 32, 83–84
    in Aeschines, *Against Ctesiphon* 147
    in Archaic poetry 82–87, 90
    in Demosthenes, *On the Crown* 148
    in Herodotus 98–102, 109, 111, 116–118
    in Sophocles' *Oedipus the King* 58–62, 64
    in Thucydides 122, 124–125, 127, 140–141
Gorgias, *Helen* 24
Gould, John 55
Greenspan, Alan 143
*Guys and Dolls* 25, 45

*Hamartia* ('Mistake') 54
*Heimarmene* ('Fate') 27, 41–44
*Heimarmene* Painter 44, 47
Hera 33, 37
Heraclitus, see Pre-Socratic Philosophers
Herodotus 93–118
Hesiod 36
    *Theogony* 45, 50
Hipponax 84
Homeric epic 27, 30–37, 39, 41–45, 80, 81, 83
    *The Iliad* 31–36, 43, 44
    *The Odyssey* 31, 32, 34, 43
*Homeric Hymn to Demeter* 45
Huxley, Aldous 17

Incompatibilism 17
Indeterminism 18

*Kairos* ('Opportunity') 48
*Kalapalo* of Brazil 72
*Karma* 7, 14–15, 53
*Ker* 36, 131

Lachesis, see *Moirai*
*Lawrence of Arabia* 1, 5, 53, 67
Lears, Jackson 158
Lot 7, 30, 32, 36, 42, 80, 83, 84, 90, 97, 98, 150, 159, 160
Luck (see *Tuche*) 2, 3, 4–5, 7, 8, 12, 13, 16, 30, 44, 66, 67, 76–77, 144, 147, 156, 158–159 and *passim*
    Lady Luck 25–27, 45, 47, 67
    Moral luck 19–22, 116, 132
    in Archaic poetry 85, 91
    in Demosthenes, *On the Crown* 146, 149–150
    in Herodotus 97, 100, 105, 108–113, 116–118
    in Thucydides 122, 127, 128–131, 132, 133, 136–140, 141

Menander
    *The Achaeans* 49
    *The Changeling* 49
    *Girl Pipers* 49
    *The Shield* 48
*Menandri Sententiae* 49
Mimnermus 79, 84
*Moira* 8–9, 13, 22–23, 27, 29, 39–43, 82, 145, 151, 152–3
    *theia moira* 41
    in Archaic poetry 82–86, 90, 91
    in Herodotus 96–100, 109
    in Homer, *Iliad* and *Odyssey* 30–35
    in Sophocles' *Oedipus the King* 55–57, 59, 60, 64, 72, 75
    in Thucydides 121
*Moirai* 35–41, 45, 47, 97, 160–161
    Cults of 37–38

*Momos* ('Blame') 36
*Moros, Morsimos* ('Fate, fated') 3, 27, 36, 41–44

Nagel, Thomas 19–20
Narrative 72–75
Necessity, see *Ananke*
Nemesis ('Retribution') 36, 44, 47, 48
*No Country for Old Men* 119–120

Obama, Barack 155–157
*Oedipus the King* 53–65
Oracle(s) 6, 34, 42, 76–77
  in Sophocles' *Oedipus the King* 54, 56–62, 64
  in Herodotus 96, 97, 98, 102, 109, 120
Orphism and mystery cults 39–41

*Parcae* ('Fates') 41
Parmenides, see Pre-Socratic Philosophers
Pausanias (travel-writer) 37–38, 45, 46
Personification 8, 10, 27–30, 47, 48, 80
Pindar 43
  Frr, 39, 40, 41 (Snell-Maehler) 45–46
  *Olympian Ode* 12 46
Plato 21, 43
  *Republic* 160–161
  *Symposium* 44
Polybius 50, 52
*Potmos* ('Fate') 27, 41, 42
Pre-Socratic Philosophers
  (Anaximander, Heraclitus, Parmenides) 22
Prototypes 68–69
Providence, divine 15

Quantum physics 17

Reinhardt, Karl 55

Responsibility, moral 17–24, 28, 68
  in Archaic poetry 77, 84, 86–87
  in Herodotus 102–105
  in Sophocles' *Oedipus the King* 55, 61
Riddles, in Sophocles' *Oedipus the King* 62–63
Risk 2–5, 82–91, 156–160

Sandell, Michael 159
Schemas 9, 69–75
  (see also Cultural Models)
Self-help 5, 15–16, 77, 157
*Serendipity* 93–94, 118
Socrates 24, 160–161
Solon 79, 81–2, 84, 85, 86–88
Sophocles
  *Oedipus the King* 53–65
  *Trachiniae* ('The Women of Trachis') 42
Spinning, images of fate 7, 35, 40–41, 83
Stoicism 21, 23, 43, 64
Strawson, Galen 19
*Suntuchie* ('Coincidence') in Herodotus 113–115

*Terminator 2* 1, 5, 53–54, 67
*Thanatos*, see Death
*Themis* ('Divine law') 36, 38, 44
Theognis 79–86, 88–92, 151
Therapy 72–74
Trauma 73–74
*Tuche* 8, 24, 26, 44, 45–52
  (see its different forms)
  of Antioch 26
  Attributes 50
  Roman period 51
  Sculptors of 46–48
  in Aeschines, *Against Ctesiphon* 146–147
  in Archaic poetry 84–5

in Demosthenes, *On the Crown*
    145–6, 147–150
in Herodotus 105–115
in Sophocles' *Oedipus the King*
    57–59
in Thucydides 122–133
*Tunchano* ('I happen') in Thucydides
    133–36
Tyrtaeus 79

Widerker, David 19
Williams, Bernard 19–21
Wiseman, Richard 4–5, 12–13, 16, 67

*Xuntuchia* ('Coincidence') in Thucydides
    128–131

Zeus 31–35, 36, 38, 40–41, 47, 57, 58, 59, 61, 81, 82, 84